NEW ENGLAND
BRUNCH

SEASONAL MIDDAY MEALS FOR LEISURELY WEEKENDS

TAMMY DONROE INMAN

Globe
Pequot

ESSEX, CONNECTICUT

*For I-Wen,
who showed me the world*

Globe Pequot

An imprint of The Globe Pequot Publishing Group, Inc.
64 South Main Street
Essex, CT 06426
www.GlobePequot.com

Distributed by NATIONAL BOOK NETWORK

Copyright © 2025 by Tammy Donroe Inman

Photography by Tammy Donroe Inman, with additional photos from Getty

All rights reserved. No part of this book may be reproduced in any form or by any electronic or mechanical means, including information storage and retrieval systems, without written permission from the publisher, except by a reviewer who may quote passages in a review.

British Library Cataloguing in Publication Information available

Library of Congress Cataloging-in-Publication Data available

Names: Inman, Tammy Donroe, author.
Title: New England brunch : seasonal midday meals for leisurely weekends / by Tammy Donroe Inman.
Description: Essex, Connecticut : Globe Pequot, [2025] | Includes index. | Summary: "More than 100 enticing recipes for homemade pancakes, muffins, doughnuts, pastries, scones, bagels, popovers, frittatas, quiches, stratas, pitcher drinks, and more. From the mountains of Maine, New Hampshire, and Vermont to the coastal communities of Massachusetts, Rhode Island, and Connecticut, the cultural and seasonal tapestry of flavors provides endless culinary inspiration for leisurely weekend brunch gatherings"— Provided by publisher.
Identifiers: LCCN 2024026491 (print) | LCCN 2024026492 (ebook) | ISBN 9781493076871 (hardback) | ISBN 9781493076888 (epub)
Subjects: LCSH: Brunches. | LCGFT: Cookbooks.
Classification: LCC TX733 .I55 2025 (print) | LCC TX733 (ebook) | DDC 641.5/2—dc23/eng/20240822
LC record available at https://lccn.loc.gov/2024026491
LC ebook record available at https://lccn.loc.gov/2024026492

∞™ The paper used in this publication meets the minimum requirements of American National Standard for Information Sciences—Permanence of Paper for Printed Library Materials, ANSI/NISO Z39.48-1992.

Contents

Introduction v

Spring
1

Summer
51

Fall
103

Winter
155

All-Season *Dim Sum*
203

Acknowledgments 238

New England Resources 240

Index 242

About the Author 249

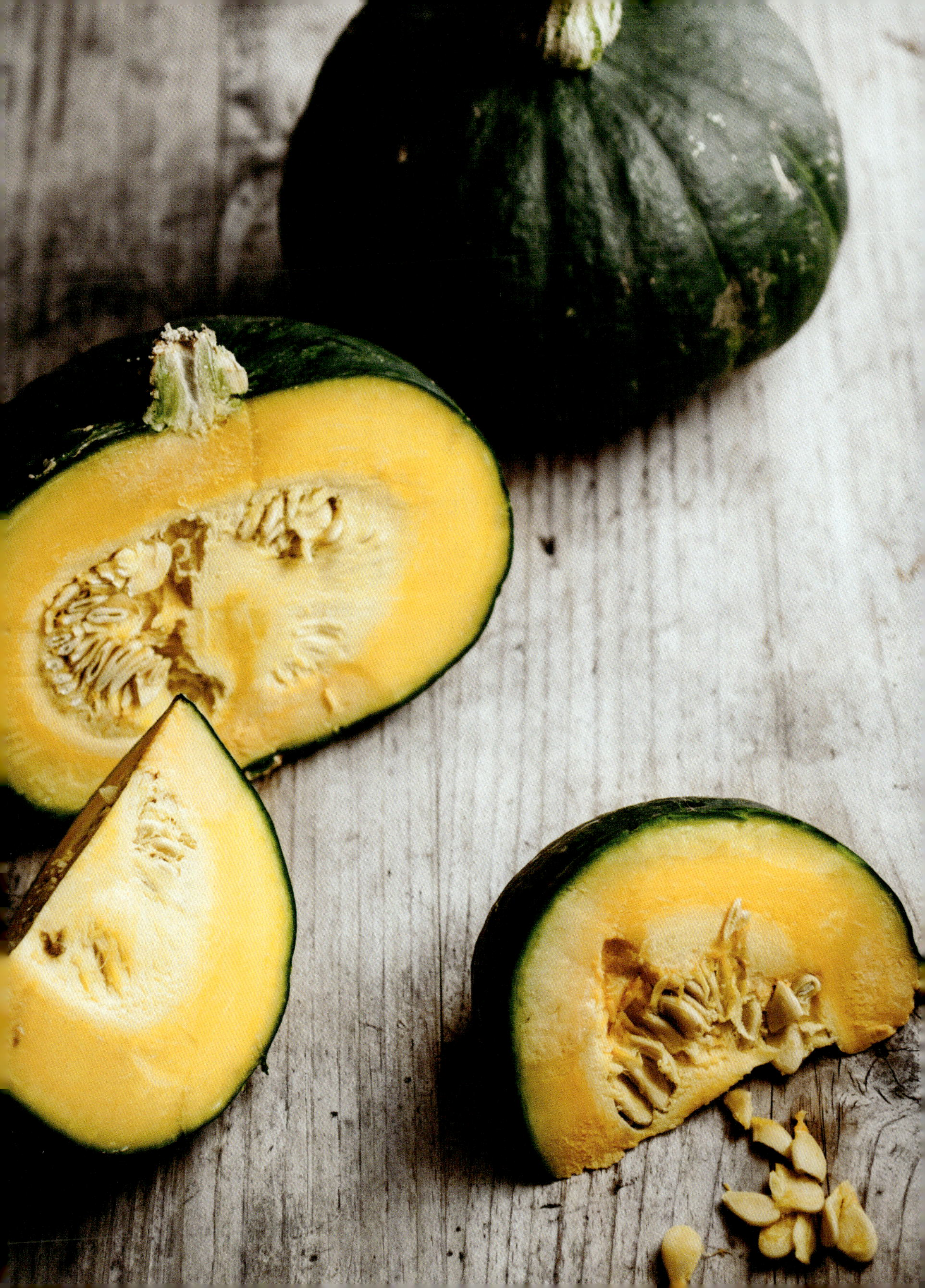

Introduction

You'll never catch me up at 5 a.m. banging pots and pans in a mad rush to prepare a fancy breakfast. I'm usually still asleep at 9 a.m. on weekends (a habit my family has long encouraged to maximize their video game play). Brunch, on the other hand, I can do. Watch me roll out of bed at an embarrassing hour, groggy and unable to form human speech, and I'll have some food on the table by noon. Maybe.

Brunch might be my very favorite meal of the week. I love its casual flexibility. It can lean more toward breakfast or lunch, savory or sweet, depending on your mood or sensibility. I have a serious sweet tooth, so that's how I tend to roll. Bring on the muffins, doughnuts, and sticky buns. But I also love savory dishes, especially if there's any sort of pork involved (I source my meat from local farms so I can observe with my own eyes how the animals are treated). A well-rounded brunch has a nice balance of seasonal fruits and vegetables. It can incorporate the coastal seafood for which New England is so well known, as well as make use of leftovers, which speaks to my Yankee frugality if not ingenuity. Furthermore, by combining two meals into one big gastronomic event, you can splurge without guilt while expending half the energy.

But, truly, it's the bounty of seasonal New England produce that gets me so excited about the prospect of brunch. I'm a New England girl, after all. Born in Maine, I was raised in New Hampshire and Massachusetts, have family ties in Connecticut, and chose to nurture my own family here, in the historic outskirts of Boston. I love getting to witness the dramatic seasonal changes play out against a multitude of diverse landscapes: rugged mountains, sprawling forests, rolling fields and pastures, rocky coastlines, quaint fishing villages, and thriving waterfront cities. Every season has its own flavor: strawberries, black raspberries, and blueberries in the summer; crisp apples and sweet pumpkins in the fall. Each state has its own indigenous ingredients: maple syrup in Vermont, cranberries in Massachusetts (though many overlap). Each region has its own special food traditions: johnnycakes (fried cornmeal pancakes) in Rhode Island, *ployes* (Acadian buckwheat crepes) in northern Maine. Who can resist a tall stack of blueberry pancakes drenched in maple syrup with crispy hash browns and homemade breakfast sausage on the side?

While restaurant brunch is a treat, you don't have to go out to experience the best of New England brunch. It's no secret that brunch is the most hated restaurant service of all time. It can often feel claustrophobic, with long lines making it awkward to linger as long as you might like. The vibe can feel like the continuation of an all-night rave, and hangovers affect both sides of the midday meal transaction. Menus can be overpriced and underwhelming. Patrons sometimes misbehave.

But brunch at home is fun. Weekends offer a chance to slow down and unwind with family and friends. Brunch allows you to set the menu and be creative using local and seasonal New England ingredients. It can be as low-key or as luxe as you like. A simple bagel spread (homemade or store-bought) is always enjoyable with a few different schmears and fresh fruit on the side. Make-your-own fruit parfaits are a fun way to celebrate summer berries with homemade granola and Greek yogurt. In the colder months, baked French toast is the way to go, dotted with cranberries or swirled with pears and chocolate-hazelnut spread. Set it up the night before, let it soak overnight, and pop it in the oven in the morning.

This cookbook celebrates my favorite meal of the week with more than 100 recipes for classic and creative dishes that feature fresh fruits and vegetables, hearty meats, seafood, and luscious libations. These brunch recipes are organized by season to allow the cook to coordinate the menu with the time of year when local produce is at its peak. In addition to historical recipes (like Boston Baked Beans on page 182), I've created new, inventive additions that reflect our thriving communities in rural Maine, Vermont, and New Hampshire, as well as the vibrant port cities of Connecticut, Massachusetts, and Rhode Island. *New England Brunch* offers enticing recipes for homemade pancakes, waffles, crepes, and French toast; syrups and preserves; muffins, biscuits, and scones; doughnuts and pastries; granola; coffee and tea cakes; bread, rolls, and bagels; eggs, sausage, and bacon; hash browns and home fries; frittatas, quiches, and stratas; soups; salads; sandwiches; beverages, and more—all year-round. There's also a dedicated chapter for all-season *dim sum*, the Chinese equivalent of brunch served with tea that's so popular in Boston's Chinatown, suburbs, and beyond. Master some of your favorite Chinese brunch recipes like Cantonese Pork and Shrimp Dumplings (*Siu Mai*), Pork and Cabbage Dumplings (*Jiaozi*), Steamed Buns (*Bao*), and Egg Custard Tarts (*Dan Tat*) in the comfort of your own home.

Starting in the springtime, ample opportunities for brunchy get-togethers abound: Easter, Mother's Day, Father's Day, bridal showers, baby showers, baptisms, graduations, you name it. The timing is excellent, as more and more fresh produce emerges, from early rhubarb, strawberries, asparagus, and spinach to the happy onslaught of berries, stone fruits, summer squash, tomatoes, and corn. Even fall and winter offer a cornucopia of cozy brunch inspiration, like pumpkins, apples, pears, and cranberries.

Raise a glass with a celebratory selection of pitcher drinks featuring fresh fruit and festive flavors in every season, like Strawberry Rhubarb Sangria, Bloody Marys, Cranberry Mimosas, and Pumpkin Eggnog. Whether you live in New England or hold a special place for it in your heart, I hope you enjoy the seasonal spirit of this regional exploration of brunch year-round.

A Brief History of New England Foodways

Here in New England, our food traditions combine indigenous customs and native crops with British ingredients and cooking techniques. Woven in along the way are the vibrant culinary traditions of nearly 400 years of immigrant influences, including the Portuguese,

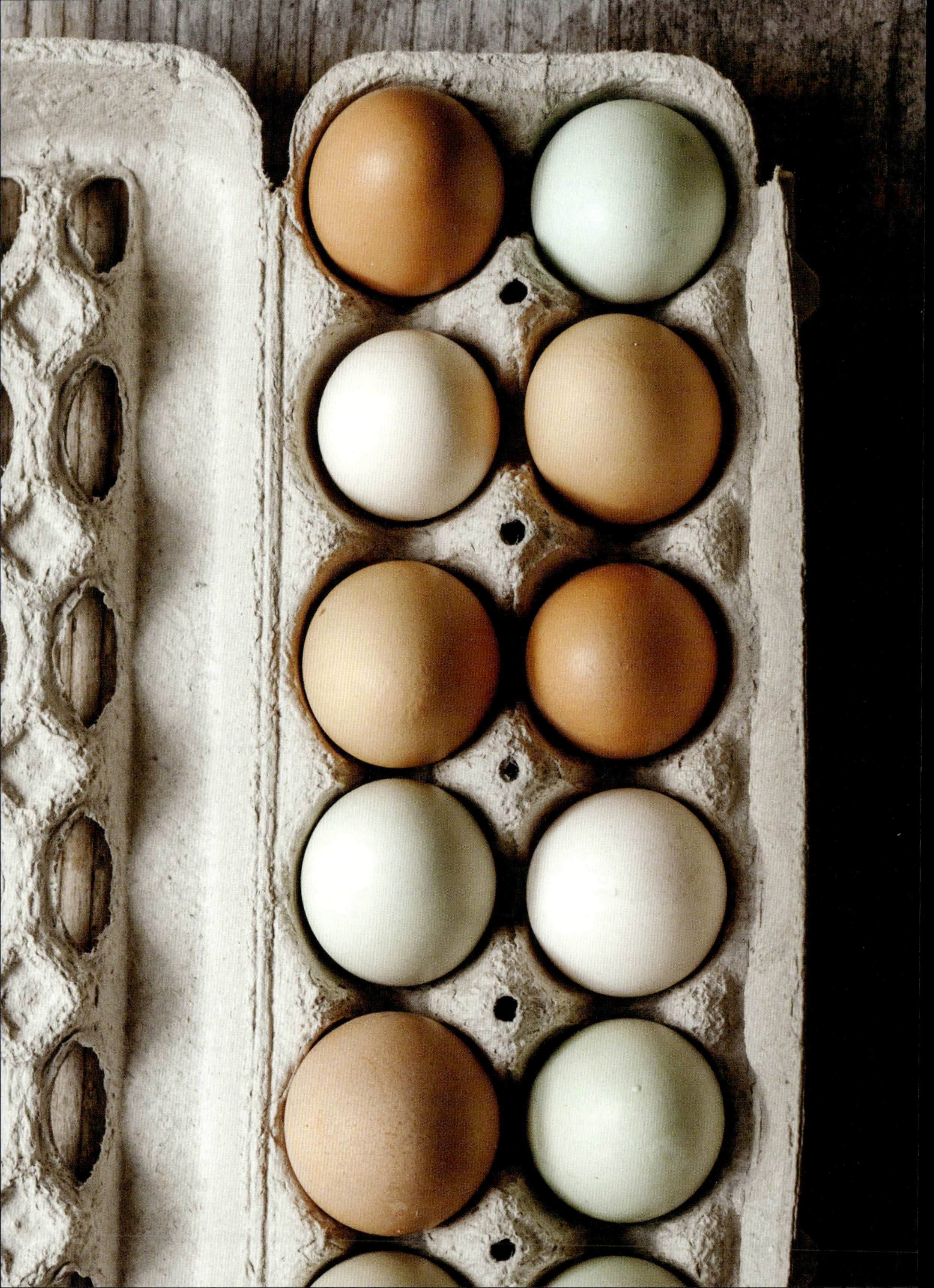

French Canadians, Irish, Italians, Jews, Chinese, Indians, Africans, and Latin Americans (among many others). The specific flavors and ingredients that feature in our most treasured food traditions tell a story about the land, the people, and the unique history that shaped the region.

The Northeast Woodlands of the United States, what we now call New England, was originally populated by numerous distinct Algonquin tribes and subtribes for more than 12,000 years, including the Abenaki and Wabanaki (including the Maliseet, Mi'kmaq, Passamaquoddy, and Penobscot) to the north; and the Mahican, Massachusett, Mohegan, Narragansett, Nipmuc, Pequot, Pocumtuc, Quiripi, and Wampanoag to the south. The Commonwealth of Massachusetts was named after a tribe that originally resided in the area, the Muhsachuweesut, which translates to "by the great hill" (referring to Great Blue Hill, just south of Boston). The state of Connecticut got its name from the Mohegan word *quinnehtukqut*, which refers to the "long, tidal river" by the same name that flows through the area.

These Native tribes had their own complete culinary repertoire perfectly suited to their environment long before anyone from across the Atlantic set foot in the region. They relied in part on foraging wild berries, nuts, seeds, and roots; fishing and clamming; and hunting wild game. The local tribes also cultivated a number of crops, the most important of which were corn, beans, and squash. These three plants were affectionately dubbed the "Three Sisters" for their complementary growing style and nurturing nutritional relationships. The tall corn provides support for the climbing beans, while the beans fertilize the soil for the heavy-feeding corn. Meanwhile, the rambling squash vines shade out weeds and keep the soil moist. Together, they create a delicious culinary trifecta that forms the basis of the regional native cuisine.

Most of our favorite corn, bean, and squash varieties are descended from native varieties. The English words for pumpkin and squash are derived from the Algonquin words *pôhpukun* (Wampanoag) and *askútasquash* (Narragansett). The origins of Boston baked beans stems from the Indigenous practice of burying a pot of beans in a rock-lined pit filled with coals (known as a "bean hole") and left to cook overnight. The New England clambake is another example of a traditional Indigenous style of cooking along the coast of Maine, Massachusetts, and Connecticut in which large quantities of shellfish are steamed on the beach in a pit dug in the sand and covered with seaweed.

To this day, it's hard to imagine anything more New England than maple syrup. It was the predominant sweetener prior to the arrival of the British, and it continues to be popular throughout the region. Each February, when warming days and cold nights cause the maple sap to run, it's collected and boiled down to concentrate its sweetness into syrup and crystallized sugar. The Native tribes would then use it year-round to sweeten cornmeal porridge (*nasaump*), cakes, and breads, as well as to season and preserve meat and fish.

When the British arrived, their supplies did not survive the cross-Atlantic trip. The Native tribes offered lifesaving hospitality by sharing their harvest, but only about half the settlers survived that first winter. Over the years, the British settlers learned from the Native Americans how to grow and grind corn, and what the local flora and fauna offered. For their part, the British had their own cooking and agricultural traditions that defined them. Puddings, cakes, and meat pies were very much a part of the British food culture, and they tried to duplicate them in the New World using the ingredients that were locally available, namely cornmeal, beans, squash, and whatever else they could grow in their gardens or forage nearby. Over time, as the colonies grew, orchard favorites like apples, pears, and rhubarb were brought over by ship as cuttings to create replicas of their English cottage gardens. They fished. They imported chickens and cows. Life became better.

We all know the rest of the story. While we celebrate Thanksgiving as a national holiday of coming together to share a meal for the common good, folks of Native American descent will tell you it's a day of mourning for Indigenous communities that have suffered diaspora, cultural fragmentation, and discrimination for generations as they were pushed off once-communal native lands.

For a century or more, agriculture continued to play a central role in New England life. But abundant fishing stocks, including cod, haddock, halibut, and flounder, had drawn fishermen from across the Atlantic to these distant shores for centuries. It's no surprise then that fishing became the first colonial industry in New England. The serpentine coastline was also home to a thriving salt industry in Revolutionary times through the Civil War. Salt was in high demand, not just for seasoning but also for food preservation in the era before refrigeration, particularly for the fishing industry.

By the early to mid-1700s, another industry had taken hold: sugar. And with it came human trafficking on a massive scale. Slaves were shipped from West Africa to the Caribbean islands in exchange for sugar and molasses, which were brought to New England to make rum. Rum was then shipped to Europe and back to Africa as payment for more slaves. This is why rum and molasses feature so prominently in old colonial recipes. It cannot be overstated how much of a role the sugar trade, and therefore slavery, played in the burgeoning economies of the New England colonies. It has been said that the sugar industry was so profitable (artificially so, because the labor was forced and unpaid), it effectively bankrolled the entire Industrial Revolution. An estimated 11 million Africans were enslaved over 400 years.

The spice trade at the turn of the eighteenth century was another industry that affected the way New Englanders cooked. These fragrant powders and whole spices, like pepper, cinnamon, cloves, nutmeg, and mace, were prized for their medicinal value as well as their flavor. Dangerous round-the-world voyages were undertaken from Salem, Massachusetts, to the Indonesian spice islands halfway around the world, positioning Salem as the center of the North American spice trade for fifty years. These exotic flavors now define some aspects of traditional Yankee cooking, like our beloved pumpkin spice.

Meanwhile, textiles and manufacturing were starting to take hold in the cities. The ensuing years saw waves of migration. The Irish Potato Famine that began in 1845 saw the Irish immigrate to Boston in massive numbers. Large groups of Azorean Portuguese, along with smaller numbers of Germans, Scots, and French Canadians, came to work at manufacturing jobs and textile mills in Massachusetts. Polish and German Jews as well as Chinese immigrants began arriving around the same time. As people moved off farms and into the cities, dairy farms and larger agricultural operations sprouted up all over the region. Another wave around the turn of the twentieth century brought Italians and Russian Jews in droves, as well as more Portuguese, Armenians, and Black migrants from the South. Each brought their food traditions with them. More recently, New England has seen an influx of immigrants from India, Southeast Asia, Africa, Latin America, and the Caribbean. It will be interesting to watch New England food continue to evolve with every new generation to come.

The Essential New England Pantry

Like anything else, the better your ingredients, the better your final product will be. I recommend prioritizing ingredients that come directly from New England producers, organic growers, small farms, community co-ops, and other local businesses. They are more likely to be invested in the quality of their products, your health, and the well-being of the environment. Produce and dairy will be fresher, and the money you spend stays in the local economy. That said, use what you like and what your budget allows. The following is a list of products I recommend keeping in stock for the recipes in this cookbook.

Maple Syrup and Sugar

Real maple syrup has a flavor no corn syrup–based pancake topping can match (though I admit I kept a bottle of the cheap stuff on hand when the kids had sleepovers, knowing that a $30 bottle of pure maple bliss was too often abandoned on empty plates in very expensive puddles). Look for Grade A real maple syrup and then choose from the following color distinctions: Golden, Amber, Dark, Very Dark. I tend to prefer the amber and darker maple syrups for their interesting flavor profiles, but they're all delicious. Keep in mind that it takes about 40 gallons of sap to make 1 gallon of maple syrup, which is why it's priced like liquid gold. Always store maple syrup in the refrigerator after opening to preserve its flavor and freshness. Maple sugar is simply crystallized maple syrup. It can be stored at room temperature and used in place of sugar. Finely ground is best; it dissolves much more easily than the coarser grinds.

Molasses and Brown Sugar

Dark, syrupy molasses is a by-product of processing sugar into pure white crystals. Molasses is what's responsible for the characteristic bittersweet flavor of Boston baked beans and brown bread, and it adds moisture and sweetness to baked goods. Brown sugar (light and

Nestlé
Carnation
BEN'S
SUGAR SHACK
100% Pure
ORGANIC
Premium Quality
PURE VANILLA
EXTRACT
MORTON & BASSETT SPICES
M&B
SPICES
SAN FRANCISCO
NO ADDED SUGAR
All Natural ◆ Gluten Free
4 fl. OZ ◆ 118 ml
GROUND
NUTMEG
MORTON & BASSETT
SAN FRANCISCO

dark) is simply white granulated sugar that contains varying amounts of molasses added back in for flavor and color. Store brown sugar in airtight containers to prevent it from drying out.

Honey

Honey is concentrated flower sugar collected by honeybees. The resulting golden syrup has a distinct flavor that can include floral, herbal, even fruity notes, depending on the types of flowers the bees have visited. You can find it jarred, in squeeze bottles, or sold in its waxy comb. If the honey recrystallizes in the jar, it's still fine to use. Just gently warm it in the microwave in 20-second bursts and stir.

Cornmeal

One of New England's most important ingredients is native cornmeal, made by drying corn kernels and pounding them into a sandy meal. Cornmeal adds a pleasant rustic texture and sweet flavor to baked goods, cornbread, and johnnycakes.

Wheat Flour

We're lucky to have a company in New England that produces high-quality baking flour. King Arthur Flour, a local, employee-owned company in Norwich, Vermont, was originally established in Boston 200 years ago and is still going strong. I keep all-purpose flour, bread flour, and whole wheat flour in stock at all times.

Oats, Buckwheat, and Rye

These three cereal grains tolerated the New England climate far better than wheat, and therefore figured prominently in colonial baking. Rolled oats are made by steaming oat groats and then rolling them into flakes, which helps them cook faster and stay fresh longer. In addition to making delicious hot cereal and granola, oats add texture and whole grain nutrients to baked goods. Buckwheat, contrary to the name, contains no wheat or gluten at all. It's especially popular in Maine, where a special Acadian variety is grown for *ployes*, a rustic crepe. Rye is a hearty flour that was often mixed into early Yankee breads like anadama bread and brown bread. It also features prominently in pumpernickel bagels.

Nuts

Walnuts have long been a component of New England baking due to Britain's established trade routes with Asia and the Middle East, where the nuts were grown. These walnuts are sweeter than New England's native black walnuts, which have a much stronger, somewhat funky flavor. But there are other delicious indigenous nuts that grow throughout New England, if you can find them, including shagbark hickory nuts, butternuts, and hazelnuts. Always taste your nuts before baking to ensure they're fresh; the oils can turn rancid over time. Storing them in the freezer extends their life.

Spices

What would New England baking be without cinnamon, allspice, ginger, cloves, nutmeg, and mace (the funny red seed coating of the nutmeg). I would also add cardamom to my list of essential spices. Pumpkin spice is now commonly found in the spice aisle of the grocery store, but you can also make your own: Try equal parts (1½ teaspoons) ground cinnamon, ginger, nutmeg, allspice, with a pinch of ground cloves. Feel free to play around with the amounts until you find your own signature blend. It has often been suggested that you replace your spices every year because they lose their potency over time, but that can get awfully expensive and rather wasteful. Instead, if your spices have been sitting around for a while, just increase the amounts until you get the intensity you're looking for.

Rum

Rum is made from fermented molasses, the by-product of sugar processing. Always a popular beverage in New England, it was also used to flavor cakes and cookies in place of vanilla. I use dark rum for the deep, caramelized flavor it has from spending time in charred oak casks.

Dried Beans

At their best, dried beans are tastier and less expensive than canned. But the truth is, dried beans that have been sitting around for years and years won't end up as tender and creamy as dried beans that are reasonably young. Buy local for peak freshness. The best beans for Boston baked beans are indigenous heirloom varieties like yellow-eye and trout (Jacob's cattle), but Marfax and navy beans are also very popular. See "New England Resources" on page 240 to stock up on dried beans from New England farms. Keep in mind that most require an overnight soak before long, slow cooking. They are delicious in soups, stews, and succotash year-round.

The Essential *Dim Sum* Pantry

Here's a list of some basic Cantonese ingredients you'll need for the homemade *dim sum* recipes in this chapter. Most of them can be found in the ethnic section of the grocery store.

For others, you may need to turn to your local Asian market, H-Mart, or online. For more information see "New England Resources" on page 240.

Tea

Dim sum is always served with pots of tea at the center of the table. Jasmine tea (*Heung Pin*), a green tea scented with jasmine flowers, tends to be the default option, but other choices include light and herbal chrysanthemum tea (*Gook Fa*); well-rounded oolong (*Tit Kun Yam*); or earthy, strong Chinese black tea (*Po-Lay*). Looseleaf tea is traditional, but tea bags may be more convenient.

High-heat oil

For wok cooking, you need an oil that won't smoke at high temperatures. Choose a neutral oil with a high smoke point, like grapeseed, peanut, vegetable, or canola oil (not olive oil) for a clean flavor that's less likely to set off your smoke alarm.

Soy sauce

Probably the most important condiment in the Chinese kitchen is soy sauce, and you probably already have a bottle in your refrigerator. Made from fermented soybeans and wheat, it adds a salty, earthy flavor to dishes. These are the three I recommend:

Regular soy sauce: Sometimes called light soy sauce, this is what most folks consider to be your regular, everyday soy sauce (like Kikkoman). Salty and medium-bodied, this is the one to have if you can tolerate gluten and salt. Otherwise, there are low-sodium versions available.

Tamari: If you're gluten-sensitive, reach for tamari instead, which is made with rice instead of wheat. It tends to be saltier than regular soy sauce, so taste the food as you season so you don't overdo it.

Mushroom soy sauce: Sometimes called dark soy sauce, this sauce contains mushroom extract. It's inky brown, much thicker than regular soy sauce, and packs an umami punch. Use it in braised dishes like the Red-Braised Pork Belly on page 221 to give it a dark, rich color and flavor. Pearl River Bridge is a brand I like.

Chili paste

It's a good idea to keep the spice level on the milder side when cooking for a group. Then serve chili paste or chili oil at the table so individuals can increase the heat to their liking. Sriracha (commonly called rooster sauce, for its logo) is a popular spicy, tangy chili sauce found in most grocery stores. Sambal oelek is an Indonesian ground chili paste that has a similar flavor but quite a bit more texture and body, which I like. Gochuchang is a bewitching Korean chili paste that includes rice and fermented soybeans. Chili oil is exactly what it sounds like: oil that's been steeped with hot peppers until spicy. Even if you don't cook any of the *dim sum* recipes, I highly recommend keeping one of these in your refrigerator to punch up fried or scrambled eggs.

Sesame oil

There are two types of sesame oil: toasted and untoasted. Toasted sesame oil is what I call for in this book. It looks darker than untoasted sesame oil and has a deeper, "roastier" flavor. I add it in small quantities to finished dishes for flavor, not as a cooking oil, because it burns too easily.

Rice wine

Shaoxing cooking wine is a mild Chinese rice wine great for cooking. It comes in both white and a sort of tawny red. If you buy just one, buy white, since it's more versatile (but the darker one has more flavor). If you can't find it, you can substitute dry, non-oaked white wine or dry sherry with good results. Rice wine is not to be confused with rice vinegar; the latter has been further fermented to have a much stronger, acidic flavor.

Rice vinegar

This is a mild type of vinegar made by fermenting rice wine to increase its acidity. Rice vinegar has a nice clean flavor that adds tangy brightness to a dish. Choose unseasoned rice vinegar instead of seasoned. The latter has lots of added salt and sugar, which aren't needed.

Black vinegar

Also made from fermented rice, Chinkiang black vinegar is stronger and more deeply flavored than white rice vinegar. It imparts a juicy, smoky acidity. I encourage you to try to find it (I like Gold Plum brand), but if you come up short, you can substitute Worcestershire sauce or balsamic vinegar, depending on which flavor profile you prefer.

Rice

The Cantonese tend to use long- or medium-grain rice instead of short-grain rice. I really like jasmine rice, a long-grain rice with a floral scent. If you make a lot of rice, I recommend buying a simple rice cooker, as the process couldn't be simpler: Measure out the rice, water, and a little salt, then set it and forget it. Rice is also made into translucent noodles and vermicelli, which are perfect if you're allergic to gluten.

White peppercorns

The Cantonese tend to use more white pepper than black pepper. It adds a slightly floral note to the peppery profile. Often you can find dedicated plastic grinders filled with white peppercorns in the spice aisle of the grocery store. If you can't find them, you can substitute black pepper instead. It will have a slightly different flavor, but it will still be delicious.

Dried black mushrooms (shiitakes)

The Chinese often employ dried mushrooms instead of fresh to impart a more concentrated flavor and texture. Soaking them in hot water softens them while simultaneously creating a flavorful broth that can enhance the overall flavor of the dish. I always save the mushroom soaking liquid and freeze it to use in place of vegetable or chicken stock. When selecting dried shiitake mushrooms, choose ones with noticeably cracked caps, which indicate high quality. Fresh shiitakes can be substituted, but the flavor will be milder and the texture less meaty.

Baking Tips and Substitutions

Here are some baking tips to help you get consistent results from this cookbook.

Flour: When measuring any flour, I recommend fluffing it up with a whisk first. This will keep your baked goods nice and light. I use measuring cups and spoons, dipping and sweeping, then leveling with the flat side of a knife. If you prefer to weigh your flour, see the Weight Conversion Table on page xxi. The all-purpose flour in most recipes can be replaced measure-for-measure with gluten-free flour with good results. The exception is pie or pastry dough, which will likely be too difficult to roll out (but you can press it into the pie plate like cookie dough or use a gluten-free pie shell instead).

Yeast: I use active dry yeast for all my baking, and that's what I call for in this book. To activate it, mix with warm water and a bit of sugar first before adding it to the rest of the ingredients. You'll be able to see the yeast bubble and foam so you know it's alive (nothing puts a wrench in your baking plans faster than expired, inactive yeast). If all you have is instant yeast, you can substitute it for active dry in equal amounts, just make sure you check the expiration date first. Do not use "Rapid Rise" yeast; it's not suitable for long, slow rises in the refrigerator, which I often call for in brunch recipes. I store my yeast in the freezer so it lasts nearly indefinitely.

Butter: Real butter is the backbone of countless amazing pastries and brunch treats. When I call for cool room-temperature butter, I mean softened to the point that the butter can easily be creamed with an electric mixer, but not so soft that it's greasy, squishy, and half-melted. An hour or two at room temperature is sufficient. If you forget to take it out of the refrigerator ahead of time, you can quickly zap a stick of butter in the microwave for 5–10 seconds on high to soften (microwave times vary, so experiment with your own). Most of my recipes call for unsalted butter. To swap in salted butter, just reduce the salt in a recipe by ¼ teaspoon per stick. Keep in mind that unsalted butter doesn't keep as well as salted butter, so store it in the freezer if you don't plan to use it within a week.

Salt: For baking, I tend to use fine sea salt or table salt because they dissolve and disperse more easily than larger grains. For stovetop cooking, I find myself reaching for kosher salt or fine sea salt. When making substitutions, remember that the size of the grind affects how many crystals fit in your measuring spoon. A teaspoon of fine sea salt will pack together more tightly and therefore be saltier than the same volume of coarse sea salt.

Milk: Whole milk is usually best for baking because of its rich flavor and 3% milkfat. Low-fat milk (1% and 2%) can also be used, but it will yield a lighter product. One exception is custard, for which I prefer to use a leaner milk, like 1%, which creates a smoother, denser texture. Skim milk contains no fat at all, so I usually avoid it for baking (but if that's all you have, go ahead and try it). You're welcome to make dairy-free substitutions as needed, but I haven't tested them out specifically.

Cream: I use heavy cream (also called heavy whipping cream) for most of my baking needs. Instead of buying a separate container of half-and-half, I just measure out half milk and half cream as needed.

Buttermilk: Real buttermilk is the tangy by-product of the butter-making process. If you can't find real buttermilk, like Kate's, at your supermarket, you can substitute cultured buttermilk, powdered buttermilk (follow the directions on the package), or use a ratio of 1 tablespoon freshly squeezed lemon juice per 1 cup milk to achieve a similar level of acidity.

Yogurt: Yogurt is another fermented milk product that adds moisture and tang to baked goods. I'm particularly fond of Cabot's whole milk Greek yogurt, which is as thick as sour cream. If a recipe calls for plain yogurt and all you have is Greek, you can thin it with milk or water to the right consistency. Similarly, if a recipe calls for Greek yogurt and all you have is plain, you can drain the yogurt in a fine-mesh sieve over a bowl in the fridge overnight to get a thicker product.

Eggs: Large eggs are the standard for baking, but if you have a mixed dozen, try to pair the smaller sizes with the extra-large sizes to approximate a large egg. Eggs incorporate best into batters and doughs when they're at room temperature. If you forget to take the eggs out ahead of time, let them sit in a bowl of warm water for 10 or 15 minutes. If you're just learning how to separate eggs, I recommend cracking the egg into a bowl and gently scooping out the yolk with your hands, letting the whites slip between your fingers back into the bowl.

Weight Conversions

You may notice that I use volume rather than weight for measurements in this cookbook. That's because these recipes don't require the sort of precision that some baking books require. Nevertheless, if you're a serious baker and you prefer to weigh out your ingredients, here are some useful conversions for this book:

- 1 cup all-purpose flour: 130 grams
- 1 cup bread flour: 130 grams
- 1 cup whole wheat flour: 140 grams
- 1 cup rye flour: 105 grams
- 1 cup finely ground cornmeal: 140 grams
- 1 cup granulated sugar: 200 grams
- 1 cup light or dark brown sugar: 210 grams
- 1 cup confectioners' sugar: 120 grams

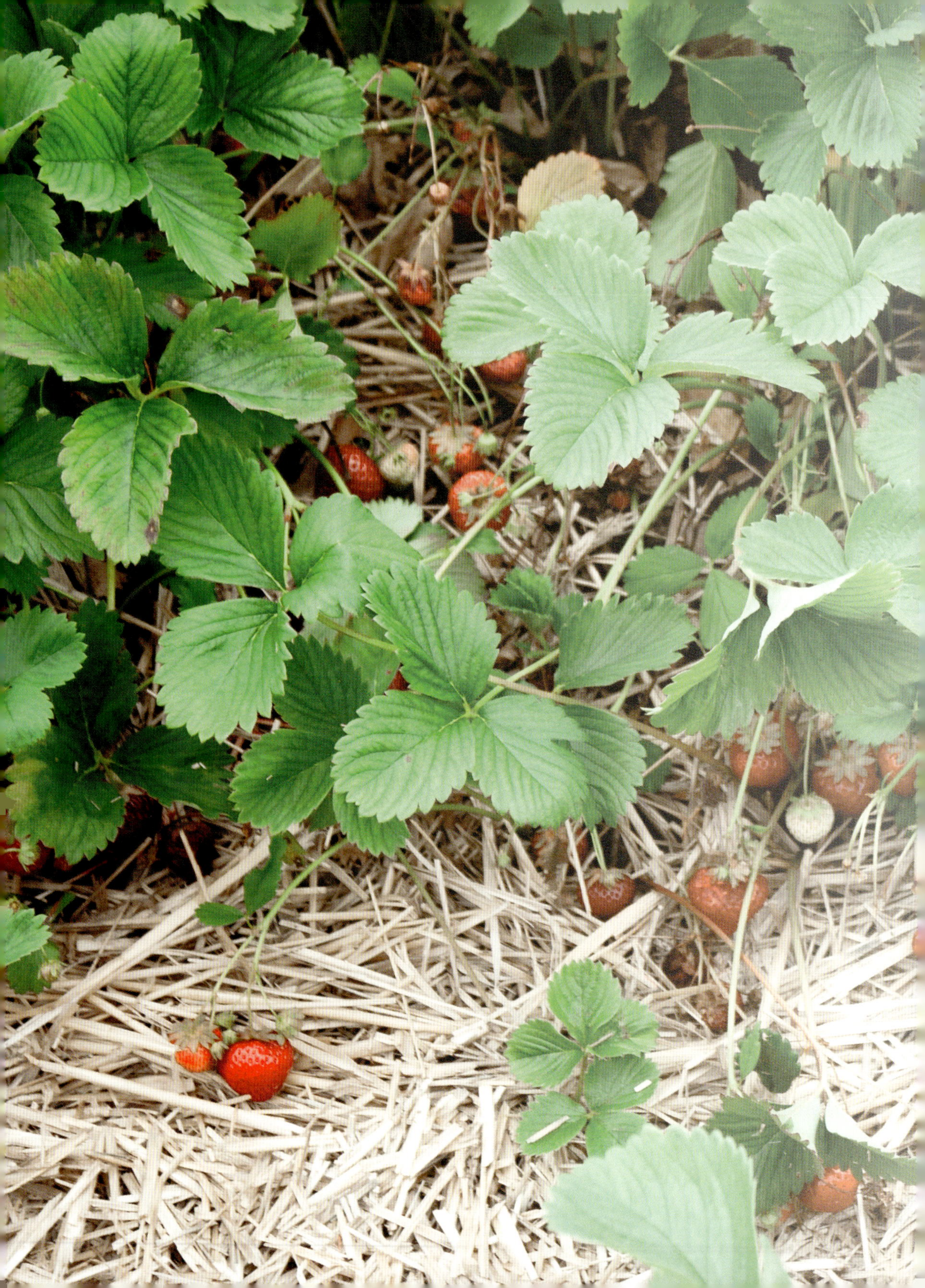

Spring

Corn Muffins 3

Whipped Maple Cardamom Butter 4

Old-Fashioned Sour Cream Doughnuts 5

Crepes with Strawberry Anise Compote 9

Dirt Bombs 12

Strawberry Rhubarb Scones 14

Portuguese Sweet Rolls 17

Stuffed Carrot Cake Muffins 19

Rhubarb Yogurt Parfaits with Ginger Granola 22

Boston Cream Doughnuts 24

Chocolate-Covered Strawberries 28

Pumpernickel Bagels 30

Asparagus Chive Frittata 32

English Muffins 34

Herbed Lobster Benedict 36

Simple Scrambled Eggs 39

Sheet Pan Bacon 40

Crispy Hash Browns 41

Simple Spring Pea Salad 42

Spinach and Feta Phyllo Crisp 45

Bloody Mary Mix 47

Strawberry Rhubarb Sangria 48

Spring, as I see it, is the beginning of brunch season. Our pantry supply of maple syrup has just been replenished for a new year of pancakes, waffles, crepes, and French toast. The receding blanket of snow gives light to the first young shoots of greenery, like chives and the first asparagus spears, flavorful ingredients that brighten up egg dishes. Tender lettuces, spinach, arugula, sweet peas, and radishes follow, creating fresh, lovely salads. And strawberries and rhubarb make their much-awaited appearance in buttery baked goods.

Springtime also offers a variety of special occasions for brunch celebrations: Easter, Mother's Day, Father's Day, graduations, bridal showers, baby showers, birthdays (not that you really need any occasion at all). A bright spring menu could include strawberry crepes with sweet mascarpone, rhubarb yogurt parfaits with ginger granola, or chocolate-covered strawberries dusted with cardamom seed. An assortment of homemade muffins or doughnuts is always a welcome sight. On the savory side, a make-your-own breakfast sandwich bar might be in order with homemade English muffins, sheet pan bacon, and scrambled eggs (don't forget the hot sauce!). Or try the showstopping-but-streamlined Lobster Benedict.

Festive get-togethers also call for festive beverages. Go sweet with the Strawberry Rhubarb Sangria or a little bit spicy with Bloody Marys. Arrange sprays of frothy spring flowers in empty honey or spice jars for simple but elegant centerpieces.

Spring Brunch Menu Ideas:

Easter Brunch: Sour Cream Doughnuts or Boston Cream Doughnuts. Asparagus Chive Frittata. Sheet Pan Bacon. Strawberry Rhubarb Sangria.

Mother's Day Brunch: Strawberry Rhubarb Scones or Chocolate-Covered Strawberries. Spring Pea Salad. Prosecco.

Father's Day Brunch: Herbed Lobster Benedict or Simple Scrambled Eggs. Sheet Pan Bacon. English muffins or Pumpernickel Bagels. Coffee or Bloody Mary.

Spring Birthday/Bridal/Baby Shower Brunch: Rhubarb Yogurt Parfaits with Ginger Granola or Crepes with Strawberry Anise Compote. Asparagus Chive Frittata. Strawberry Rhubarb Sangria or Prosecco.

Graduation Brunch: Dirt Bombs. Bagels and cream cheese. Fresh strawberries and Greek yogurt. Sheet pan bacon. Sparkling nonalcoholic apple cider.

Corn Muffins

We're starting off our New England brunch journey with corn, a staple of Native American cooking. These whole-grain muffins are great to make in the spring as we await all the beautiful fruit that would also be delicious in these muffins: blueberries and raspberries in the summer, sugar-dusted cranberries in the fall. I love splitting corn muffins across the equator and frying them in butter until golden brown. But for a more sophisticated brunch affair, try whipping some Maple Cardamom Butter (next page) to slather onto warm muffins fresh from the oven.

SERVINGS: MAKES 12

- 2½ cups all-purpose flour
- 1 cup yellow cornmeal
- 2 teaspoons baking powder
- ½ teaspoon baking soda
- 1 teaspoon fine sea salt
- ½ cup (1 stick) unsalted butter, melted
- ½ cup canola or vegetable oil
- ¾ cup light brown sugar, firmly packed
- 3 large eggs, at room temperature
- ½ cup sour cream, at room temperature
- 1 cup milk, at room temperature

Preheat the oven to 350°F. Grease or line a standard 12-cup muffin tin with liners.

In a medium bowl, combine the flour, cornmeal, baking powder, baking soda, and salt. Stir well. In a large bowl, stir together the melted butter, oil, and brown sugar with a sturdy wooden spoon. Beat in the eggs, one at a time. Add the sour cream and stir until combined. Gradually whisk in the milk. Then stir the dry ingredients into the wet just until combined. Divide the batter between the muffin cups (a 1.5-ounce cookie scoop works great).

Bake 25–28 minutes until the muffins are just starting to brown and the tops spring back when gently pressed. Let cool 15 minutes before serving. Leftovers can be covered and stored at room temperature for 3–4 days.

Whipped Maple Cardamom Butter

This delectable topping is great spread on warm corn muffins, English muffins, or scones.

MAKES 1 CUP

- 1 cup (2 sticks) unsalted butter, at room temperature
- 2 tablespoons maple syrup (preferably dark amber)
- ¼ teaspoon fine sea salt
- ¼ teaspoon ground cardamom

Use a handheld electric mixer to whip the softened butter until fluffy. Add the maple syrup 1 tablespoon at a time, whipping well and scraping down the bottom and sides of the bowl as necessary. Add the salt and cardamom. Whip well.

The butter can be stored at room temperature, where it will stay nice and soft, for about 2 days. For longer-term storage, keep in the refrigerator for about a week. Just be sure to take it out 1–2 hours ahead of time to soften at room temperature. (You can always rewhip if necessary.)

Old-Fashioned Sour Cream Doughnuts

I remember the glory days of Dunkin' Donuts when the doughnuts were actually good. Sadly, those days are gone—but rest assured, you can still make delicious doughnuts at home. These old-fashioned cake doughnuts are craggly and delicious, the way they should be. They remind me of the sour cream doughnuts from the Hole in One on Cape Cod, which my in-laws always have on hand when we bring the kids down for a visit. Here I've done my best to re-create what I love about those doughnuts, including the tantalizing way the glaze drapes itself into the nooks and crannies, crisping up mid-drip. See the variations below for Blueberry, Pumpkin Spice, and Chocolate Honey-Dipped versions. This recipe also makes killer plain doughnuts if you want to skip the glaze.

SERVINGS: MAKES ABOUT 8 DOUGHNUTS AND HOLES

Doughnuts

- 2 cups all-purpose flour
- 1 teaspoon baking powder
- ½ teaspoon baking soda
- 1 teaspoon salt
- ½ teaspoon ground nutmeg
- 2 tablespoons unsalted butter, softened
- ½ cup granulated sugar
- 2 large eggs, at room temperature
- ⅔ cup sour cream, at room temperature
- Vegetable or canola oil, for frying

For the doughnuts: Sift the flour, baking powder, baking soda, salt, and nutmeg together in a medium bowl.

With an electric mixer fitted with the whisk attachment, mix the butter and sugar together for about 1 minute on medium speed until sandy. Add the eggs, one at a time, scraping down the bottom and sides of the bowl as necessary. Whisk for about 2 minutes more until light and fluffy. Switch to the paddle attachment or use a wooden spoon to beat in one-third of the dry ingredients just until combined. Alternate adding half the sour cream and half the remaining dry ingredients, mixing on low or stirring by hand just until combined. Cover the bowl with plastic wrap and refrigerate for 30 minutes to 1 hour.

Heat the oil (2–3 inches deep) in a large, heavy-bottomed pot until a candy thermometer reaches 350°F–375°F.

Turn out the dough onto a well-floured counter, sprinkle with more flour, and roll out to a thickness of ½ inch. Using a 3¼-inch biscuit cutter or drinking glass, cut out as many circles as you can, flouring the cutter to prevent sticking. Gently pat the scraps together and reroll to make additional doughnuts. Use a 1¼-inch biscuit cutter to cut out the centers. (Don't have a cutter that size? Poke a hole with your finger and twirl the doughnut around on the floured counter.)

Add the dough to the hot oil in batches of 2 or 3, being careful not to crowd the pot and drive the oil temperature down. After

Glaze

3 cups confectioners' sugar, sifted

1½ tablespoons honey

4–6 tablespoons hot water

a few seconds, the doughnuts will float to the top. Fry for 75–90 seconds, until golden brown and cracked. Flip and fry the other side for 60–75 seconds until golden. Transfer to a rack set over a pan lined with paper towels to drain. For best results, glaze as soon as possible while still warm.

For the glaze: Sift the confectioners' sugar into a large bowl to remove any lumps. Whisk in the honey and 6 tablespoons of the hot water. Dribble in only as much additional water as it takes to make a smooth, runny glaze that still coats the back of a spoon well. If the slurry ends up too runny, add more confectioners' sugar. Dip the warm doughnuts into the glaze, one side at a time, letting the excess run off for a few seconds. Allow the doughnuts to dry completely on a rack until the glaze crisps up, at least 15–20 minutes.

Doughnuts are best consumed the day they're made. Store uncovered in a cool, dry place until ready to serve (humidity will cause the glaze to melt). However, if necessary, extras can be stored for a day or two in the refrigerator, covered with a dishtowel. To refresh day-old doughnuts, pop them in the microwave one at a time for 5–10 seconds on low just until warm, before the glaze starts to melt.

A note on frying: Be careful to minimize splashing when you place the doughnuts into the hot oil. Bring the dough as close to the oil as possible without burning yourself, and, when you let it go, make sure the top falls toward the back of the pot so it splashes away from you. The same goes for the doughnut holes. Don't plop them all in—use a slotted spoon and lower the dough balls into the oil, then wiggle the spoon out from underneath.

Variations

Blueberry Doughnuts: Omit the nutmeg and replace with cinnamon (or finely grated lemon zest). Add ½ cup fresh wild blueberries to the dough along with the last of the dry ingredients (you can also use frozen berries, defrosted and drained). Serve plain or glazed.

Pumpkin Spice Doughnuts: Substitute ⅔ cup pumpkin or squash puree for the sour cream. Replace the nutmeg with 1½ teaspoons pumpkin spice (to make your own, see page xv). Serve plain or glazed.

Chocolate Honey-Dipped Doughnuts: Reduce the flour to 1½ cups, increase the baking soda to 1 teaspoon, and omit the nutmeg. Add ½ cup natural unsweetened cocoa powder to the mix along with the 1 teaspoon baking powder and 1 teaspoon salt. In a small bowl or measuring cup, whisk together ⅔ cup sour cream, ¼ cup strong coffee (or ¼ cup hot water mixed with ½ teaspoon espresso powder), 2 tablespoons melted butter (instead of softened), and 1 teaspoon vanilla. With an electric mixer fitted with the whisk attachment, mix 2 large eggs and ½ cup granulated sugar together for about 2 minutes, scraping down the bottom and sides of the bowl as necessary. Switch to the paddle attachment or use a wooden spoon to alternate adding the dry and wet ingredients, mixing on low or stirring by hand just until combined. Cover the bowl with plastic wrap and refrigerate for 30 minutes. Proceed with heating the oil and shaping the doughnuts.

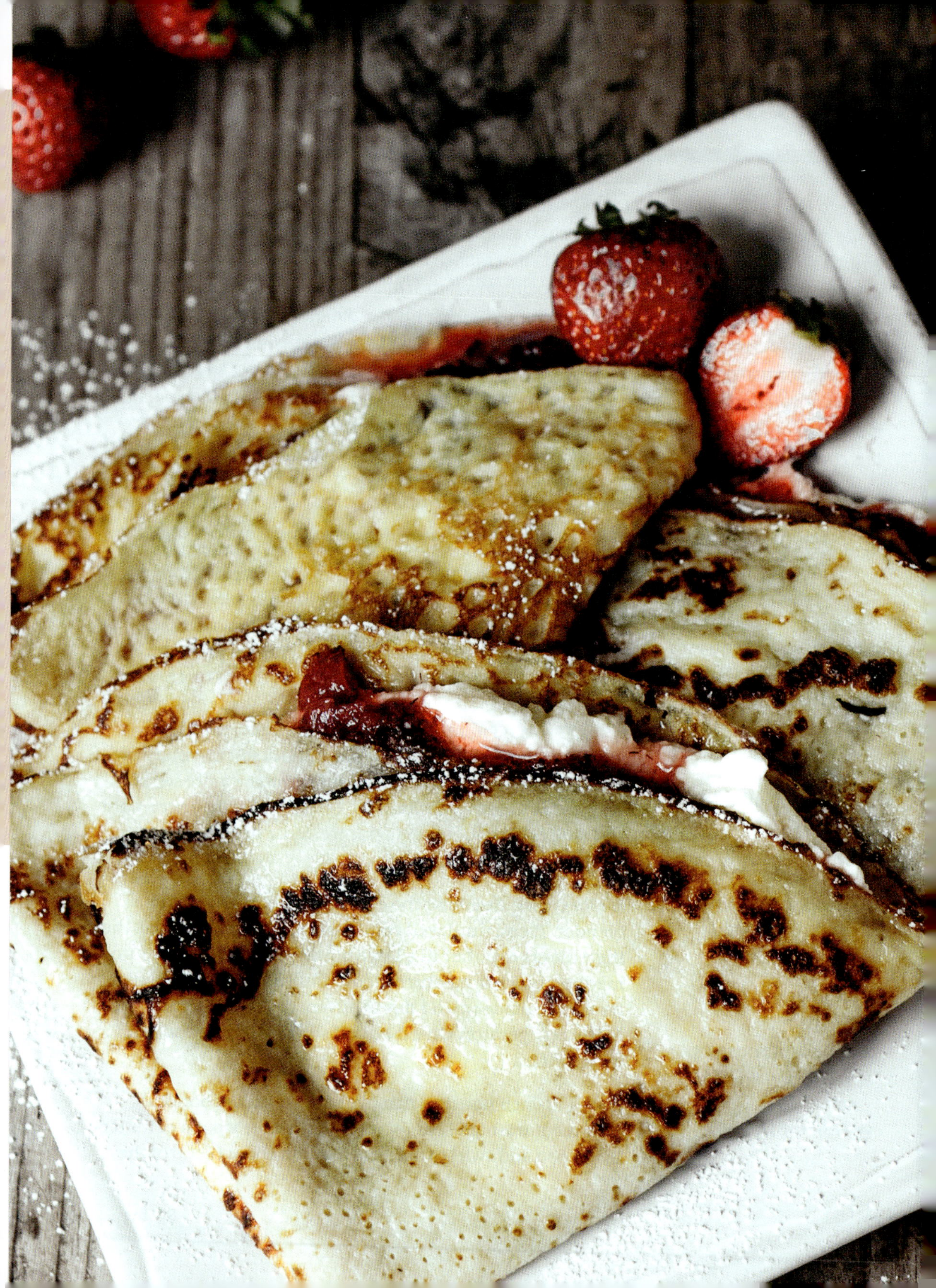

Filling

¼ cup granulated sugar
1 cup cold heavy cream
8 ounces mascarpone
Fresh strawberries, for garnish

batter and immediately swirl the pan to coat the entire bottom. Cook 1–2 minutes, until the edges are lacy and crisp and the underside of the crepe is a mottled golden brown. With a spatula, flip from the center and cook 30 seconds more until set. Let cool.

For the filling: Stir the sugar into the cream to dissolve. In a medium bowl, whip the mascarpone briefly to loosen, 5–10 seconds. Gradually, about ¼ cup at a time, add the cream to the mascarpone and whip with an electric mixer fitted with a whisk attachment on high just until soft and pillowy, 5–10 seconds. (If it ends up too thick, stir in more heavy cream by hand, 1 tablespoon at a time, until soft.)

To assemble: Spread some whipped mascarpone on one-half of a crepe. Top the mascarpone with Strawberry Anise Compote. Fold the crepe in half, then in half again. Set on a platter garnished with fresh strawberries.

The crepes can be stored in a stack, covered, in the refrigerator for up to 2 days. The whipped mascarpone is best when made fresh. Assemble right before serving.

Dirt Bombs

The name for these incredible muffins coated in cinnamon sugar comes from the wet fistfuls of sand kids used to hurl at one another on the beach (at least that's what my husband tells me). These muffins have been a mainstay at the Cottage Street Bakery in Orleans, Massachusetts, for years. Think of them as the best apple cider doughnuts you've ever had, but in muffin form. Everyone loves them, and they're easy to make. The next time you're heading to the Outer Cape, stop by and grab some before they run out. If they do, you can console yourself with a cranberry almond poppyseed muffin, another fan favorite.

SERVINGS: MAKES 12

3 cups all-purpose flour

1 tablespoon baking powder

½ teaspoon salt

½ teaspoon ground nutmeg

¼ teaspoon ground cardamom

¾ cup (1½ sticks) unsalted butter, at room temperature

1 cup granulated sugar

2 large eggs, at room temperature

1 cup whole milk, warmed to room temperature

Topping

1 cup (2 sticks) unsalted butter, melted

¾ cup granulated sugar

2 teaspoons ground cinnamon

Preheat the oven to 400°F. Grease a standard-size 12-cup muffin tin very well with butter (don't use muffin liners).

Sift the flour, baking powder, salt, nutmeg, and cardamom in a medium bowl.

With an electric mixer, cream the butter and sugar in a large bowl until light and fluffy, 2–3 minutes. Mix in the eggs, one at a time. Alternate the dry ingredients and the milk in two additions, mixing just until incorporated. Scrape down the bottom and sides of the bowl as necessary. Don't overmix or the muffins will be tough. Divide the batter between the 12 muffin wells, filling to the top.

Bake 20–25 minutes, until the tops are golden and a toothpick inserted into the center comes out clean. When the muffins are still warm, but cool enough to handle, turn them out onto a wire rack set over a sheet pan.

For the topping: Add the melted butter to one small bowl. Mix the sugar and cinnamon in a separate bowl. Dip the muffins (top, sides, bottom) in the butter. Use a pastry brush to touch up the spots you miss. Immediately roll the muffins in the cinnamon-sugar. Serve warm or at room temperature.

Leftovers can be covered and stored at room temperature for several days (but there will be no leftovers).

Strawberry Rhubarb Scones

These beautiful scones celebrate the long-awaited arrival of strawberries and rhubarb, a gardener's favorite spring pairing. Separately, they're delicious—together, they're magical. Striped with a glaze flavored with maple syrup and cardamom, these scones would be perfect to serve at a Mother's Day brunch alongside the Simple Spring Pea Salad (page 42).

SERVINGS: MAKES 8

Scones

- 2 cups all-purpose flour
- 1 tablespoon baking powder
- ¼ cup granulated sugar
- ½ teaspoon fine sea salt
- ¼ teaspoon ground cinnamon
- ¼ teaspoon finely grated lemon zest
- 6 tablespoons cold unsalted butter, cut into 6 pieces
- 1 cup heavy cream
- 1 cup chopped strawberries (¾-inch pieces)
- 1 cup chopped rhubarb (½-inch pieces)

Glaze

- 1 cup confectioners' sugar, sifted
- 2 tablespoons maple syrup
- 1 tablespoon water
- 2 teaspoons freshly squeezed lemon juice
- ½ teaspoon ground cardamom

Preheat the oven to 425°F. Grease a large 12 × 17-inch baking sheet or line it with parchment paper.

In the bowl of a food processor, combine the flour, baking powder, sugar, salt, cinnamon, and lemon zest. Process the mixture for a few seconds to blend. Add the cold butter and process 15–20 seconds, until the butter pieces are the size of small peas. (You can also cut the butter into the dry ingredients with a pastry blender or your fingers.)

Dump the mixture into a large bowl. Add the cream to the dry ingredients and fluff with a fork until it all comes together into a shaggy dough. Add the strawberries and rhubarb. Gently bring the dough together. Turn it out onto a floured surface and, with floured hands, fold the dough over on itself several times until it holds together. Gently pat the dough into a ¾-inch-thick disk. Cut it into 8 wedges like a pizza. Transfer the scones to the prepared pan and space them out at least 2 inches apart.

Bake 22–26 minutes, until the tops brown and the centers of the scones are set. Remove the pan from the oven and transfer the scones to a rack to cool.

For the glaze: Whisk together the confectioners' sugar, maple syrup, water, lemon juice, and cardamom. The glaze should be runny but still coat the back of a spoon. If it's too thin, add more sugar. If it's too thick, stir in water a few dribbles at a time until it reaches the right consistency. When the scones are cool, drizzle the glaze over the tops with a fork or a zip-top bag sealed tight with the tip of a corner snipped off. Let the icing air-dry for about 20 minutes.

Scones are best eaten the day they're made, but they can be stored, loosely covered, at room temperature for 2–3 days. The moisture in the fruit will cause the scones to soften over time.

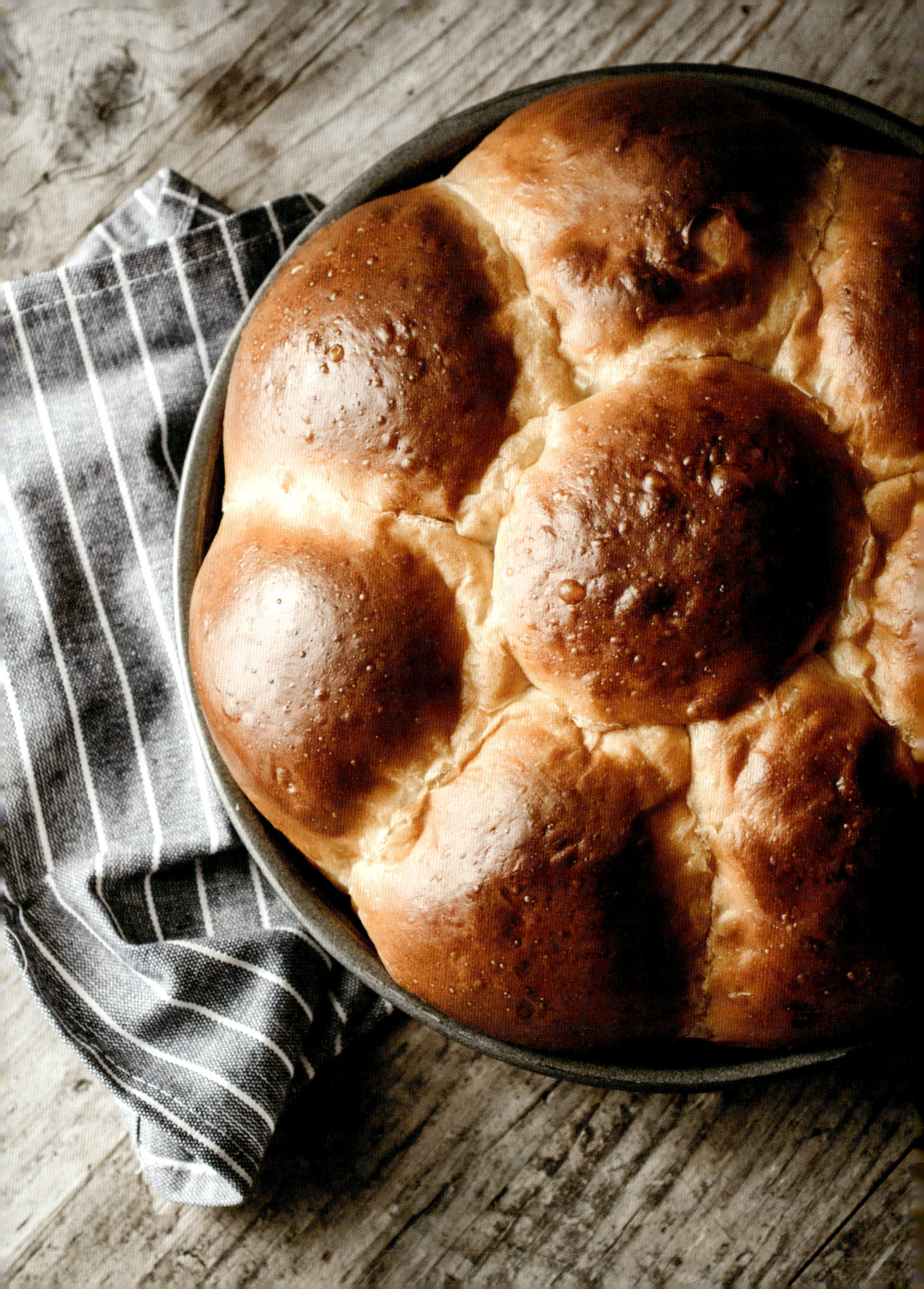

Portuguese Sweet Rolls

If you want your house to smell amazing as your guests arrive, have these sweet, pillowy rolls ready to pull out of the oven. The aroma is to die for. This traditional sweet bread hails from the Azores, an archipelago off the coast of Portugal where so many of New England's Portuguese community originated. These tender, fluffy rolls are often served at Christmas or Easter, but it's a simple enough bread to pull off on an everyday weekend too. Serve them warm, with butter and jam, alongside eggs and bacon or red flannel hash. Or try them with the Lobster Salad Sliders recipe on page 74. In the latter case, you'll want to omit the sugar topping and make twice as many smaller rolls (spread out between two cake pans) so you get the right ratio of bun to filling. Or do one pan plain and one pan sugared.

SERVINGS: MAKES 8 LARGE ROLLS OR 16 SMALL SLIDER ROLLS

- 2¼ teaspoons active dry or instant yeast
- ¼ cup warm (not hot) water
- ⅓ cup granulated sugar, plus ½ teaspoon for the top
- 4 tablespoons unsalted butter, at room temperature
- 2 large eggs, divided
- 3–3½ cups bread flour
- ½ cup warm (not hot) milk
- ½ teaspoon fine sea salt

In a small measuring cup, stir together the yeast, warm water, and a pinch of sugar to wake up the yeast.

In the bowl of a stand mixer fitted with a paddle attachment, cream the sugar and butter together on medium speed until fluffy, 1–2 minutes. Scrape down the bottom and sides of the bowl as necessary. Add the two egg yolks and mix well, about 30 seconds. Reserve 1 tablespoon of the egg whites in a ramekin for the topping. Add the remaining egg whites to the dough mixture along with 1 cup of the bread flour. Mix on low speed until combined. Add the yeast mixture and, starting on low speed, mix well, increasing the speed to medium until smooth. Add another 1 cup of the bread flour and, with the mixer running on low, gradually add the warm milk in a steady stream. Add the third cup of flour and the salt. Mix until the dough starts to come together in a shaggy dough. With a clean finger, touch the dough. If it's still sticky, mix in the last ½ cup of flour a little at a time until the dough feels tacky but no longer sticks.

Switch out the paddle for the dough hook and run on medium speed for 5 minutes to knead. (Don't leave the mixer unattended—the kneading motion can cause the machine to waddle over to the edge of the counter and dive off.) The bread can also be made with a handheld mixer or by hand and then kneaded with oiled hands to prevent sticking, but this is a messier process as the dough is quite soft.

Spring 17

Pour a bit of oil into a large bowl and rub it around with your hands. Scrape the dough into the bowl and, with your oiled hands, form it into a tight ball by gathering the sides of the ball and pulling them underneath. Roll the ball around in the bowl so it's coated in oil; set it seam side down. Cover the bowl with plastic wrap and let the dough rise until doubled in bulk, about 1 hour.

Grease a 9-inch cake pan and line with a circle of parchment paper. (If making slider rolls, grease and line two cake pans.)

Once the dough is doubled, punch it down with oiled hands. Cut the dough into 8 even pieces and form them into balls. Arrange them in the cake pan with one ball in the center and plenty of space in between. (If making slider rolls, cut the dough in half, form two balls, and cut each into 8 even pieces. Arrange them in two cake pans.) Cover and let rise until doubled, 45 minutes to 1 hour.

Preheat the oven to 350°F. Gently brush the tops of the rolls with the egg white mixed with 1 teaspoon water. Sprinkle with sugar, unless making slider rolls. For the bigger rolls, bake 30–35 minutes, rotating the pan once midway through baking, until the bread starts to split along the creases between the rolls. For sliders, bake 25–30 minutes. Let cool. Serve warm or at room temperature.

Once cool, rolls can be stored in a sealed plastic bag for 3–4 days at room temperature. Leftovers make great French toast.

Stuffed Carrot Cake Muffins

My family loves carrot cake, and I've included decadent recipes for it in both of my previous cookbooks, New England Desserts *and* Wintersweet. *This muffin recipe is a healthier version of the all-American carrot cake with cream cheese frosting. Here, the cream cheese—only lightly sweetened—is in the center. I've added dates for natural sweetness and walnuts for texture (if you don't like nuts, you can use rolled oats instead). To increase the whole-grain factor, I've added some whole wheat flour, but you could also use spelt or buckwheat. You could even substitute frost-sweetened, spring-dug parsnips for the carrots. For best results, make the cream cheese centers at least a day ahead of time so they can fully freeze (they bake up creamier that way). Or you can serve cream cheese on the side.*

SERVINGS: MAKES 12

Filling
- 8 ounces cream cheese, at room temperature
- 2 tablespoons confectioners' sugar
- 2 tablespoons heavy cream

For the filling: Beat the cream cheese and confectioners' sugar in a medium bowl with an electric mixer until smooth. Scrape down the sides of the bowl as needed. Mix in the cream, 1 tablespoon at a time. Portion the cream cheese into tablespoon-sized dollops (I use a ½-ounce cookie scoop), and set them spaced apart in a wide, flat, freezer-safe container with a lid (you should have at least 12 dollops). Freeze until firm, 3-plus hours or overnight.

Preheat the oven to 400°F. Grease or line the cups of a standard 12-cup muffin tin.

Spring 19

Rhubarb Yogurt Parfaits with Ginger Granola

I love the taste of cooked rhubarb all on its own. Its bright pink color is fun to showcase, layered with yogurt and gingery granola, in little jars or pedestal bowls. If you find yourself with rhubarb that's more green than pink, you can spruce it up with a handful of strawberries, raspberries, or a drop of red food coloring. I like to use chia seeds to bind the granola into light, crispy clumps; if you don't have chia seeds, you can stir in 2 unbeaten egg whites. All these components can be made a day or two ahead of time, then assembled right before serving. Save any extra granola for breakfast during the week.

SERVINGS: 4–6

Rhubarb Compote

- 1½ pounds rhubarb, stalks trimmed, cut into ½-inch pieces
- 1 cup granulated sugar
- 2 tablespoons freshly squeezed lemon juice
- 1 teaspoon vanilla extract

Ginger Granola

- 3 cups rolled oats
- 2 cups Grape-Nuts cereal
- ¼ cup light brown sugar, firmly packed
- 2 tablespoons whole flaxseed
- 1½ teaspoons fine sea salt
- ½ teaspoon ground cinnamon
- ¼ teaspoon ground ginger

For the rhubarb compote: Combine the diced rhubarb, sugar, lemon juice, and vanilla in a small saucepan. Cook over medium-low heat, stirring occasionally, 7–10 minutes, until the rhubarb is soft but still holds its shape. Remove from the heat and transfer the mixture to a medium bowl. Let cool. Cover and refrigerate overnight.

Preheat the oven to 300°F. Brush a large, rimmed 12 × 17-inch baking sheet with 1 tablespoon oil.

For the granola: Stir together the oats, Grape-Nuts, brown sugar, flaxseed, salt, cinnamon, and ginger in a large bowl. In a medium bowl, whisk together the oil, maple syrup, and vanilla. Add the wet ingredients to the dry. Mix well with a wooden spoon. In a small bowl or ramekin, stir together the chia seeds and water. Let them sit 5 minutes, until the water is absorbed and the seeds form a gray gel. Stir it well to loosen, then add it to the granola mixture, being careful to mash the chia gel into the dry ingredients until it's no longer visible. Spread the granola evenly on the prepared pan and press it flat with a spatula.

Bake 25–30 minutes, flipping the mixture twice during the baking time, and re-flattening it with a spatula. Remove from the oven and let it cool on the pan without stirring for 30 minutes to 1 hour. (It might still seem slightly damp, but it will firm up on sitting.) Loosen the mixture from the

- ½ cup grapeseed, vegetable, or canola oil, plus 1 tablespoon for the pan
- ⅓ cup maple syrup
- ½ teaspoon vanilla extract
- 1 tablespoon chia seeds
- 2 tablespoons water
- 3 tablespoons chopped crystallized ginger (optional)

Yogurt

- 3 cups plain yogurt (or Greek yogurt thinned with a little milk)

pan with a spatula and let it cool completely, then add the chopped crystallized ginger, if desired.

To assemble the parfaits: Layer the yogurt, rhubarb compote, and granola in thin layers (the more layers, the better for the prettiest presentation). Top with fresh strawberries or raspberries, if desired. Don't assemble the parfaits too far in advance or the granola will get soggy. You can even set out the components and let people assemble their own parfaits (there's no wrong way to layer the ingredients).

Granola can be stored in sealed jars for up to 3 weeks. The rhubarb compote can keep, covered, in the refrigerator for up to 5 days.

Boston Cream Doughnuts

These doughnuts, inspired by the famous Parker House Hotel's Boston cream pie, are a decadent combination of pillowy, yeasted dough filled with vanilla custard and topped with shiny chocolate ganache. Make the filling the day before so it's plenty cold and perfectly set. Start the dough the night before you plan to serve the doughnuts so the dough can slowly rise overnight in the refrigerator. Then allow 2–3 hours the next morning to shape, proof, fry, fill, and glaze the doughnuts. Once the glaze has set, serve the doughnuts with coffee, fresh fruit, and a side of bacon.

SERVINGS: MAKES 8–9

Dough

- 1½ teaspoons active dry yeast
- ¾ cup milk, warmed (not hot)
- 1 cup all-purpose flour
- 1 cup bread flour
- 1 teaspoon table salt or fine sea salt
- 2 tablespoons granulated sugar
- 3 large egg yolks
- 4 tablespoons unsalted butter, warmed to room temperature
- Vegetable or canola oil, for frying

For the dough: Stir the yeast into the warm milk. Let sit for 5 minutes to activate.

Meanwhile, in the bowl of a stand mixer (preferably fitted with the paddle attachment), combine the all-purpose flour, bread flour, salt, and sugar. Add the egg yolks and the milk mixture to the dry ingredients. Mix on low. Once the liquid is absorbed, increase the speed to medium and add the butter 1 tablespoon at a time. Once the butter is incorporated, continue mixing on medium to medium-high for 6–8 minutes, until the dough starts to pull away from the sides of the bowl. The dough will be very sticky and elastic.

Oil a large bowl. Scrape the dough into the oiled bowl with a scraper and turn the dough around in the bowl so it gets coated in oil on all sides. Cover the bowl tightly with plastic wrap and refrigerate 12–15 hours.

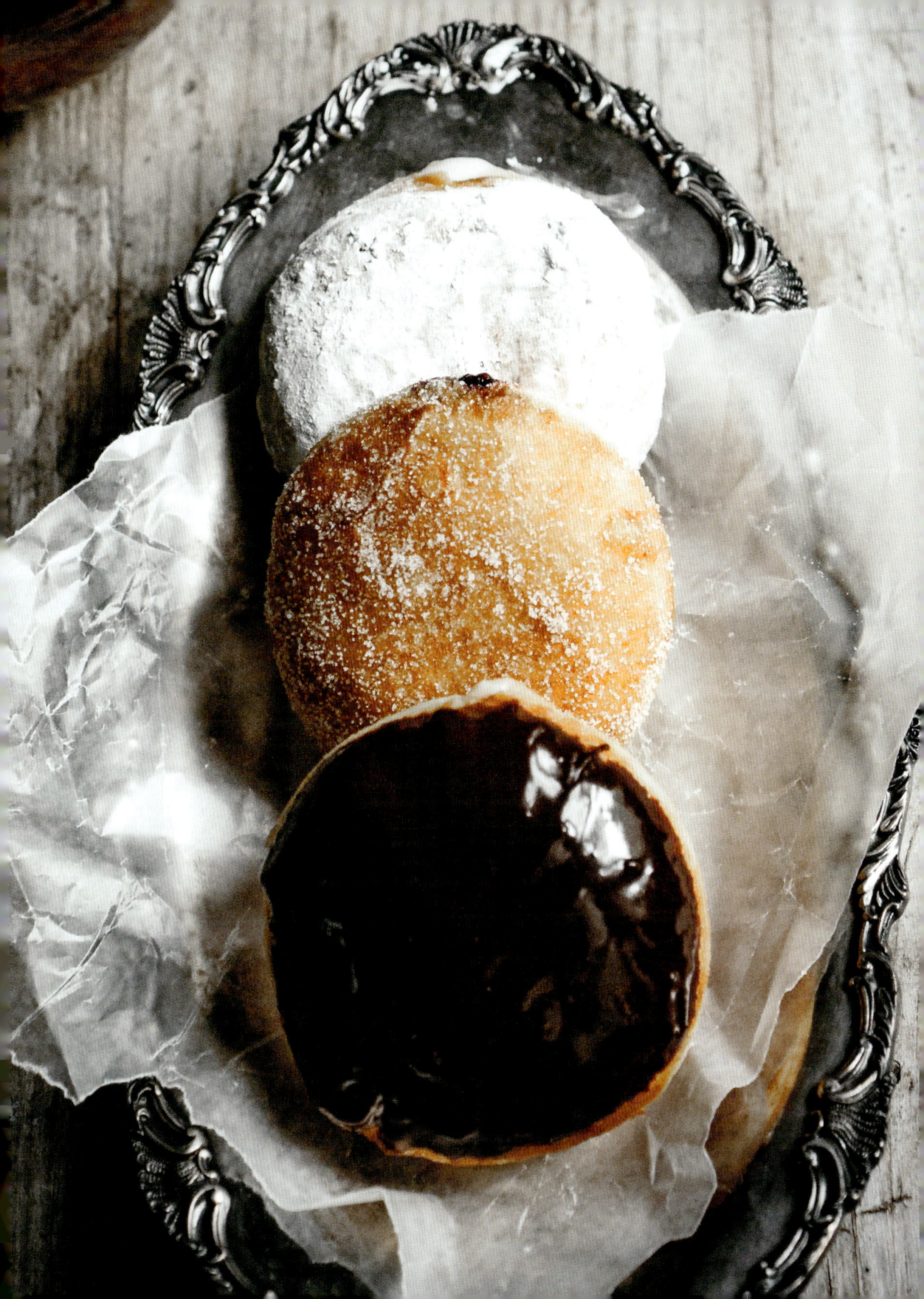

Filling

½ cup granulated sugar

3 tablespoons cornstarch

¼ teaspoon table or sea salt

2 large egg yolks

2 cups milk

2 tablespoons unsalted butter

2 teaspoons vanilla extract

Glaze

½ cup heavy cream

1 cup semisweet chocolate chips, divided

For the filling: Whisk together the sugar, cornstarch, and salt in a medium saucepan off heat. Whisk in the yolks and a generous splash of milk until no lumps remain. Gradually whisk in the rest of the milk. Set the pot over medium heat. Bring to a simmer, whisking the sides and bottom of the pot frequently to prevent lumps as the mixture thickens. Simmer 1–3 minutes, whisking constantly, until it achieves a pudding-like consistency. Remove the pan from the heat and add the butter. Switch to a wooden spoon and stir until the butter melts. Stir in the vanilla. Immediately transfer to a heatproof bowl. Cover with plastic wrap pressed right up against the surface to prevent a skin from forming. Poke several holes in the film with a toothpick to allow the steam to escape. Refrigerate overnight until cold and set.

For the doughnuts: The next morning, cut a sheet of parchment paper into 12 squares (you will only need 9, but these are the perfect size, and I save the extras for future doughnuts). Set 9 squares on a sheet pan and spray with nonstick spray. Set aside.

Remove the dough from the refrigerator. Scrape out the dough onto a lightly floured counter and gently press it ½ inch thick. Using a 3-inch round biscuit or cookie cutter, cut the dough into circles and transfer each one to a square of oiled parchment paper. Arrange them back on the sheet pan, cover with plastic wrap, and let proof 30–45 minutes in a warm place until puffed.

Meanwhile, add the vegetable or canola oil to a large Dutch oven or heavy stainless steel pot to a depth of 2–3 inches. Set over medium heat and insert a candy thermometer. Set up a cooling rack with a double layer of paper towels over a sheet pan nearby.

Once the oil temperature reaches 350°–375°F, transfer the proofed doughnuts one at a time to a slotted spoon, peeling off the parchment backs, and gently lower them into the hot oil. Fry about 3 at a time for 2–3 minutes per side, until golden brown. Drain on paper towels. Adjust the burner as needed to maintain the optimum temperature window so the doughnuts don't get too greasy (temperature too low) or have undercooked centers (temperature too high). Let the doughnuts cool completely.

To make the chocolate glaze: Heat the cream with half the chocolate chips in the microwave for 30 seconds to 1 minute (or in a small saucepan over medium-low heat), stirring occasionally until melted. Remove from the heat. Stir in the rest of the chocolate chips until completely smooth.

To assemble the doughnuts: Use a sharp-tipped paring knife to cut an X in the side of each doughnut, then push the knife gently into the center. (I also fan the blade slightly inside the doughnut to make room for more cream. Just be careful not to go all the way through to the other side.)

Use a piping bag fitted with a long nozzle, if you have one (I use Wilton tip #230). If not, use what you have or use a zip-top plastic bag with the corner snipped off. Fill the bag three-fourths of the way with the chilled vanilla cream. Insert the tip of the pastry bag into the hole in the side of each doughnut and squeeze slowly until the doughnuts are full. (If you fill them too much, the cream will leak out of the hole when doughnuts are set on their sides.)

Dip the filled doughnuts, top side down, in the chocolate glaze and then let them sit chocolate-side-up until set. If the chocolate firms up too soon, just microwave gently for 15 seconds or so and stir until loosened.

Keep doughnuts refrigerated until ready to serve. Doughnuts are best eaten the day they're made, but these can keep covered in the refrigerator for several days.

Variation

Bavarian Cream: Omit the chocolate glaze. Let the doughnuts fully cool before sugaring. One at a time, dredge each doughnut in a bowl with 1 cup confectioners' sugar (sifted, if lumpy). Shake off the excess. Follow the instructions to fill each doughnut with vanilla cream.

Chocolate-Covered Strawberries

Fresh, local strawberries are a delectable treat unto themselves. But if you want to add that special something to a Mother's Day brunch or bridal shower, try these chocolate-covered strawberries. You can make them with white or dark chocolate. Sprinkle them with flaky sea salt, chopped nuts, or my personal favorite: dusting them with crushed green cardamom seed. Cardamom pods can be found at Indian and South Asian markets (do not substitute black cardamom pods, which have a smoky flavor). Try to source strawberries locally or from an organic grower to minimize pesticide exposure (strawberries are known to soak up pesticides like a sponge—no thank you). I don't enjoy tempering chocolate and avoid it at all costs. Instead I use a lazy microwave method whenever possible, which allows you to melt the chocolate without taking it out of temper (meaning the chocolate retains a specific chemical structure that yields a shiny finish and pleasing snap). Every microwave is different, however, so you will need to experiment with your own. Go by visual cues rather than specific times. When in doubt, be conservative with the heat, and stir often.

SERVINGS: MAKES ABOUT 16

- 1 pound fresh, ripe strawberries
- 4 ounces dark chocolate (70%), finely chopped (not chocolate chips)
- 4 ounces white chocolate, finely chopped (not chocolate chips)
- Crushed whole green cardamom seed (pods removed)
- Finely chopped, toasted hazelnuts or walnuts
- Flaky sea salt

Wash and dry your strawberries well, letting them continue to dry on a dishtowel or double layer of paper towels. Line a baking sheet with parchment paper.

Add the chopped dark chocolate to a small, microwave-safe bowl. Heat on high power in 15-second increments, stirring in between. Once the chocolate pieces start to melt, decrease the cook time to 10 seconds and stir for at least 10 seconds in between each burst of heat to give the chocolate a chance to melt from the residual heat. When the chocolate is mostly liquid with a few unmelted pieces of chocolate, reduce the cook time to 5 seconds, being sure to stir well between bursts, until fully melted. The idea is not to overheat the chocolate and take it out of temper. Use immediately.

One by one, dip half the strawberries into the melted chocolate, holding on to the green tops, tipping them while rotating until they're fully coated almost up to the top. Let the excess chocolate drip off; set strawberries on the parchment-lined pan. Immediately sprinkle the chocolate with toppings, if desired, before the chocolate sets. If drizzling with white chocolate, let the chocolate set first. Transfer the remaining melted chocolate into a zip-top plastic bag and seal it.

Repeat the process for the chopped white chocolate in a separate small, microwave-safe bowl. When the remaining strawberries are dipped and sprinkled, transfer the remaining melted white chocolate into a zip-top plastic bag and seal it.

Once the chocolate has set, you can drizzle the strawberries with contrasting chocolate. Make sure the chocolate in the zip-top bags hasn't solidified again. If it has, put the bags in the microwave and heat for 3–4 seconds, squishing the chocolate around in the bags with your hands to distribute the heat. You want the chocolate to be melted and fairly runny, but not hot. Snip the very tip of one corner of each bag. Drizzle some of the strawberries with chocolate (for a professional look, drag the drizzle past the sides of the strawberries onto the parchment paper before reversing direction).

Store the strawberries in the refrigerator to chill and allow the chocolate to fully set. Chocolate-covered strawberries are best eaten the day they're made. Keep leftovers in the refrigerator for a day or two, but they'll start to release their syrupy juices over time.

Pumpernickel Bagels

New England isn't exactly famous for its bagels, sandwiched as it is between two bagel meccas, New York City and Montreal. But you can absolutely find delicious bagels all over New England, particularly in the Boston area; Portland, Maine; and Burlington, Vermont. Bagels were originally created by Jewish bakers in what is now Poland, where historical borders shifted often between Russia, Prussia, Austria, and Germany. Written records from Krakow mention bagels as early as 1610, but bagels didn't arrive in the United States until the late nineteenth century, when Polish, Russian, and German Jews immigrated to the East Coast in large numbers. Bagels differ from other types of bread in that the circular rings of dough are boiled before baking, giving them their signature chew and crackly crust. Pumpernickel is one of my favorite flavors. As with the other bagel recipes in this book, I've spread the work out over two days so you can have fresh bagels on the morning of Day 2 instead of the evening of Day 1.

SERVINGS: MAKES 8

- 1 tablespoon active dry yeast
- ½ teaspoon light brown sugar, firmly packed
- 3½ cups bread flour, divided
- 1½ cups pumpernickel or dark rye flour, divided
- 1⅓ cups warm water, plus ¼ cup warm water for the yeast
- 3 tablespoons molasses (not blackstrap)
- 2 tablespoons caraway seeds
- 2 tablespoons unsweetened dark cocoa powder
- 1 tablespoon kosher salt, plus more for boiling water
- 1 tablespoon barley malt syrup (or molasses)

In a small bowl, combine the yeast, brown sugar, and ¼ cup warm (not hot) water. Let sit until foamy while preparing the other ingredients.

To a large bowl (with or without the help of a stand mixer fitted with the paddle attachment), add 2 cups bread flour and 1 cup pumpernickel flour. Add 1⅓ cups warm water; mix to blend. Add the yeast mixture and blend well. Add the molasses, caraway seeds, and cocoa powder; mix well. Add 1 cup bread flour along with the kosher salt; mix well. Gradually add ½ cup pumpernickel flour and mix until you get a stiff dough. Depending on your flour, you may need to add up to ½ cup additional bread flour until you have a very stiff dough that isn't at all sticky.

At this point, turn the dough onto the counter and knead for 10–15 minutes until smooth, or switch out the paddle attachment for a dough hook and run on medium-low for the same amount of time (do not leave the mixer unattended—the motion tends to cause the machine to inch dangerously close to the counter's edge).

Place the dough in a clean, oiled bowl and cover with plastic wrap or a damp towel. Let rise at room temperature until nearly doubled in bulk, about 1½–2 hours.

Line a rimmed 12 × 17-inch baking sheet with parchment paper. Punch the dough down all over to degas it. Turn it out onto the counter in a round disk. Cut the dough into eighths, like a pizza. Shape the bagels by forming each piece of dough into a tight ball, pushing your thumb through the center to form a hole, and, using both pointer fingers revolving around each other, gently stretch out the hole in the center. Set the bagels on the prepared pan with at least 1 inch of space between them. Cover the baking sheet with plastic wrap and refrigerate overnight, 12–18 hours, until puffed but not quite doubled in bulk.

The next morning, set a large pot half full of water to boil (cover the pot for faster heating). Preheat the oven to 425°F. Line a second pan with parchment paper.

Remove the bagels from the refrigerator. The bagels should have puffed slightly, but not yet doubled in bulk. With scissors, cut the parchment paper around the bagels without jostling them too much so they don't lose air. They should each be resting on their own little mat of parchment paper.

When the water comes to a rolling boil, add a generous pinch of salt and the malt syrup (or molasses). Stir with a wooden spoon to dissolve. Gently slip the bagels into the boiling water, parchment paper on top, 2 or 3 at a time. Set the timer for 30 seconds and gently peel the parchment paper off. It should lift off easily. Flip the bagels over and simmer 30 seconds more. Remove bagels with a slotted spoon and place them on the prepared pan to dry slightly. Repeat with the remaining dough.

Bake the bagels for 18–22 minutes on the middle rack of the oven until golden brown. Remove from the oven and let cool before serving. Leftovers can be stored in a sealed plastic bag at room temperature for a few days; freeze, tightly wrapped, for longer storage.

Asparagus Chive Frittata

My husband makes the best frittatas, bar none. Broccoli and cheddar. Spinach, peppers, and feta. I've hesitated to learn his secret because even food writers need some time off from cooking once in a while. Then again, why should I be the only one who gets to enjoy spectacular frittatas? So I asked him to spill the beans, so to speak, and now I'm teaching you. I created the spring version with asparagus, chives, and a few handfuls of Gruyère, which has now been added to the family repertoire.

SERVINGS: 4–6

1 bunch asparagus

2 tablespoons olive oil, divided

8 large eggs

2 tablespoons milk

1 tablespoon sliced chives, divided

½ teaspoon kosher salt

Black pepper and garlic powder to taste

½ cup shredded Gruyère cheese

Snap off the tough, woody ends of the asparagus where they naturally break (near the bottom third of the stem). Cut the remaining stalk into bite-sized pieces.

Heat an 8- or 10-inch, oven-safe sauté pan over medium heat. Add 1 tablespoon olive oil and swirl to coat the bottom of the pan. Add the asparagus and cook, stirring occasionally, until crisp-tender, starting to brown in spots, but still bright green (about 4–6 minutes, depending on thickness). Transfer the asparagus to a plate and wipe out the pan.

In a large bowl, whisk the eggs with the milk. Add half the chives, the salt, and a few shakes of black pepper and garlic powder. Whisk well. Stir in the asparagus with a wooden spoon until well distributed.

Heat the medium sauté pan over medium heat. Swirl in the remaining 1 tablespoon olive oil. Pour the egg mixture into the pan all at once. Let cook undisturbed until the edges start to set. With a spatula, gently lift an edge, tip the pan, and let the uncooked egg run underneath. Continue this process all around the pan until there's no more runny liquid. If the center seems loose, you can do the same thing in the center. Once the egg is almost, but not fully, cooked, preheat the broiler to high. Add the cheese in several small piles around the frittata so it melts and pools.

Place the pan in the oven and broil on high, keeping a close eye on it, until the cheese is melted and starting to brown, 3–5 minutes. Remove from the oven and sprinkle with the remaining chives. Serve warm.

English Muffins

Englishman Samuel Bath Thomas opened a New York City bakery in 1880 that popularized these individual yeast-leavened breads so common in British cookery. Closer to English crumpets than American muffins, they've charmed generations of Americans ever since. But this version has converted me to homemade forevermore, thanks to the ample nooks and crannies that cradle soft butter and jam. English muffins are cooked on a griddle or hot pan rather than in the oven. It may seem like there's not enough yeast in this recipe, but the long room-temperature overnight fermentation means there's plenty of time for the yeast to bubble away. Just remember to start the dough the night before. They're spectacular simply buttered but can also be transformed into fantastic diner-style breakfast sandwiches or fancy-schmancy Herbed Lobster Benedict (page 36).

SERVINGS: MAKES ABOUT 8

- 2½ cups all-purpose flour
- ½ teaspoon table salt or fine sea salt
- ¼ teaspoon active dry or instant yeast
- ⅔ cup milk, heated to lukewarm in the microwave
- ½ cup warm water
- 1 tablespoon unsalted butter, melted
- Cornmeal

The night before serving: Whisk together the flour, salt, and yeast in a large bowl. In a small bowl, combine the warm milk, water, and melted butter. Stir the wet ingredients into the dry until they just come together into a shaggy dough. Scrape down the sides of the bowl and cover tightly with plastic wrap. Let the dough sit out at room temperature overnight for 12–18 hours.

In the morning: The dough should have doubled in size. Set a sheet of parchment paper on the counter and dust with a handful of cornmeal. Scrape the dough onto the paper. Dust with flour, cover with the plastic wrap, and let rest for 10 minutes.

Pat down the dough about ¾ inch thick. Using a 3-inch biscuit or cookie cutter dusted in flour, cut out rounds and set them on the free areas of the parchment paper, adding more cornmeal if necessary to prevent sticking. Scraps can be pressed together to make more muffins. Dust the tops of the muffins with a little flour and cover with plastic wrap. Let them proof for 40–45 minutes, until they are puffed but haven't yet doubled in bulk. Cut the parchment around the muffins into little squares to help transfer them to the griddle.

Heat a large nonstick or cast iron skillet or griddle over medium-low heat. In batches of 4, tip off any extra cornmeal from the parchment and gently transfer the muffins to the dry pan, parchment side up. Gently remove the parchment paper (if it sticks, use a spatula to help scrape the dough from the bottom of the paper). Cook on one side, covered with a pot lid, checking after 2 minutes. You may need to rotate the muffins a half-turn for even browning. Cook 2–4 minutes more until golden brown. Flip the muffins with a spatula and cook, covered, checking after 2 minutes to see if they need rotating. Cook 2–4 minutes more, until golden brown and the centers are fully cooked through (a thermometer inserted into the center should read 200°F). Let the muffins cool slightly on a rack while making the second batch, first wiping the excess cornmeal from the pan.

For best results, split the English muffins with a fork instead of cutting them with a knife. Perforate the sides with the tines of the fork, and then pry them apart before toasting. Leftovers can be stored in an airtight bag in the refrigerator for about a week. They can also be frozen, tightly wrapped, for at least a month.

Variations

Cinnamon Raisin: Stir 1 cup raisins and 2 teaspoons ground cinnamon into the dry ingredients before adding the wet ingredients. Let them proof a full hour before cooking.

Cranberry: Stir 1 cup dried cranberries and 1 teaspoon ground allspice into the dry ingredients before adding the wet ingredients. Let them proof a full hour before cooking.

Herbed Lobster Benedict

Honestly, I usually find eggs Benedict to be a little rich. What makes this version work for me, besides the succulent lobster and fried eggs, is the garlic-rubbed English muffin with a slice of heirloom tomato under it all, a dollop of lemony hollandaise, and a confetti-like sprinkling of herbs on top. I love chives and summer savory, but tarragon or lemon thyme would also work nicely. If you're too scared or lazy to make the hollandaise, I think it's just as good without it—just squeeze a little lemon juice over the top before serving (there's plenty of butter on the lobster and runny egg yolk to self-sauce). Then again, nothing says "brunch diva" like lobster and a perfectly made hollandaise. Why not give it a try? Vegetarians might consider replacing the lobster with steamed or roasted asparagus spears.

SERVINGS: 6

Lobster

2 (1½-pound) cooked lobsters (or 1 pound frozen lobster meat, defrosted)

6 tablespoons unsalted butter

Hollandaise

½ cup (1 stick) unsalted butter, melted

2 large eggs yolks

2 teaspoons freshly squeezed lemon juice, plus more to taste

1 tablespoon water

Pinch of finely grated lemon zest

Shake or two of Tabasco sauce (optional)

Salt and white pepper to taste

Assembly

3 whole English muffins, store-bought or homemade (see recipe on page 34)

Olive oil

6 large eggs

2 ripe tomatoes

1 small clove garlic

2 teaspoons chopped fresh chives

1 teaspoon chopped fresh summer savory

Salt and paprika to taste

For the lobster: Using a dishtowel to protect your hands, break the lobster tail, claws, and front arms from the rest of the body by quickly snapping in the direction in which you feel the most resistance. With a sharp chef's knife, firmly cut down the center of the underside of the tail. Wrap the tail in a dishtowel and, holding the sides of the tail firmly, bend the tail backwards to open. Unwrap and pull the meat out. With lobster crackers, crack the claws and knuckles. Pull out the cooked lobster meat with a pick, again using a dishtowel so the sharp shells don't cut your skin. Chop the lobster meat into bite-sized chunks and set aside in a small bowl. (If using frozen lobster, defrost and set aside in the refrigerator.)

For the hollandaise: Melt the butter in the microwave or a saucepan on the stove. Pour it into a measuring cup for easier pouring and let it cool while preparing the rest. Whisk the egg yolks, lemon juice, water, and pinch of salt in a small glass bowl that can nest in a small saucepan over an inch of simmering water without the bottom touching the water. Over low heat, whisk the yolks constantly until they foam and double in volume (it happens quickly—sometimes less than 1 minute). Immediately remove the bowl from the heat and dribble in a tiny bit of melted butter (say, ⅛ teaspoon) while whisking enthusiastically. Continue dribbling and whisking until you've incorporated about half the butter. Then you can whisk in the rest more quickly until combined. If it's too thick, add another 1 tablespoon water. (For this preparation, I like it thick enough to dollop, but you may prefer it runnier). Stir in the lemon zest, Tabasco (if desired), and salt and pepper to taste. To keep the hollandaise warm before serving, store it in an insulated thermos preheated with hot water (just dump out the water and add the sauce); it will hold for 2 hours or so.

When ready to serve: Melt 6 tablespoons butter in a small pan and gently heat the lobster over low heat. Remove from the heat and cover to keep warm.

To assemble: Split and toast the English muffins. When they are crispy, halve a garlic clove and rub the cut side all over the nooks and crannies while the muffins are still warm. If you have help, you can assign someone this task and to slice the tomatoes while you take care of the eggs.

Fry the eggs in a little olive oil in a nonstick pan. You can fry them individually over easy, but for a crowd it's usually easier to crack them one at a time into the pan, letting them settle into their own quadrants. Cook about 2 minutes over medium heat until the outer whites set. Then add a tablespoon or two of water and cover until the inner whites are set but the yolks are still a little runny. Then cut through the cooked whites with a spatula so everyone gets a yolk. Alternatively, you can use a spatula to cut through the whites of the partially cooked eggs and flip each egg individually, so some are over easy and some are well-done. Season with salt and pepper.

On each buttered English muffin half, set a slice of tomato, a fried egg, and one-sixth of the buttered lobster over the top. Add a dollop of hollandaise and sprinkle liberally with chopped herbs and perhaps a pinch of paprika. Serve immediately.

How to Poach Eggs

If you'd rather poach eggs the traditional way, here's what to do. Fill a medium saucepan halfway with water. Add a pinch of salt to the water and bring to a bare simmer (little bubbles rising to the surface occasionally). One at a time, crack an egg into a ramekin, keeping the yolk intact. Gently pour the egg into the simmering water close to the surface. Repeat for the remaining eggs, keeping plenty of space between them. Cover with a lid and cook about 4 minutes or so, until the whites are set but the yolks are still runny. Remove with a slotted spoon to a shallow baking dish. Partly cover to keep warm until ready to serve.

Troubleshooting Hollandaise

A broken hollandaise happens to everyone at one time or another, but don't throw it away. You can rescue it by restarting with a tablespoon of boiling water in a clean bowl and gradually whisking in the broken sauce, a few drips at a time, adding more and whisking well all the while until it comes together. Keep warm in a preheated thermos.

Simple Scrambled Eggs

Why include a recipe for something as simple as scrambled eggs? Because I've made a lot of bad scrambled eggs in my day, mostly due to over-stirring and/or overcooking. If you don't already have a favorite way to make scrambled eggs, try this method. It's a lot like making an omelet, and it will break you of your habit of over-stirring if you fall into my camp. Plus, you can easily make little patties of perfectly scrambled eggs for breakfast sandwiches this way. A nonstick pan is nonnegotiable, like well-seasoned cast iron or carbon steel. This recipe serves two to four in a 10-inch pan, but it can be doubled or tripled in a 12-inch pan as needed.

SERVINGS: 2–4

- 4 large eggs
- 1 tablespoon milk
- 1 tablespoon chopped chives or garlic chives (optional)
- Salt and pepper to taste
- 1 tablespoon butter, salted or unsalted

In a medium bowl, whisk together the eggs and milk until bubbly, about 1 minute. Whisk in the chives, if using, and salt and pepper to taste.

Heat a nonstick pan over medium heat. Melt the butter in the pan and swirl to coat. Add the egg mixture and swirl to cover the entire bottom of the pan. Let sit undisturbed for 10–15 seconds. Use a spatula to push the cooked edges toward the center, then tilt the pan so the uncooked egg runs onto the exposed bottom of the pan. Repeat until there's no more runny egg. Use the spatula to flip the eggs to cook the other side. At this point, you can break up the eggs into smaller clumps with the spatula or keep them in breakfast sandwich–size patties. Cook only until there's no more raw egg visible so they don't dry out. Immediately transfer eggs to a shallow bowl or casserole dish to prevent overcooking. Cover to keep warm.

Sheet Pan Bacon

It took me a while to convert from cooking bacon in my trusty cast iron skillet to this simple oven-baked method, purely because I'm attached to my habits. But the truth is, the process is much faster for large batches, less messy, and comes out just as good if not better. Whether you like your bacon shatteringly crisp or just shy of crispness (when it still has a little juice), you may never go back to stovetop bacon again. To double the recipe, use a second baking sheet and rotate the pans in the oven halfway through. Save the residual rendered bacon fat from the pan in a small jar in the refrigerator for frying eggs and vegetables, or for the Broccoli and Brie Quiche (page 78), which uses the flavorful bacon fat in the crust.

SERVINGS: 4–6

1 pound sliced bacon

Preheat the oven to 375°F.

Arrange the bacon slices side by side on a rimmed 12 × 17-inch baking sheet (they can overlap slightly, as they will shrink). Bake on the middle rack of the oven for 15 minutes. Flip the strips of bacon and move the inner slices to the outside of the pan and vice versa for more-even cooking. Continue baking to your desired doneness, checking often, about 5 minutes more for thin bacon and 10–15 minutes for thick-cut bacon.

Transfer the bacon to a large plate lined with paper towels. Serve warm or at room temperature. Any leftovers can be stored in a sealed sandwich bag or covered container in the refrigerator.

Crispy Hash Browns

I like to make these hash browns in a cast iron pan as one giant potato pancake, then cut it into wedges. That way, I can maximize the surface of the pan and I don't have to mess around with forming and flipping individual patties. When done right, it will be a crisp golden brown on each side with a thin layer of tender potato in between. Serve with scrambled eggs or Asparagus Chive Frittata (page 32) with Maple Breakfast Sausage (page 186).

SERVINGS: 6–8

- 1 pound Yukon gold potatoes (2–3 medium), unpeeled
- ½ teaspoon kosher salt
- ¼ cup vegetable, canola, or grapeseed oil, divided

Grate the potatoes using the large holes on a box grater. Transfer the grated potatoes to a large bowl. Add enough warm water to cover and fully submerge the potatoes. Stir in the kosher salt. Let sit 10 minutes.

Set a 10-inch cast iron skillet (or other heavy-bottomed, non-stick skillet) over low heat to preheat. Set a plate lined with two layers of paper towels near the stovetop.

Drain the grated potatoes in a colander. Squeeze out the excess moisture over the sink, one handful at a time.

Add 2 tablespoons of the oil to the preheated skillet and tilt to fully coat the bottom. Scatter the grated potato evenly across the pan all the way to the edges. Use a spatula to press firmly on the top. Cover the pan with a lid or a sheet pan. Increase the heat to medium-low and cook 15–20 minutes, until the lacy edges have browned and the bottom of the potato pancake is golden brown and crispy all the way across. Check often, adjusting the heat as necessary to avoid burning.

Loosen the edges all around with a spatula and lift the potato pancake out of the pan (it should be crisp enough to hold itself together in one piece, but you can use a second spatula if needed). Add the remaining 2 tablespoons of oil to the skillet and tilt to coat. Gently flip the potato pancake into the skillet to cook the other side, making sure not to splash yourself with oil. Continue to cook uncovered for 10–15 minutes more, until the second side is golden brown and crisp. Transfer to the paper towel–lined plate to cool slightly. Cut into wedges with a pizza cutter, sprinkle with salt, and serve immediately. These are best eaten the day they're made.

Simple Spring Pea Salad

A beautiful salad can really elevate brunch, as well as remove some of the guilt of indulging in a smorgasbord of baked goods. This one is especially pretty with its shades of green, purple, pink, and white. Spring is the perfect time for tender lettuce, spinach, peas, radishes, red onions, and herbs. I use three kinds of peas here: sugar snap, snow peas, and English shelling peas (plus some tendrils and shoots), but you can use whatever you have. Herbs are a must—mint, dill, tarragon, parsley, or chives would all work well here. I like to serve this with the optional chicken salad (make it a day ahead for best flavor), but you could top it with grilled chicken instead or skip the chicken entirely.

SERVINGS: 4

Salad

- 4 ounces English shelling peas (or ½ cup frozen peas)
- 1 medium head lettuce or 12 ounces mixed lettuces and spinach
- 2–3 ounces sugar snap peas
- 2–3 ounces snow peas
- 2–3 radishes
- ⅛ cup very thinly sliced red onion, loosely packed
- ¼ cup herbs (mint, dill, tarragon, chives, or parsley), lightly packed

Dressing

- 2 tablespoons white wine vinegar
- 2 teaspoons Dijon mustard
- ⅓–½ cup extra-virgin olive oil
- Salt and black pepper, to taste

Set a small pot of water to boil for the shelling peas. Set a medium bowl half full of ice water nearby. Snap off the tops of the shelling peas and open the pods along the seams. Remove the peas and collect them in a small bowl. Discard the pods. (Snap peas and snow peas don't need to be shelled or precooked.)

Boil fresh shelling peas for 2–4 minutes and frozen peas for about 1 minute, until tender and sweet. Skim the green peas from the top with a slotted spoon before they wrinkle. Place them in the bowl of ice water to preserve their bright green color. Drain when cool.

For the salad: Wash and dry the greens in a salad spinner. Trim the stems from the snap and snow peas, and cut them in half diagonally. Very thinly slice the radishes and onions. Combine the greens, snap and snow peas, cooked and cooled shelling peas, sliced radishes and onions, torn herbs, and pea shoots or tendrils in a salad bowl (or compose on individual plates).

For the dressing: Whisk or use an immersion blender to combine the white wine vinegar, Dijon mustard, and 1 tablespoon of the olive oil. Slowly add the remaining olive oil, whisking or blending until well emulsified. Season to taste with salt and pepper. Don't dress the salad until the very second before serving.

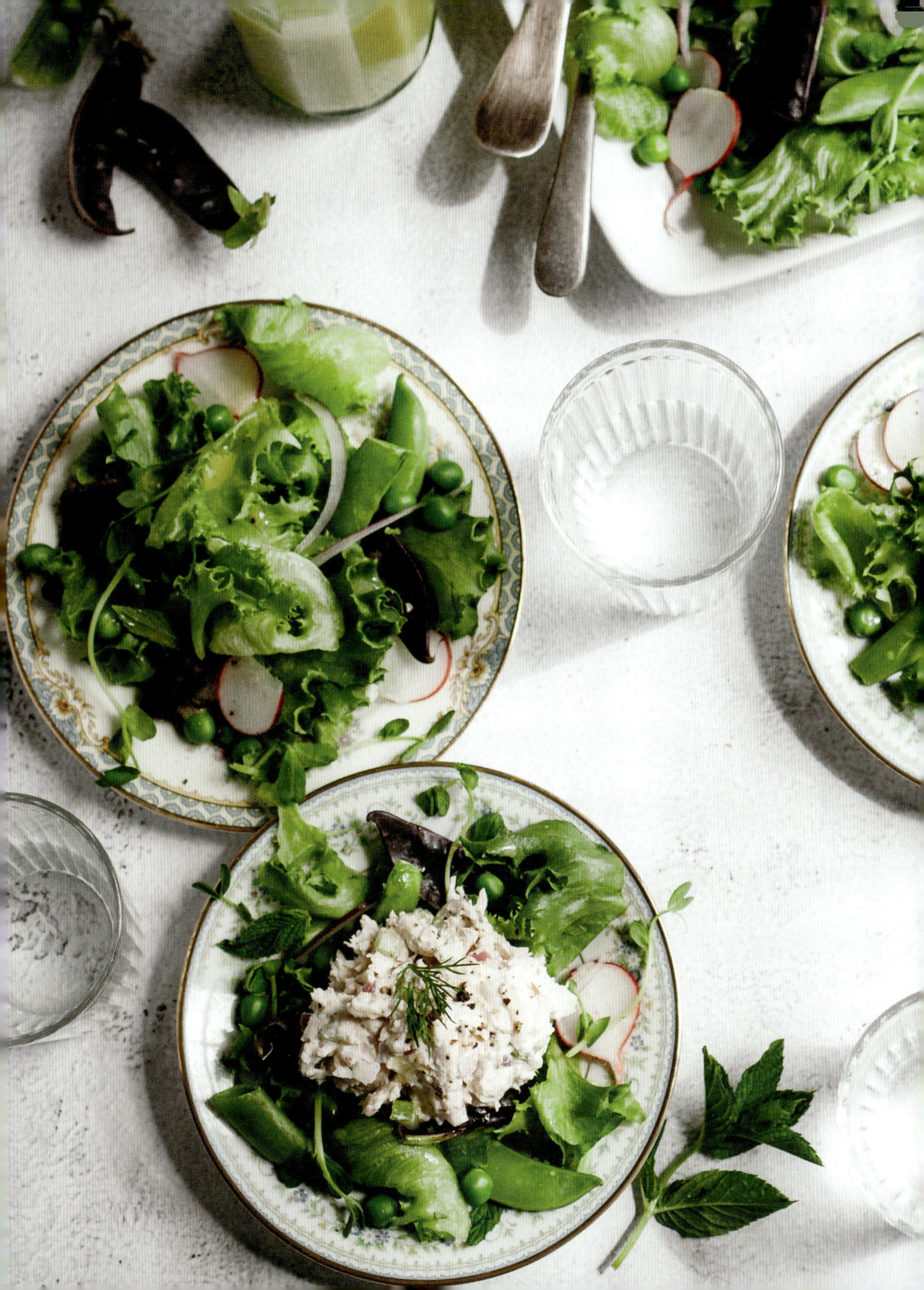

Chicken Salad

Servings: 4

- 1 tablespoon extra-virgin olive oil
- ½ pound skinless, boneless chicken breast
- Salt and pepper
- ¼ cup minced red onion
- ¼ cup minced celery stalks
- 1 tablespoon chopped chives
- ⅓ cup mayonnaise
- 1 teaspoon Dijon mustard
- Garlic powder, to taste

Preheat the oven to 400°F. Add the olive oil to a rimmed sheet pan.

Rinse and dry the chicken breasts. Coat them in the olive oil on the pan. Sprinkle with salt and pepper. Roast for 18–20 minutes, depending on thickness, until the juices run clear and the internal temperature reaches 165°–170°F. Remove the chicken from the oven and let it cool to room temperature.

Add the cooked chicken breasts to the bowl of a stand mixer fitted with a paddle attachment. Turn the mixer on low speed to gently beat the chicken into bite-sized shreds, 1–2 minutes. (Don't beat too long or you'll end up with chicken paste.) Alternatively, you can shred the chicken with a fork and knife.

To the shredded chicken, add the onion, celery, chives, mayonnaise, mustard, garlic powder, salt, and pepper. Mix well and taste for seasoning. Cover and chill in the refrigerator until ready to serve.

Spinach and Feta Phyllo Crisp

Here's a flavorful, vegetable-forward dish perfect for springtime brunch. Based on the Greek dish spanakopita, it pairs cheesy greens with crisp, buttery phyllo pastry. But I veered way off course by adding lots of fragrant Indian spices, so it ends up more in saag paneer *territory. In addition to spinach, you can also use Swiss chard and beet greens. Since these tender greens cook down to a fraction of their original size, I recommend bulking up with frozen spinach. I limit the phyllo layers to just the top, where they stay nice and crispy, scrunching up the sheets into loose rosettes for a pretty presentation. Don't forget to defrost the phyllo dough overnight in the refrigerator. This dish can also be made well ahead of time and frozen until ready to bake. Just increase the cooking time as needed.*

SERVINGS: 4–6

- 2 pounds spinach
- 2 tablespoons olive oil
- 1 medium leek (white and light green parts only), diced into ½-inch pieces
- 2 cloves garlic, minced
- 2 teaspoons ground cumin
- 1 teaspoon ground coriander
- 1 teaspoon turmeric
- ¼ teaspoon cayenne or Aleppo pepper
- ¼ cup chopped fresh parsley or cilantro
- ¼ cup chopped fresh dill

If using fresh greens, wash, trim the stems, and cut them into manageable pieces. Add to a large saucepan with the water clinging to the leaves. Cover the pot and cook over low heat, stirring occasionally, until wilted (2–3 minutes). You may have to do this in batches. Transfer to a sieve to drain and cool completely. Then chop. (If using frozen spinach, defrost according to the package instructions.)

Gather the spinach in a sieve, a dish towel, or cheesecloth. Squeeze as dry as possible over the sink. Set aside in a large bowl.

Heat the olive oil in a large skillet over medium-low heat. Sauté the leeks for 3–4 minutes until softened. Add the garlic and ground spices. Cook for 1 minute more. Stir in the parsley and dill until wilted. Make sure any liquid in the pan has cooked off, then remove from the heat and let cool completely.

Gently pull the spinach apart. Add the cooled leeks mixture to the bowl of spinach. Stir until well distributed. Mix in the lightly beaten eggs, yogurt, and salt. Add the feta. Season with black pepper. Mix well.

- 2 large eggs, lightly beaten
- ½ cup Greek yogurt
- ¾ teaspoon kosher salt
- 1 cup crumbled feta cheese
- 8 sheets phyllo dough, defrosted overnight in the refrigerator
- 4 tablespoons unsalted butter or ghee

Preheat the oven to 350°F. Grease an 8-inch square or 9-inch round baking pan. Spread the spinach mixture evenly in the prepared pan.

Melt the butter and let sit undisturbed for 5–10 minutes.

Lay the defrosted stack of phyllo dough on a sheet of plastic wrap or waxed paper on the counter. Cover with a slightly damp dish towel.

If using melted butter instead of ghee, pour off the pure yellow fat from the melted butter into a small bowl or ramekin, discarding the foamy white liquid at the bottom. (Melted ghee is ready to use as is.)

Working with one sheet of phyllo at a time, brush the butter over one side with a pastry brush. Crumple up the sheet into a loose rosette, brush any dry spots with butter, and place on top of the spinach filling. Continue buttering and crumpling up the dough, spacing out the rosettes just enough to leave space for slicing, until the entire top is covered. (You won't use the whole box of phyllo dough, but it can be portioned, rewrapped, sealed in an airtight bag, and refrozen.)

Bake 40–45 minutes, until the top is crisp and golden. If the phyllo rosettes aren't quite golden and crisp enough, you can slide the pan under the broiler for a few minutes, but keep an eye on them so they don't burn. Remove from the oven and let cool 15 minutes before serving.

This dish is best enjoyed the day it's made, but leftovers can be covered and stored in the refrigerator for 1–2 days. For best results, don't microwave. Reheat in the bottom half of the oven, uncovered, until heated through, but remove before the top browns too darkly.

Bloody Mary Mix

During the recipe-testing process, I learned something important about myself: I really, really don't like Bloody Marys! At least not Bloody Marys spiked with alcohol. Hence, the following is my personalized vodka-less Bloody Mary mix, but feel free to embellish to your heart's desire. During the height of summer, using garden-fresh tomatoes feels right to me. I use a combination of 1½ pounds (3–4) medium cored tomatoes (no need to peel) and 3 ounces tomato paste in a blender instead of store-bought tomato juice. Some New England folks add clam juice to the mix too, but I'm not quite there yet.

SERVINGS: 6–8

- 3 cups tomato juice
- 2 cups V8 vegetable juice
- 3 tablespoons lemon juice or white vinegar
- 2 teaspoons Worcestershire sauce
- 1½ teaspoons kosher salt
- 1½ teaspoons granulated sugar
- 1 teaspoon onion powder
- ¾ teaspoon prepared horseradish
- ¼ teaspoon celery seed or celery salt
- ⅛ teaspoon ground black pepper
- Tabasco sauce, to taste
- Celery stalks, for garnish

In a pitcher, combine the tomato juice, V8, lemon juice or white vinegar, and Worcestershire sauce. Stir well. Add the salt, sugar, onion powder, horseradish, celery seed or salt, black pepper, and a few dashes of Tabasco. Stir again. Taste and adjust the seasonings to your taste (if using low-sodium V8, you may need a bit more salt). If using fresh tomatoes, you can add more water to thin it to your desired consistency. Chill in the refrigerator. To serve, pour into highball glasses over ice and garnish with a celery stalk. For those partaking of alcohol, add 1 ounce vodka to each glass.

Spring 47

Strawberry Rhubarb Sangria

This sensational, not-too-sweet adult pitcher drink is the perfect way to toast the arrival of spring. It's got plenty of juicy, boozy strawberries as well as tart, refreshing rhubarb. Be sure to sugar the fruit early in the morning (even the night before) so there's enough time to pull out the flavorful fruit juices. The rest practically takes care of itself.

SERVINGS: 6

- ½ pound strawberries (about 1½ cups), cut into ¾-inch pieces
- 1 (6-inch) piece rhubarb, cut into small cubes (about ¼ cup)
- ¼ cup granulated sugar
- 1 (750 milliliter) bottle Prosecco
- 1½ cups red wine, like Cabernet Sauvignon
- Splash of triple sec, Cointreau, or Grand Marnier

Combine the strawberries and rhubarb with the sugar in a medium bowl. Cover and refrigerate at least 4 hours to give the sugar a chance to pull out the fruit juices. You should have at least ⅓ to ½ cup syrup.

Add the fruit and its juices to a pitcher. Pour in the Prosecco and red wine. Add a splash of orange liqueur and stir well. Chill several hours. When ready to serve, fill wine glasses halfway with ice cubes and pour in the sangria, making sure to include plenty of boozy fruit.

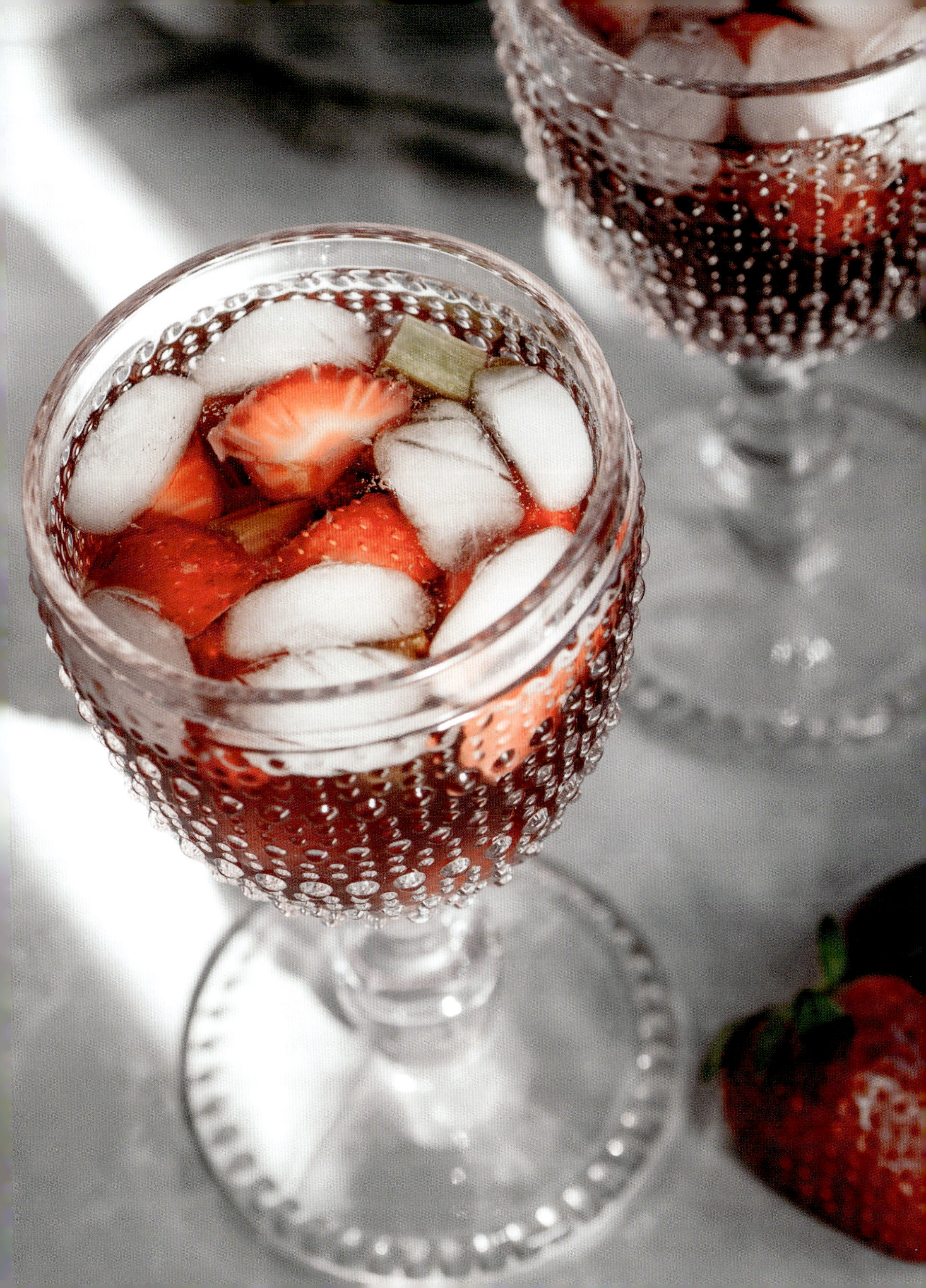

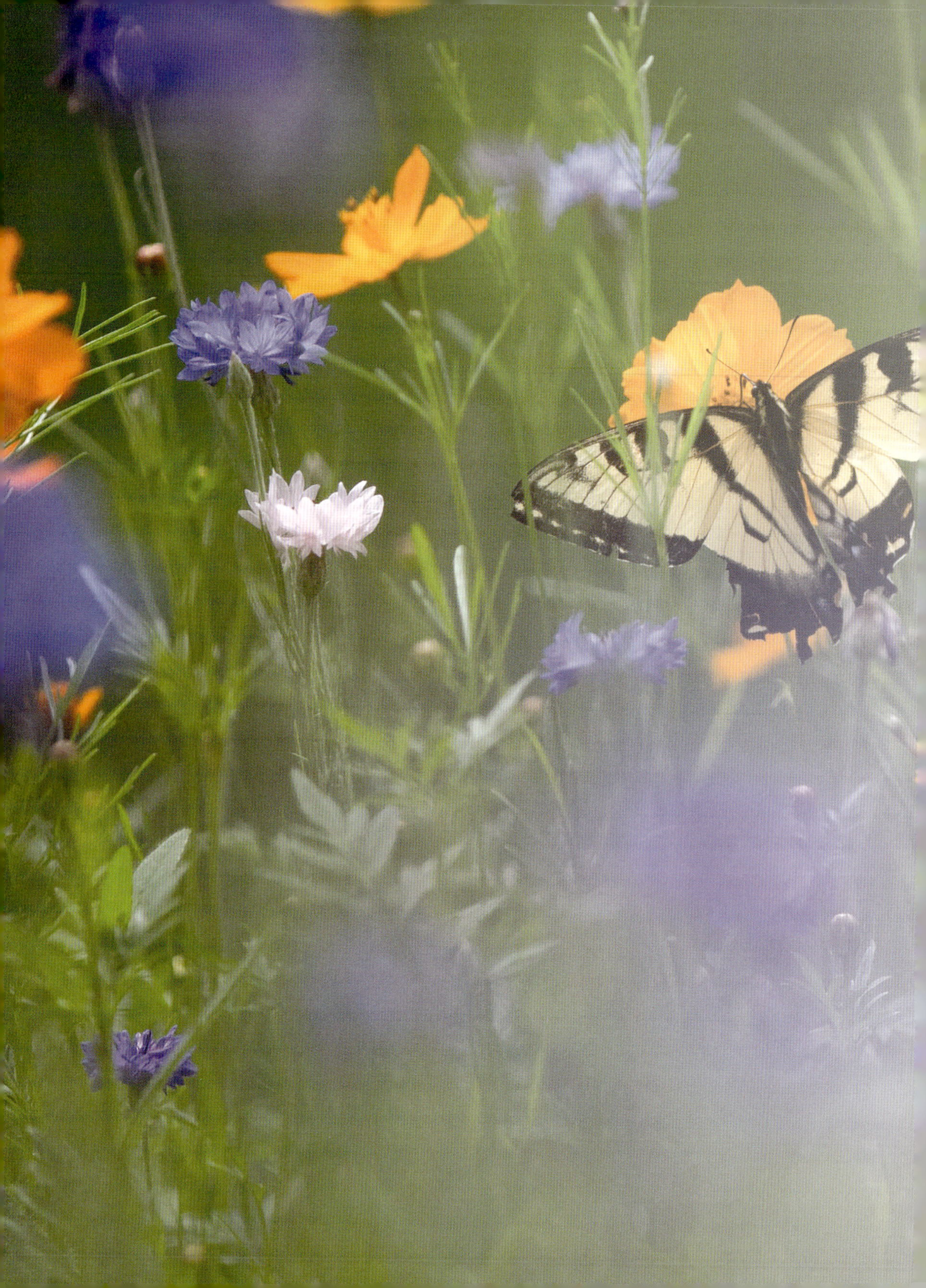

Summer

Classic Blueberry Muffins 54

Sourdough Waffles 56

Black Raspberry Ricotta Dutch Baby 58

Blueberry Buttermilk Pancakes 60

Jelly Doughnuts 62

Mixed-Berry Jam 65

Sweet Cherry Puff Tarts 66

Wild Blueberry Maple Syrup 69

Zucchini Earl Grey Tea Cake 70

Blackberry Marjoram Scones 72

Lobster Salad Sliders 74

Saltwater Pickles 77

Broccoli and Brie Quiche 78

Sweet and Spicy Skillet Cornbread 82

Eggplant and Red Pepper Shakshuka 84

Rhode Island Johnnycakes with Shrimp, Zucchini, and Sweet Corn 86

Herbed Heirloom Tomato Tart with Whipped Ricotta 88

Three Sisters Succotash 91

Cod Cakes with Preserved Lemon and Dill Sauce 92

Cherry Tomato Burrata Salad 94

Peach-Berry Sangria 95

Blueberry Lemonade 96

Mint Watermelon Gimlets 98

Lavender Lemon Martinis 100

You can't beat the summertime for alfresco brunch. While the afternoons can be steamy, the late morning is usually tolerable, particularly in the shade, especially if a sea breeze gently wafts in from the east. Whether you're on the ocean, lakeside, or the deck of an urban triple-decker, weekend brunch is totally doable. The cooking can happen in the morning or the night before so the oven is off during the hottest part of the day. Or eliminate the oven altogether and focus on stovetop favorites like pancakes, waffles, and eggs.

The perpetual smorgasbord of fresh, local summer fruit like blueberries, raspberries, peaches, cherries, plums, blackberries, and melon offer endless inspiration for baked goods, seasonal preserves, and fruity sangrias and cocktails. While you'll find the usual classic New England brunch options here, like blueberry muffins, jelly doughnuts, and buttermilk pancakes, there are also some unusual entries that round out the seasonal menu, like the Black Raspberry Ricotta Dutch Baby, Sweet Cherry Puff Tarts, and Blackberry Marjoram Scones. Refreshing beverages for sipping—a must in the dog days of summer—are inspired by the local bounty and include Blueberry Lemonade, Peach-Berry Sangria, and Weekend Watermelon Gimlets. But often, you don't need to do anything to the fruit at all. A bowl of fresh strawberries or cherries is a complete dish on its own, or pile them high on homemade sourdough Belgian waffles.

On the savory side, summertime means tomatoes, zucchini, and sweet corn coming out of our ears. I'm a sucker for a good pie crust, so the Broccoli and Brie Quiche is a must-try, as is the Heirloom Tomato Tart with Whipped Ricotta. Coastal New Englanders will enjoy incorporating seasonal seafood into their brunch dishes, like Lobster Salad Sliders, Cod Cakes with Lemon and Dill Sauce, and Rhode Island Johnnycakes with Shrimp, Zucchini, and Sweet Corn, a savory riff on the Native American and colonial staple.

Whether brunch is the main event, a jumping-off point for the rest of your day, or a pleasant prequel to an afternoon siesta, you'll have a smile on your face regardless.

Summer Brunch Menu Ideas:

Summer Birthday/Bridal/Baby Shower Brunch: Broccoli and Brie Quiche. Sweet Cherry Puff Tarts. Fruit Salad. Lavender Lemon Martinis or Peach-Berry Sangria.

Summer Picnic Brunch: Classic Blueberry Muffins or Blackberry Marjoram Scones. Sheet Pan Bacon. Three Sisters Succotash. Blueberry Lemonade.

Oceanside Brunch: Lobster Salad Sliders. Saltwater Pickles. Cape Cod potato chips. Mint Watermelon Gimlets or Lavender Lemon Martinis.

Summer Garden Brunch: Blackberry Marjoram Scones or Jelly Doughnuts. Herbed Heirloom Tomato Tart with Whipped Ricotta. Peach-Berry Sangria or Mint Watermelon Gimlets.

Savory Summer Brunch: Sweet and Spicy Skillet Cornbread. Eggplant and Red Pepper Shakshuka or Cherry Tomato Burrata Salad. Blueberry Lemonade.

Classic Blueberry Muffins

Ask any Bostonian of a certain age and they'll tell you the best blueberry muffins in the world were made by baker John Pupek at the Jordan Marsh at Downtown Crossing in Boston (the store was shuttered in 1996 and replaced by Macy's). These muffins are based on that same recipe, though I've taken some small liberties, like replacing the shortening with butter. The secret is to use the small, wild, lowbush blueberries (like the ones grown in Maine), not the plump highbush blueberries, which turn into big blobs of purple goo. If you can't find the little ones fresh, you can buy Wyman's flash-frozen wild blueberries in the freezer section of the grocery store any time of year; they work perfectly.

SERVINGS: MAKES 12

¾ cup (1½ sticks) unsalted butter, at room temperature

1½ cups granulated sugar, plus 2 tablespoons for the tops

2 large eggs, at room temperature

2 teaspoons vanilla extract

2½ cups all-purpose flour, plus 2 tablespoons for the berries

1 tablespoon baking powder

½ teaspoon table salt or fine sea salt

⅔ cup milk, at room temperature

3 cups wild blueberries (thawed, if frozen)

Preheat the oven to 400°F. Grease or line a standard 12-cup muffin tin.

In a large bowl, beat the butter with an electric mixer fitted with a paddle attachment on medium speed for 1 minute, until smooth and creamy. Scrape the bottom and sides of the bowl as needed. Add the sugar and beat 1–2 minutes more until fluffy. Add the eggs one at a time, beating well after each addition. Beat 2–3 minutes more to aerate. Mix in the vanilla.

Add the flour, baking powder, and sea salt to the butter mixture. Mix on low while streaming the milk slowly down the side of the bowl until just combined.

If your berries aren't very juicy, take ½ cup and mash them with a fork. Mix the remaining berries with 2 tablespoons of flour. (If your berries are extremely juicy, such as defrosted frozen blueberries, strain them over a bowl to eliminate most of the juice. Mix all the berries with the 2 tablespoons of flour.) Add the whole and mashed blueberries to the bowl and mix just until dispersed. Divide the batter equally between the muffin cups. Sprinkle generously with sugar if desired.

Bake 5 minutes at 400°F. Then reduce the heat to 375°F and bake about 22–26 minutes more. Let cool. Store leftovers in an airtight container for 3–4 days.

Sourdough Waffles

This started as a random internet recipe I printed out many years ago, and I've been playing with it ever since, making little tweaks and scribbling notes that look like the ravings of a madman. Below is the translation. This recipe is completely delicious and a wonderful way to use up sourdough discard. It has completely ruined me for waffles anywhere else, and it's insanely easy to make. For best results, start the night before with a very simple overnight rise at room temperature—not in the refrigerator. The rest of the prep is a snap, just allow plenty of time to supervise the waffle-maker. These waffles also freeze very well, so you can pop individual waffles into the toaster, Eggo-style, a dangerous perk indeed.

SERVINGS: MAKES ABOUT 6

- 2 cups all-purpose flour
- 1½ cups warm water
- 1 cup sourdough starter (or discard)
- 2 large eggs
- 1 tablespoon water
- ½ teaspoon baking soda
- ½ cup vegetable, canola, or grapeseed oil
- 3 tablespoons granulated sugar
- 1 teaspoon kosher salt
- Fresh fruit
- Greek yogurt or whipped cream
- Maple syrup

The night before serving: Stir together the flour, water, and sourdough starter (or discard) in a large bowl. Cover with plastic wrap and let sit overnight in a warm place (an hour can work in a pinch).

In the morning: Whisk the eggs in a medium bowl. Stir the water and baking soda together in a ramekin and whisk it into the eggs. Add the oil, sugar, and salt. Whisk well. Stir the egg mixture into the sourdough batter with a wooden spoon.

Preheat a waffle iron according to the manufacturer's instructions. Pour the batter onto the hot iron (about 1 cup for my Belgian waffle iron) and close the top. The batter will expand as it heats. Cook for 3–5 minutes or until it reaches your desired brownness, which for me is very golden-brown and crispy. Serve immediately as they come off the iron. Or make them ahead and spread out the cooked waffles on sheet pans or individual plates instead of stacking, which deflates their airiness and reduces their crispness. Reheat in a 325°F oven if needed.

Serve with fresh fruit, Greek yogurt or whipped cream, and maple syrup. Leftovers can be covered and stored in the refrigerator for 3–4 days or frozen up to 1 month.

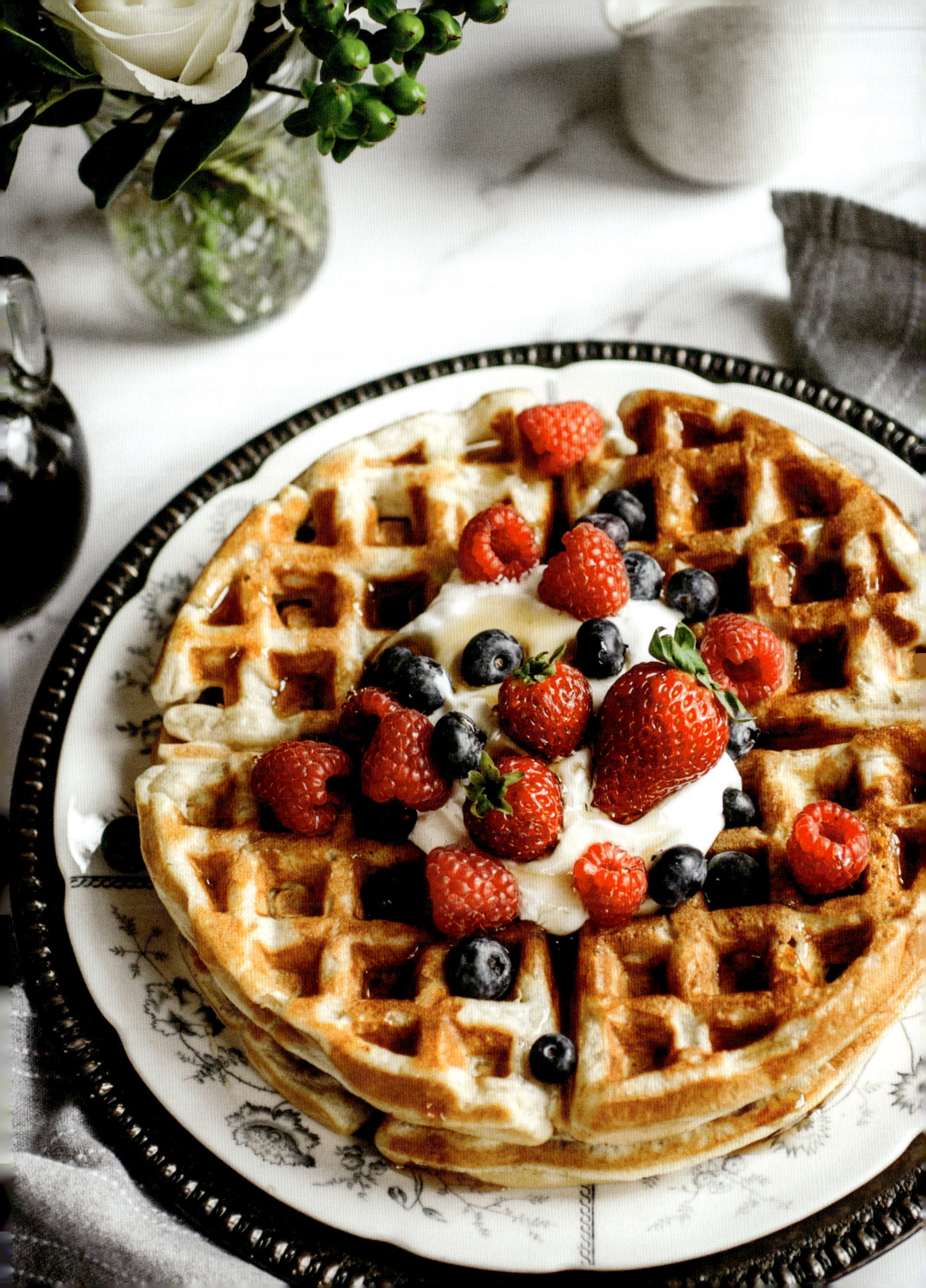

Black Raspberry Ricotta Dutch Baby

In the summertime, when fresh berries are abundant, sometimes you just want to let them be. That's where a Dutch baby comes in. My friend Erin taught me how to make Dutch babies in college. I had never tasted anything like it: a fluffy, custardy pancake that curled up crisply around the edges to create a tantalizing, edible vessel for fruit and syrup. Here I add a handful of black raspberries to the batter (you can substitute wild blueberries), which turn soft and jammy in the oven. The rest can be added on top with a plethora of other fresh berries. This particular pancake is pillowy with ricotta and has a bright, lemony zing. If you're not a fan of ricotta, you can leave it out—the recipe will still work. You can make one giant Dutch baby in a 10-inch cast iron pan or make individual servings in four small cast iron pans. Just dust the pancake(s) with powdered sugar, pile with fruit and whipped cream or Greek yogurt, and serve maple syrup on the side for sweet summer simplicity.

SERVINGS: 4–6

3 large eggs

½ cup milk, warmed

½ cup all-purpose flour

¼ cup ricotta

2 tablespoons melted butter

3 tablespoons granulated sugar

1 teaspoon vanilla extract

¼ teaspoon table salt or fine sea salt

Pinch of ground cinnamon

Finely grated zest of 1 lemon (about ½ teaspoon)

Juice of 1 lemon (about 2 tablespoons)

1 tablespoon cold butter

½ cup black raspberries (fresh or frozen)

Confectioners' sugar

Additional fresh berries, to serve

Greek yogurt or whipped cream

Maple syrup

Preheat the oven to 450°F. Set a 10-inch cast iron skillet or other nonstick, oven-safe skillet in the oven to preheat (10 minutes is just right—much longer, and the bottom of the pancake might get too brown).

In a large mixing bowl, whisk the eggs for 15 seconds until frothy. Add the milk, flour, ricotta, melted butter, sugar, vanilla, salt, and cinnamon. Whisk until mostly smooth. Add the lemon zest and lemon juice, and whisk briefly until smooth. (This can also be done in a blender.)

Remove the hot skillet from the oven with mitts. Add the remaining 1 tablespoon cold butter to the pan and swirl to coat the bottom and sides. Pour in the batter. Scatter the black raspberries on top. Return the pan to the oven and bake 16–20 minutes, until puffed, golden brown, and the center springs back when gently pressed (smaller skillets will take less time). Let cool slightly.

Dust with powdered sugar. Serve with fresh berries, Greek yogurt or whipped cream, and maple syrup. Dutch babies are best eaten the day they're made, but leftovers can be covered and stored in the refrigerator for 1–2 days. Gently reheat in the microwave.

Blueberry Buttermilk Pancakes

Buttermilk pancakes are a classic New England weekend brunch. Tiny Maine blueberries make them even better, but don't let me limit your imagination. Try raspberries, sliced strawberries, or chopped-up peaches, nectarines, or plums in your summer pancakes. Switch out the whole wheat flour for spelt flour or buckwheat flour. Keeping powdered buttermilk in your pantry is a good way to ensure you always have the means to whip up tangy buttermilk pancakes whenever your cravings strike. But in a pinch you can always mix 2 cups regular milk with 2 tablespoons lemon juice or apple cider vinegar to get the right acidity. If none of these options works for you, just use regular milk and switch out the baking soda for 2 tablespoons baking powder for an epic rise.

SERVINGS: MAKES 6–8

- 4 large eggs
- 2 cups buttermilk, slightly warmed in the microwave
- 6 tablespoons unsalted butter, melted
- ¼ cup vegetable oil
- 1½ cups all-purpose flour
- 1 cup whole wheat flour
- 2 tablespoons light brown sugar, firmly packed
- 1 teaspoon baking soda
- 1 teaspoon fine sea salt
- 1½ cups blueberries, fresh or frozen (defrosted and drained)
- Butter for the pan

Whisk the eggs in a large bowl until foamy. Add the buttermilk, butter, and oil. Whisk to combine. Sift the dry ingredients over the wet ingredients in the bowl. Whisk until smooth.

Heat a nonstick frying pan or griddle over medium heat until hot (test by flicking some water into the pan; the water droplets should sizzle vigorously and disappear). Add some butter and swirl it around the pan until melted. Pour the batter into evenly-sized circles (I use a ⅓-cup scoop). Sprinkle the blueberries over the batter. Cook 2 to 4 minutes per side, until tiny bubbles start to pop on the surface of the pancakes and the bottoms are beautifully brown. Repeat with remaining batter.

Stack the pancakes with pats of butter in between. Cover them with aluminum foil or an inverted bowl to keep warm. Serve with maple syrup and fresh fruit, if desired. Store leftovers well wrapped in the refrigerator for 3–4 days.

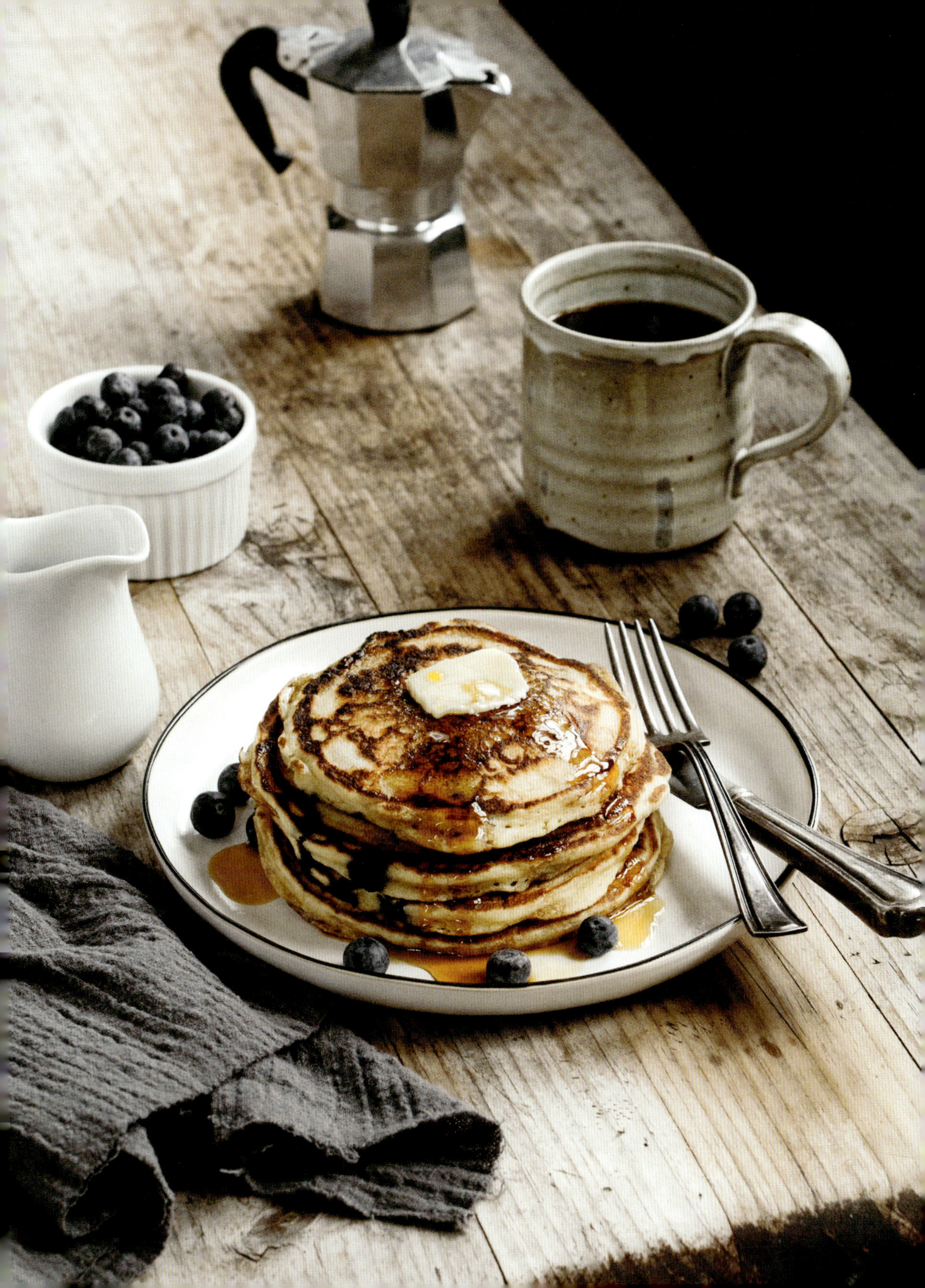

Jelly Doughnuts

I absolutely love a good jelly doughnut. You can use your own homemade preserves, your favorite farmers' market flavor, or the Mixed-Berry Jam on page 65. Try to choose a jam that isn't too chunky, which can clog up the tip of the pastry bag. Also, if you're making the jam from scratch, start at least a day before you plan to use it in your doughnuts so it's cold and set. Start the dough the night before, too, so the dough has time for a slow overnight rise in the refrigerator. Then allow a 2- to 3-hour window the next morning to shape, proof, fry, sugar, and fill the doughnuts. I like jelly doughnuts sugared, but if you prefer them glazed, see the Honey Glaze recipe on page 6.

SERVINGS: MAKES 8–9

Dough

1½ teaspoons active dry yeast

¾ cup milk, warmed to room temperature

1 cup all-purpose flour

1 cup bread flour

1 teaspoon table salt or fine sea salt

2 tablespoons granulated sugar

3 large egg yolks

4 tablespoons unsalted butter, warmed to room temperature

Vegetable or canola oil, for frying

Coating and Filling

1 cup granulated sugar

½ cup fruit jam

For the dough: Stir the yeast into the warm milk. Let sit for 5 minutes to activate.

Meanwhile, in the bowl of a stand mixer (preferably fitted with the paddle attachment), combine the all-purpose flour, bread flour, salt, and sugar. Add the egg yolks to the dry ingredients with the milk mixture. Mix on low. Once the liquid is absorbed, increase the speed to medium and add the butter 1 tablespoon at a time. Once the butter is incorporated, continue mixing on medium to medium-high for 6–8 minutes, until the dough starts to pull away from the sides of the bowl. The dough will be very sticky and elastic.

Oil a large bowl. Scrape the dough into the oiled bowl with a scraper and turn the dough around in the bowl so it gets coated with oil on all sides. Cover the bowl and refrigerate 12–15 hours.

The next morning, cut a sheet of parchment paper into 12 squares. (You will need only 9, but these are the perfect size.) Set 9 squares on a sheet pan and spray with nonstick spray. Set aside.

Remove the dough from the refrigerator. Scrape out the dough onto a lightly floured counter and gently press it ½ inch thick. Using a 3-inch round biscuit or cookie cutter, cut the dough into circles and transfer each one to a square of oiled parchment paper. Cover with plastic wrap and let proof for 30–45 minutes in a warm place until puffed.

Meanwhile, add the vegetable or canola oil to a large Dutch oven or heavy stainless steel pot to a depth of about 3 inches. Set over medium heat and insert a candy thermometer. Set up a cooling rack with a double layer of paper towels over a sheet pan nearby.

Once the oil temperature reaches 350°–375°F, transfer the proofed doughnuts one at a time to a slotted spoon, peeling off the parchment backs, and gently lower them into the hot oil. Fry about 3 at a time for 2–3 minutes per side, until golden brown, flipping once. Drain on paper towels. Adjust the burner as needed to maintain the optimum temperature window so the doughnuts don't get too greasy

Summer

(temperature too low) or have undercooked centers (temperature too high).

Let the doughnuts cool for about 20 minutes. Remove the paper towels from the cooling rack. Add the granulated sugar to a medium bowl. While still warm, dip each doughnut in the sugar on all sides until fully coated. Return to the rack to cool completely.

To fill the doughnuts, use a sharp-tipped paring knife to cut an X in the side of each doughnut, and extend the knife all the way to the center. (I also fan the blade across the interior of the doughnut to make room for more jelly. Just be careful not to go all the way through to the other sides.)

Use a piping bag fitted with a long nozzle, preferably one more than ½ inch wide at the small end to accommodate any chunks in the jam. If you don't have that size, use what you have or use a zip-top plastic bag with the corner snipped off. Fill the bag three-fourths of the way up with jam and twist the top closed. Insert the tip of the pastry bag into the hole in the side of each doughnut and squeeze slowly until the doughnuts are full (if you overfill them, the jelly will leak out of the hole when the doughnuts are set on their sides).

These doughnuts can be kept at room temperature until ready to serve. Doughnuts are best eaten the day they're made, but these can keep a few days longer covered in the refrigerator.

Mixed-Berry Jam

This is the perfect summer jam for toast, yogurt parfaits, or jelly doughnuts. I like to use a mix of strawberries, blueberries, raspberries, and blackberries, but use whatever you have. It will be a little bit seedy, a little bit chunky, just the way I like it. If making doughnuts, be sure to mash the fruit especially well during the cooking process so there are fewer chunks to clog the piping nozzle.

SERVINGS: MAKES ABOUT 1 PINT

- 12 ounces mixed berries, fresh or frozen
- 1 teaspoon freshly squeezed lemon juice
- 1½ cups granulated sugar, divided
- ¼ cup powdered pectin

Mash the berries, lemon juice, and 1 tablespoon of the sugar in a small saucepan over medium heat. Cook 3–5 minutes, until the berries release their juices and come to a hard boil. Add the rest of the sugar and the pectin all at once. Stir well. Bring back to a hard boil and cook for 1–2 minutes, until the mixture is thick and syrupy (let a bit of jam drip off the edge of a wooden spoon; if it sheets, meaning two drips combine into one before slipping off, it's ready). Remove from the heat and pour into two half-pint jars. Cover and let cool. Chill in the refrigerator overnight to set. (The jam can be stored in the fridge for up to 1 month).

Sweet Cherry Puff Tarts

I'm very fond of leftover pie for breakfast. These little tartlets have a similar vibe, slightly less sweet than your average fruit pie, and packaged up, Danish-like, with a cream cheese drizzle. I've included instructions for how to make your own rough puff pastry, but you could use store-bought puff pastry to save time (I like Dufour). Just be sure to set it in the refrigerator the night before to defrost. If you don't have a cherry pitter, you can use a chopstick to push out the pit through the stem end. Or gently mash each cherry on a cutting board with the broad side of a chef's knife, then pull apart the cherry and discard the pit (it's messy work—don't wear white for this). Pitted frozen cherries are also perfectly acceptable.

SERVINGS: MAKES 9

Pastry

- 2 cups all-purpose flour
- 1 teaspoon table salt or fine sea salt
- 1 cup (2 sticks) cold unsalted butter, cut into quarters
- 6–10 tablespoons ice water, or as needed
- 1 teaspoon melted butter

For the pastry: Mix the flour with the salt in the bowl of a food processor. Add half the butter and process about 20 seconds, until the butter pieces stop jumping around like popcorn. Add the rest of the butter and process 8–10 seconds, until the largest chunks of butter are about grape-sized. (If you don't have a food processor, you can cut the butter into the flour with your fingers or a pastry blender.) Add ¼ cup of ice water and process for a few seconds. Add more ice water, 1 tablespoon at a time, pulsing the motor several times after each addition, until the dough holds together when gently squeezed. Use only as much water as you need.

Gather the dough mixture together on the counter and gently fold the dough over itself two or three times until it holds together. Flour your counter and rolling pin well. Roll out the dough into a 12 × 12-inch square. (To coax out some corners from a circle of dough, use the left side of your rolling pin to roll the right side of your dough, and the right side of the pin to roll the left side of the dough so the sides become even with the middle.) Fold the 12 × 12-inch square in half like you're closing a book so you have a tall 6 × 12-inch rectangle. Next, fold the bottom third of the dough up and the top third of the dough down, as if you're folding a business letter. Wrap and refrigerate for 30 minutes to relax the dough.

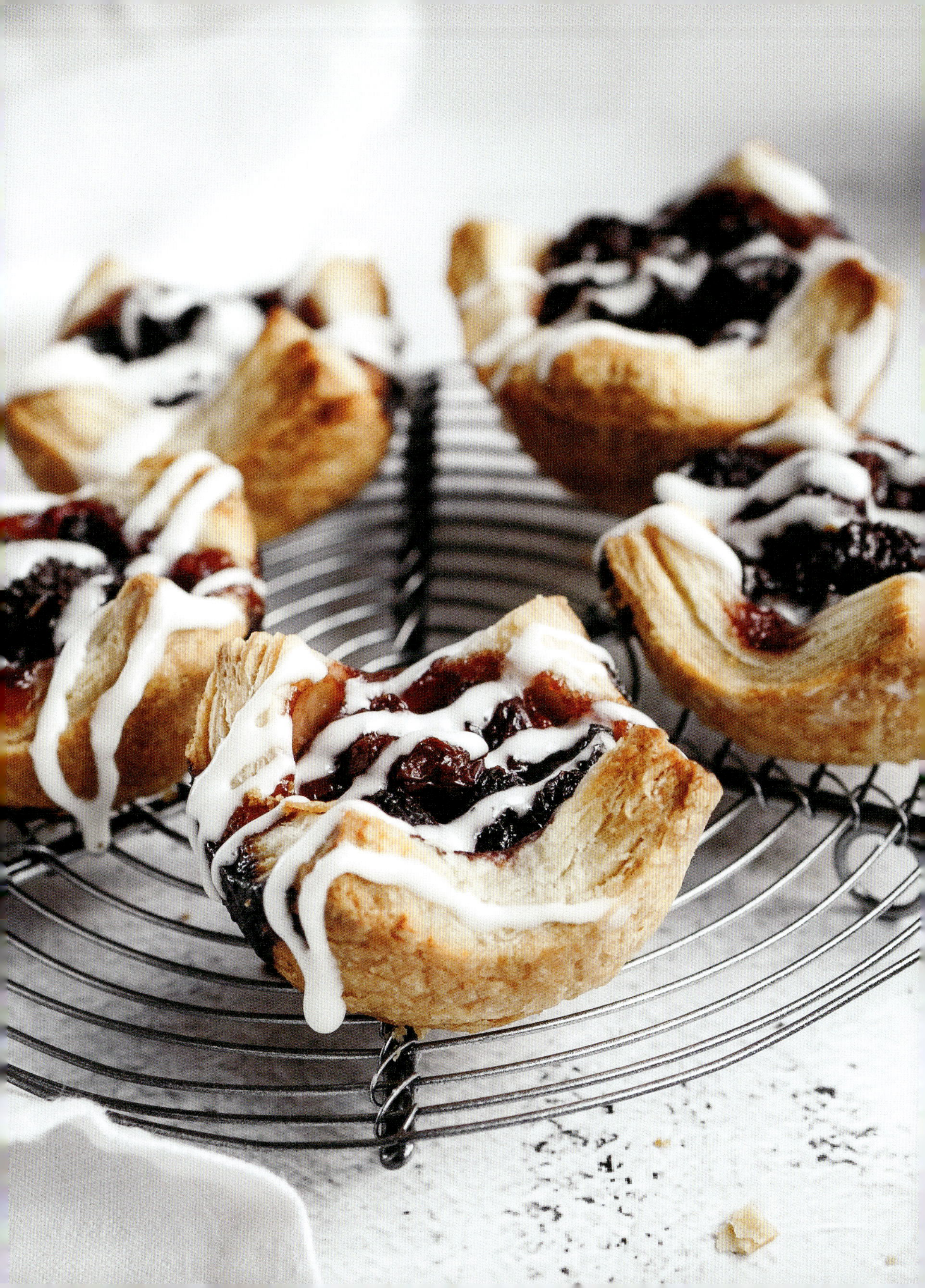

Filling

2 cups fresh sweet cherries, stemmed and pitted (or 12 ounces frozen cherries, defrosted and drained)

¼ cup granulated sugar

1 tablespoon cornstarch

1 teaspoon lemon juice

1 teaspoon vanilla extract

⅛ teaspoon almond extract

Drizzle

1 ounce cream cheese, at room temperature

½ cup confectioners' sugar, sifted

1 tablespoon cold water

Preheat the oven to 400°F. Grease a standard 12-cup muffin tin.

Pit the cherries (over the sink, if possible) and tear them in half. Place them in a medium bowl and set aside.

On a floured surface with a floured rolling pin, roll out the dough about ¼ inch thick to a 12 × 12-inch square. Cut into 4-inch squares with a sharp paring knife or bench scraper. Set the squares in the wells of the prepared muffin tin. The corners should be pointing upward. Make sure each piece of dough is touching the bottom of the pan (not hovering in the air) so that it bakes properly. Set in the refrigerator briefly to chill while mixing the filling.

For the filling: To the bowl of cherries, add the sugar, cornstarch, lemon juice, vanilla, and almond extract. Stir well.

Portion about 1 heaping tablespoon of cherry filling into the center of the dough. Brush the melted butter on the exposed dough. Set the muffin pan in the oven with a sheet pan resting on the rack underneath to catch any spills. Bake 30–35 minutes, until the pastry is golden brown and the filling is bubbly (err on the side of baking longer to ensure that all the layers of dough are fully baked). Remove from the oven and let cool 10–15 minutes. When cool enough to handle, remove the tartlets from the pan with an offset spatula or spoon and transfer to a cooling rack set over a baking sheet. Let cool completely before icing.

For the drizzle: Using an electric mixer, beat the cream cheese until fluffy. Add the sugar and whip on low until combined. Increase the speed and continue to mix until there are no more lumps. Add ½ tablespoon cold water and mix. Dribble in enough of the remaining tablespoon of water to create the desired consistency: thick enough to hold its shape, but thin enough to drizzle. Scoop the mixture into a small zip-top bag and zip it shut. Snip off a bottom tip of the bag and drizzle the glaze over the tops of the tartlets. Let sit at room temperature or the refrigerator for about 30 minutes, until the icing sets.

These are best served the day they're made, but leftovers can be covered and stored in the refrigerator for 1–2 days.

Wild Blueberry Maple Syrup

This is hardly a recipe—more of a concept—but absolutely worth mentioning. Adding berries to maple syrup tones down the sweetness while adding dimension to pancakes, French toast, and waffles. Tiny Maine lowbush blueberries, which you can buy frozen all year long, are perfect for this, but any berry will do (increase the cooking time based on size). Maple syrup cooked with fruit won't have as long a shelf life as pure maple syrup, so make only as much as you'll use within a week or two. This is especially delicious poured over the fabulous New England Cornmeal Custard Cake (page 162). Try stirring it into oatmeal or yogurt too.

SERVINGS: 8–12

- 1 cup maple syrup
- ½ cup frozen wild blueberries
- 1 tablespoon unsalted butter (optional)
- Squeeze of fresh lemon juice

Add the maple syrup and blueberries to a small saucepan and bring to a boil. Turn the heat down to medium-low and simmer 10–12 minutes, stirring occasionally, until the berries burst but still hold their shape. The liquid should turn from gray to deep violet and be thick enough to coat the spoon. Remove from the heat and stir in the butter, if desired, and the lemon juice. Let cool and pour into a small pitcher, jar, or gravy boat. Serve warm or cold. Store covered in the refrigerator for a week or two, labeled and dated.

Zucchini Earl Grey Tea Cake

Keep this recipe front of mind when your garden's overrun with zucchini. Here I've gussied up zucchini bread with the addition of an Earl Grey tea glaze. I particularly love this cake with walnuts, but you can leave them out if you prefer or if allergies are a concern. This recipe makes two loaves, so you can serve one and freeze the other (or give it away). The glaze makes enough to fully cover one cake or lightly drizzle over two, but there's enough tea to make a larger batch if you'd like. The remaining triple-strength tea can be frozen and defrosted to make more icing as needed (it's great for muffins and scones too).

SERVINGS: MAKES 2 LOAVES

Cake

- 2 cups all-purpose flour
- 2 teaspoons baking powder
- ¼ teaspoon baking soda
- 1 tablespoon ground cinnamon
- 1 teaspoon table salt or fine sea salt
- 3 large eggs
- 1½ cups granulated sugar
- 1 cup vegetable oil
- 2 teaspoons vanilla extract
- 2 cups shredded zucchini, from 1 large or 2 small zucchini
- 1 cup chopped walnuts, plus more finely chopped for garnish

Preheat the oven to 375°F. Grease or line two medium loaf pans (either 8½ × 5 × 2¾-inch or 7½ × 4 × 2-inch) with parchment paper.

In a medium bowl, whisk together the flour, baking powder, baking soda, cinnamon, and salt. Set aside.

In a large bowl, whisk the eggs well. Add the sugar, oil, and vanilla extract; whisk well. Add the shredded zucchini, walnuts, and dry ingredients to the bowl. Stir with a wooden spoon until combined. Divide the batter between the two prepared pans.

Bake in the middle of the oven for 45–50 minutes, until the tops are browned and a toothpick inserted into the centers comes out clean. Remove from the oven. Let cool completely.

Add the 3 tea bags to the boiling water and let steep for 3 minutes. Remove the tea bags and chill the tea in the refrigerator several hours until cold.

For the glaze: Sift the confectioners' sugar into a small bowl with the salt. Start by adding 1 tablespoon of the cold tea to the sugar mixture and whisk well. Dribble up to 1 tablespoon more tea as needed, whisking all the while. The icing should be loose enough to drizzle, but thick enough to coat the cake without running off. If it's too thin, sift in another tablespoon of confectioners' sugar. If it's too thick, add more tea a few drops at a time. Freeze the remaining tea for future use.

Glaze

3 Earl Grey tea bags
½ cup boiling water
1 cup confectioners' sugar, sifted
Pinch of finely grated lemon and orange zest (optional)
Pinch of sea salt

Pour or drizzle the glaze over the top of the cake. Sprinkle with finely chopped walnuts, if desired. Let sit in the refrigerator for 15 minutes to set.

Serve at room temperature. Leftovers can be covered and stored in the refrigerator for 4–5 days.

Blackberry Marjoram Scones

These terrific summery scones come together quickly, so you can pop them in the oven in the morning before it gets too hot. Cornmeal gives them a rustic texture, while the marjoram, an unusual addition to baked goods, perfumes the dough with a velvety, savory scent that pairs well with blackberries. The lemony glaze ties it all together and makes the flavors pop.

SERVINGS: MAKES 8

Dough

1½ cups all-purpose flour
½ cup cornmeal
¼ cup granulated sugar
1 tablespoon baking powder
½ teaspoon table salt or fine sea salt
6 tablespoons cold unsalted butter, cut into 6 pieces
1 cup heavy cream
¾ cup blackberries (cut in half if too large)
1½ tablespoons roughly chopped fresh marjoram

Glaze

⅓ cup confectioners' sugar, sifted
1 tablespoon lemon juice
Pinch of lemon zest

Preheat the oven to 425°F. Grease a 12 × 17-inch baking sheet or line it with parchment paper.

In the bowl of a food processor, combine the flour, cornmeal, sugar, baking powder, and salt. Process the mixture for a few seconds to blend. Add the cold butter and process 15–20 seconds, until the butter pieces are the size of small peas. (You can also cut the butter into the dry ingredients with a pastry blender or your fingers.)

Dump the mixture into a large bowl. Add the cream to the dry ingredients and fluff with a fork until it all comes together into a shaggy dough. Add the blackberries and marjoram. Gently bring the dough together. Turn it out onto a floured surface and, with floured hands, fold the dough over itself several times until it holds together. Gently pat the dough into a ¾-inch-thick disk. Cut it into 8 wedges like a pizza. Transfer the scones to the prepared pan and space them out at least 2 inches apart.

Bake 18–24 minutes, until the tops are golden and the centers of the scones are set. Remove the pan from the oven and transfer the scones to a rack to cool.

For the glaze: Whisk together the confectioners' sugar, lemon juice, and lemon zest. The glaze should be runny but still coat the back of a spoon. If it's too thin, add more sugar. If it's too thick, stir in lemon juice or water a few dribbles at a time until it reaches the right consistency. When the scones are cool, drizzle the glaze over the tops with a fork or a zip-top bag sealed tight and the tip of a corner snipped off. Let the icing air-dry for about 20 minutes.

Scones are best eaten the day they're made, but they can be stored, loosely covered, at room temperature for 2–3 days. The moisture in the fruit will cause the scones to soften over time.

Lobster Salad Sliders

Lobster rolls are a New England tradition. I like mine heavy on the lobster, light on the mayo, and top-loaded into a butter-toasted hot dog bun. Here I've switched things up a bit by using Portuguese sweet rolls as slider buns, which are lighter than brioche but just as delicious. I recommend hollowing out the top bun a bit to make room for more lobster. But if making your own bread is a bridge too far, you can buy your own slider rolls or fall back on the traditional split-top buns, cut in half for slider portions (lobster can be very rich for some). All the components for this meal can be made the day before, which makes this a relatively easy, if indulgent, brunch spread. Recipe can be doubled.

SERVINGS: 4

Lobster Salad

- 12 ounces lobster meat, fresh or frozen (from about 3 [1½-pound] lobsters)
- 4 scallions (white and light green parts), minced
- 1 celery stalk, finely diced
- 2–4 tablespoons mayonnaise, to taste
- ¼ teaspoon fine sea salt
- Squeeze of lemon juice
- Pinch of cayenne pepper
- Freshly ground black pepper, to taste

Sliders

Make one-half recipe Portuguese Sweet Rolls (page 17), which makes 8 slider rolls (one pan). Omit the sugar on top.

If using fresh lobster, follow the instructions on page 76 to cook and extract the tail, claw, and arm meat. Chop into bite-sized pieces. In a medium bowl, combine the lobster, scallions, celery, mayonnaise, salt, lemon juice, and cayenne. Refrigerate until well chilled, at least 4 hours.

To serve: Gently pull the rolls apart and hollow out the centers of the tops a bit, pulling out some of the bread to make room for more lobster filling. To toast the buns, melt a little butter in a medium nonstick sauté pan over medium heat. Place the cut side of the rolls onto the pan and let cook until golden and toasty, about 30 seconds to 1 minute. (For split-top hot dog rolls, toast the outside of the buns, then cut them in half crosswise.) Serve the rolls on a platter along with the lobster salad, and let folks serve themselves.

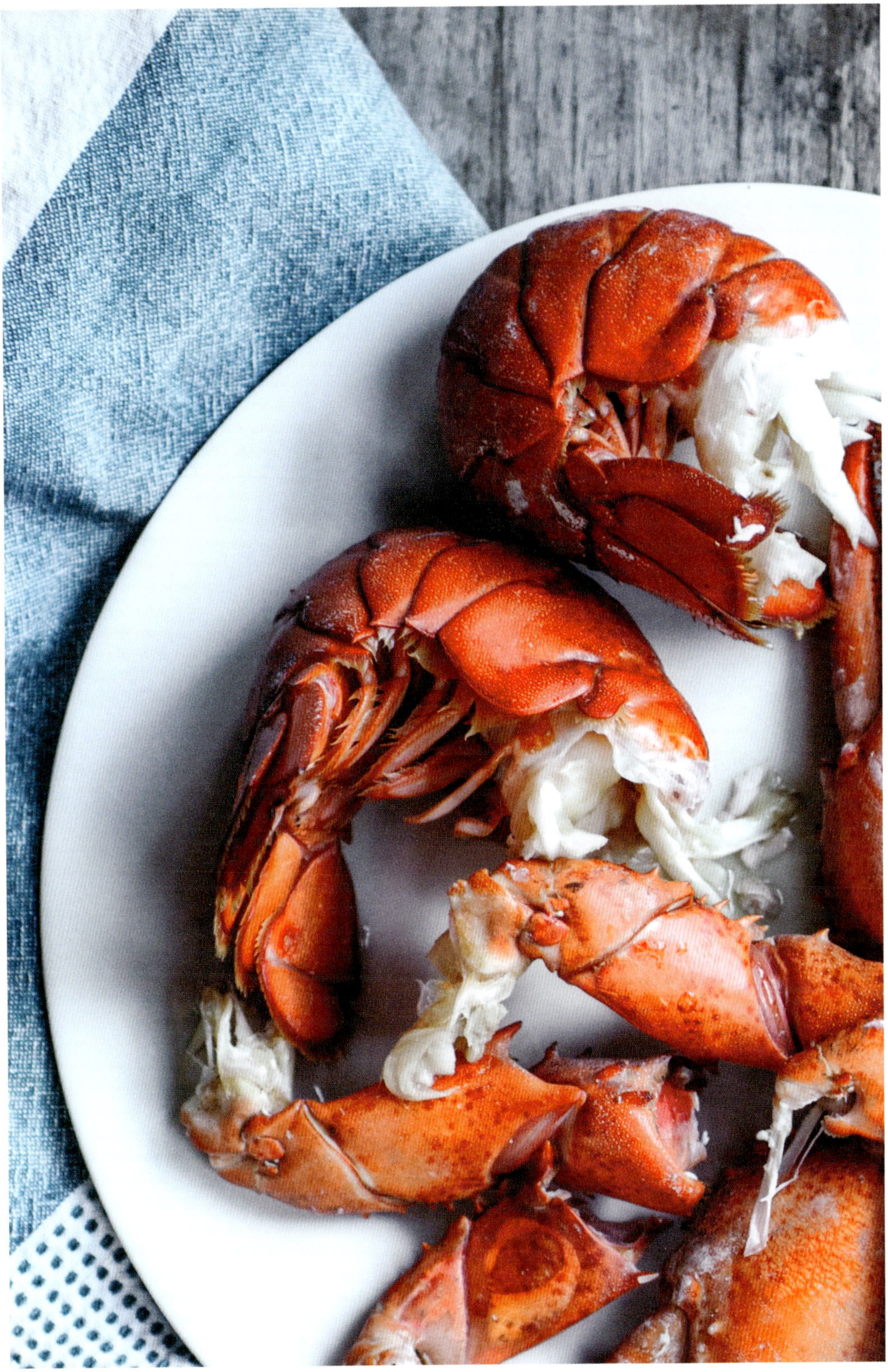

How to Cook Lobster (and Extract the Meat)

Bring a large stockpot three-fourths full of water to a boil with the lid on. Once boiling, add a tablespoon of salt. Cook the lobsters, covered, for 8–10 minutes, until the lobster shells are fire engine red and the meat is white, not translucent.

Remove the lobsters from the pot with tongs and set them on a cutting board until cool enough to handle. Using a dish towel to protect your hands, pull the tail and front legs from the rest of the body. Continue using the dish towel to twist the front legs at the joints to break them apart into knuckles and claws. Use lobster crackers to crush the shells and a pick to coax out the meat. Rinse off any shell fragments and dry the meat well with a clean tea towel.

For the tail, remove the green tomalley and pink roe. Flip the tail so the red shell is on the bottom. Using a sharp knife or kitchen shears, cut lengthwise down the underside of the tail. Pull the tail open and remove the meat. Cut into bite-sized chunks. (I don't find it worth the time to remove the meat from the smaller legs. Instead, I freeze the lobster carcass and use it to make bisque or chowder.)

Handling Seafood Humanely

I'm an omnivore that loves animals, so I do my best to reduce their suffering. I don't believe cooking lobsters alive is humane. Instead, I use a modified version of *Ikejime*, the Japanese method of killing lobster and other seafood for consumption, which is considered the fastest and most humane method (it also maintains the quality of the meat).

I keep the lobsters in their bags in the soundproof refrigerator so they don't get stressed out. Then I take one out, holding it by the back of the carapace, and use a sharp chef's knife to quickly sever the spinal cord and brain to prevent it from feeling any pain or awareness. Then I add the lobster to the pot immediately and repeat for the next lobster. You can learn more about *Ikejime* online. If you're squeamish, I recommend having your fishmonger precook the lobsters to order (or buy ones that are already precooked in the case).

Saltwater Pickles

These bright, crisp refrigerator pickles are one of my favorite ways to serve garden-fresh cucumbers in the summertime. There's no vinegar in the brine, only salt, so they lack the tart tang of supermarket dills. Nor do they feature the funky fermentation of deli dills, since they're barely allowed to ferment at all. Instead, they retain a pleasant, briny flavor reminiscent of the sea or a freshly shucked oyster. They pair with any kind of sandwich, but particularly the Lobster Salad Sliders (page 74).

SERVINGS: MAKES 2 PINT JARS

- 3–4 medium pickling cucumbers (about 1 pound), spines rubbed off sideways with a dish towel
- 2 cups cold water
- 1 tablespoon fine sea salt
- 1 teaspoon dill seed, divided
- 12 black peppercorns, divided
- 2 bay leaves, divided
- 2 sprigs fresh dill
- 1 small garlic clove, smashed, peeled
- Red chile flakes, to taste (optional)

Slice off the ends the cucumbers. Cut them into spears about three-fourths the height of the jar and no more than ¾ inch wide.

In a large measuring cup, stir the salt into the water until fully dissolved.

To each of two clean pint jars, add ½ teaspoon dill seed, 6 peppercorns, 1 bay leaf, 1 sprig of dill, half a garlic clove, and a sprinkle of red chile flakes. Pack the cucumber spears into the jar tightly so they don't float to the top when the water is added. Pour the water into the jars, covering the cucumbers by about 1 inch (you may not need all the water, and that's okay).

Screw on the lids and refrigerate (note the date on a label). Chill overnight. Keep refrigerated for 1–2 weeks. If the liquid turns cloudy, the pickles are past their prime and should be discarded.

Broccoli and Brie Quiche

Broccoli is one of my all-time favorite vegetables, and this deep-dish quiche is chock-full of it along with melty chunks of brie. This quiche recipe differs from most in that the crust contains bacon fat in addition to butter, giving it a salty, savory flavor that doesn't overpower the filling. (To learn how to render bacon fat, see the Sheet Pan Bacon recipe on page 40.) If you don't eat meat, you can replace the bacon fat with more butter. If you're gluten-free, just leave out the crust and make a frittata instead (see the technique on page 33). You can also swap out the fillings to your heart's content (see the summer squash and red pepper variation on page 81). Look to your garden or the local farmers' market for inspiration. Just be sure to cook the meat and vegetables until fully cooked and tender before adding to the quiche. If serving the quiche the same day you're making it, allow a full four hours from start to finish to allow for chilling the dough, blind-baking the crust, and baking the quiche. Or the prep can be split over two days: Make the dough the day before, chill it, roll it out, assemble it in the pie dish, then freeze it. The next morning, pull it out of the freezer and follow the instructions for blind-baking.

SERVINGS: 6–8

Crust

- 2 cups all-purpose flour
- ½ teaspoon fine sea salt
- ½ cup (1 stick) cold unsalted butter, cut into 8 pieces
- 2 ounces (4 tablespoons) cold rendered bacon fat (or butter)
- 4–5 tablespoons ice water

For the crust: Combine the flour and salt in the bowl of a food processor. Add the cold butter and bacon fat, and process 15–20 seconds, until the butter pieces stop jumping around like popcorn. With the motor running, add the ice water through the feed tube, 1 tablespoon at a time, until the dough starts to come together. Add only as much water as you need, and don't overprocess. The dough should hold together when gently squeezed. (If you don't have a food processor, you can work the butter and bacon fat into the flour mixture with a pastry blender, fork and knife, or your fingers.)

Gather the dough together, folding it over itself two or three times to make sure it holds together. Form the dough into a disk and wrap it in wax paper, plastic wrap, or reusable wrap. Let it rest in the refrigerator for 30 minutes and up to 1 hour.

Meanwhile, fill a medium pot with 1 inch of water. Set a metal steamer basket on the bottom of the pot, cover the pot with a lid, and set over medium-high heat. Bring to a simmer.

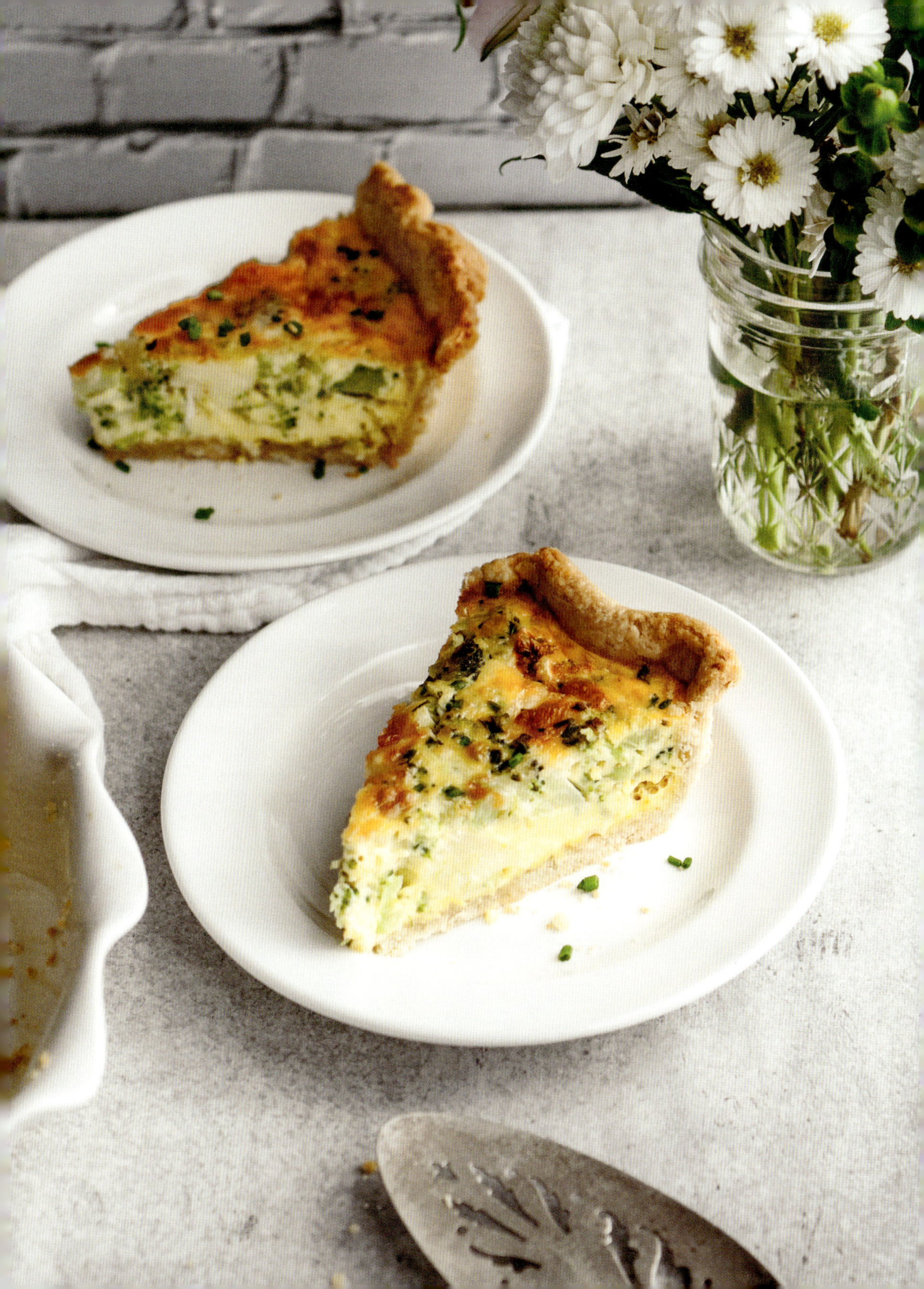

Filling

½ pound (3–4 cups) fresh broccoli florets

6 large eggs

¾ cup milk

¾ cup heavy cream

½ teaspoon kosher salt

Freshly ground black pepper, to taste

3 ounces brie (⅓ cup), cut into ½-inch cubes

¼ cup shredded cheddar

Fresh chives, chopped, for garnish

Cut the broccoli into florets about 1 inch across the top. Add the broccoli to the steamer basket, cover, and steam over medium heat for 4–5 minutes. The broccoli should be bright green and easily pierced with a fork. (You can also steam the broccoli in the microwave. Add the florets to a medium bowl with 2 tablespoons water. Cover with a plate and heat on high for 2–4 minutes, stirring once in between, until tender. Microwave times vary.) Remove the broccoli with tongs and let cool on a cutting board. Once cool, cut the broccoli into bite-sized pieces.

Preheat the oven to 375°F. Grease a 9- to 10-inch deep-dish pie dish or springform pan.

Flour your counter and rolling pin well. Roll out the disk of pie dough to 13 or 14 inches in diameter (slightly less than ¼ inch thick). Using a bench scraper or spatula to loosen the dough from the counter, flip one side of the dough over the rolling pin, center over the pie dish, and unfurl over the top. Without stretching the dough, nudge it into place, trim the excess, and form a shapely edge. Poke the dough all over the bottom with a fork to prevent the crust from puffing up too much. Set a sheet of parchment paper touching the dough and nestle a second, smaller cake pan or pie plate inside to help the dough hold its shape. (I prefer this method to using pie weights, but feel free to use weights, dried beans, or rice if you don't have a pie plate that fits.)

Bake for 20 minutes. With oven mitts, carefully remove the inner pan and parchment paper from the crust; bake 10–15 minutes more, until the crust around the edges is golden and the bottom crust looks dry. Remove from the oven and let cool.

For the filling: Whisk the eggs in a large bowl. Stir in the milk, cream, salt, black pepper, and steamed, chopped broccoli with a wooden spoon. Add the cubes of brie, separating them so they don't stick together, and mix well. Pour the filling into the crust; top with shredded cheddar. (Depending on the height of your pie plate, you may have extra filling. Simply pour into a small, buttered casserole dish and bake as a frittata.)

Place on the middle rack in the preheated oven with a sheet pan underneath to catch any drips. Bake 45–50 minutes, until the crust is golden brown and the center is fully set (use the tip of a paring knife to probe the center to be sure). If the top starts to get too brown, lay a piece of aluminum foil over the top of the quiche. Remove the quiche from the oven and sprinkle with chives. Let cool 20 minutes; serve warm or at room temperature.

The quiche is best the day it's made, but leftovers can be covered and stored in the refrigerator for 3–4 days. The quiche can be reheated in the microwave.

Variation

Summer Squash and Red Pepper Quiche: Make the crust and let it chill. Meanwhile, dice 1 small yellow onion and sauté it in 1 tablespoon olive oil over medium heat for 4 minutes until soft. Add 1 cup cubed zucchini, 1 cup cubed yellow squash, ¼ cup diced red bell pepper, and 1 teaspoon chopped fresh thyme. Sauté 3–5 minutes, until the vegetables are soft. Set aside and let cool. Continue with the filling instructions, reducing the milk to ½ cup, replacing the broccoli with the squash mixture, and replacing the brie and cheddar with ½ cup shredded Gruyère (saving some cheese to sprinkle over the top). Continue as directed.

Sweet and Spicy Skillet Cornbread

This savory cornbread combines just the right amount of honey with hot and sweet peppers to keep it moist and flavorful with a slow burn. I love the flavor of fresh poblano peppers, but use whatever mild, fresh peppers you like, from cubanelles and Hungarian wax peppers to Italian frying peppers and bell peppers. I save the hot peppers, like jalapeños and serranos, for the top, scattered more heavily in some places than others so folks can choose their spice level (or pick them off as needed—be advised, seeds still contain lots of heat). If spice isn't your thing, just leave out the hot peppers and stick to sweet. Cooking cornbread in a skillet gives it crispy edges, and it can be conveniently served right from the pan. A drizzle of hot honey on top sweetens the deal. This cornbread is delicious served with Warm Tomato Basil Bisque (page 147).

SERVINGS: 8–12

1 tablespoon olive oil or bacon fat

½ pound poblano peppers (about 2), cut into ½-inch pieces

1½ cups all-purpose flour

1½ cups cornmeal

¼ cup granulated sugar

2 teaspoons baking powder

½ teaspoon baking soda

1 teaspoon fine sea salt

2 eggs, beaten

4 tablespoons unsalted butter, melted

¼ cup honey

1 cup buttermilk, slightly warmed

4 scallions, thinly sliced

1–2 jalapeño or serrano peppers, thinly sliced

Hot honey (optional)

Preheat the oven to 400°F.

Melt the olive oil or bacon fat in a 10-inch cast iron or other nonstick, oven-safe skillet over medium-low heat. Cook the diced peppers, stirring frequently, until the skins blister and the peppers soften slightly but still hold their shape, 8–10 minutes. Remove the peppers to a small bowl, but reserve the fat in the pan.

In a large bowl, whisk together the flour, cornmeal, sugar, baking powder, baking soda, and salt. Make a well in the center. Add the beaten eggs, butter, honey, and buttermilk. Stir with a wooden spoon. Add the scallions and sautéed peppers. Mix until well dispersed.

Scrape the batter into the prepared pan and spread evenly. Scatter the sliced hot peppers on top. Place the skillet on the top rack of the oven and bake 20–25 minutes, until the top cracks and a toothpick inserted into the center comes out clean. Let cool slightly. Serve warm or at room temperature, drizzled with hot honey, if desired. Leftovers can be covered and kept at room temperature for 3–4 days.

Eggplant and Red Pepper Shakshuka

Shakshuka, eggs poached in a spiced tomato sauce, originated in northern Africa. Sephardic Jews from Libya and Tunisia brought it to Israel in the mid-twentieth century. The Moors probably also brought it to southern Italy, where a twist on this dish translates to "Eggs in Purgatory." Whether you're Jewish or Italian or none of the above, you've probably come across this dish somewhere in New England; if not, you should. Here I've included other heat-loving nightshades like red peppers and eggplant in the mix to make a delectable summer sauce that makes excellent use of the garden. Serve this tasty dish with a little bread to mop up the sauce and runny yolks, such as Focaccia with Rosemary, Red Onion, and Olives (page 134) or Portuguese Sweet Rolls (page 17).

SERVINGS: 6

- ½ pound eggplant, cut into ½-inch dice (peeled or unpeeled)
- 3 tablespoons extra-virgin olive oil
- 1 pound red bell peppers (about 2 medium), cut into ½-inch dice
- 1 medium yellow onion, cut into ¼-inch dice
- 4 garlic cloves, minced
- 1 tablespoon tomato paste
- 1 (28-ounce) can crushed tomatoes
- ¾ pound fresh tomatoes (about 2 medium), cut into ½-inch dice
- 2 tablespoons capers, drained
- 1 tablespoon harissa (or a pinch of red pepper flakes and a splash of red wine vinegar)

For the eggplant: Scatter the cubes in a medium sieve set over a plate and scatter ½ teaspoon salt over the top. Let sit while preparing the other ingredients.

Heat the olive oil in a large 12-inch skillet over medium heat. Cook the peppers, stirring frequently, for 5–6 minutes, until they start to soften. Add the onions and continue sautéing until the vegetables are soft, about 4 minutes more. Stir in the eggplant, first squeezing it dry with a paper towel, one handful at a time. Add the garlic and tomato paste. Stir for about 1 minute, until the pan goes dry. Add the canned and fresh tomatoes, ½ cup water, capers, harissa, salt, oregano, allspice, and black pepper. Stir well, then continue cooking, uncovered, stirring occasionally, 25–30 minutes, until the peppers and eggplant soften and the sauce is thickened but not dry (you can always add a bit more water, if necessary).

One at a time, make 6 deep wells in the sauce with the back of a big spoon and crack an egg into each one, trying to keep the yolk intact. You want most of the egg sunken into the sauce so the yolks stay runny, not sitting on top, where they will cook up firm (unless you prefer your eggs that way). Season the eggs with salt and black pepper. Cover the pan, reduce the heat to medium-low, and cook until the eggs whites are set but the yolks are still runny, 5–10 minutes.

- 2 teaspoons kosher salt, plus ½ teaspoon for salting the eggplant
- ½ teaspoon dried oregano
- ⅛ teaspoon ground allspice
- 6 large eggs
- 2 ounces crumbled feta cheese
- Freshly ground black pepper
- Aleppo pepper (optional)

Scatter the feta on top, sprinkle with Aleppo pepper, and serve immediately.

The eggs are best eaten the day they're made, but any leftover sauce can be stored for 3–4 days in the refrigerator and served with more eggs or tossed with pasta.

Rhode Island Johnnycakes with Shrimp, Zucchini, and Sweet Corn

Johnnycakes, fried corn cakes made with stone-ground white flint corn, are a Rhode Island specialty. They were originally made by the Algonquin tribes of the region, but the British settlers adopted the practice, calling them "journeycakes" because they traveled well. Eventually, as is common in the regional vernacular, the "r" was dropped, giving us "johnnycakes." They can be made thick or thin, as a sweet preparation served with maple syrup or with savory toppings instead. Here I opt for the thicker West Bay style of johnnycakes as a savory foil for garlicky shrimp, zucchini, and summer's sweetest corn. For a vegetarian option, swap out the shrimp for beans. You can buy traditional stone-ground johnnycake cornmeal from Kenyon's Grist Mill in Rhode Island, where they've been grinding white corn for johnnycakes since 1886 (see page 241 for mail-order info). But they can also be made with regular supermarket cornmeal—you just may need to add a bit more water.

SERVINGS: 4–6

Johnnycakes

2 cups white cornmeal
2 teaspoons granulated sugar
1 teaspoon fine sea salt
3–4 cups boiling water
Corn oil (or vegetable, canola, or grapeseed), to fry
Butter, to fry

Topping

2 tablespoons olive oil
2 small zucchini, diced into ¾-inch pieces
1 pound raw shrimp (large or medium), peeled, deveined
4 cloves garlic, sliced
1 jalapeño pepper, seeds removed, chopped (optional)
½ teaspoon paprika
2 ears sweet corn, kernels removed
4 tablespoons unsalted butter
Freshly squeezed lemon juice, to taste
2 tablespoons chopped fresh basil, parsley, or cilantro
Salt and black pepper, to taste

Preheat the oven to 200°F.

For the johnnycakes: Stir the cornmeal, sugar, and salt together in a large bowl. Gradually stir in 3 cups of the boiling water until fully absorbed and mixture is no longer lumpy. You want the consistency to be thick but not doughy. Different brands or grinds of cornmeal may absorb liquid differently—rely on visual cues, and add more of the remaining 1 cup of hot water a little at a time until the mixture is slightly looser than mashed potatoes.

Heat one or two large nonstick pans, cast iron skillets, or a griddle over medium-low heat until hot. Add 1 tablespoon oil and 1 tablespoon butter to the pan. Swirl fats when melted and, with a spoon, dollop about 1 heaping tablespoon-worth of the batter onto the pan and smoosh it with the back of the spoon into a patty about 2 inches in diameter. Working in batches, continue forming patties about 2 inches apart. Cook about 4–5 minutes per side, until golden brown and crisp. You may need to rotate the cakes 180 degrees halfway through the cooking time on each side before flipping to ensure even browning. When you flip the johnnycakes, gently press with the spatula to get more batter in contact with the hot pan. Add more oil and butter as needed to get that golden, crispy crust. Drain on a plate lined with paper towels. Sprinkle with salt. Set in the warm oven on a rack set on a sheet pan until the topping is ready to serve.

For the topping: Wipe out the pan and heat the olive oil. Cook the zucchini over medium heat, stirring occasionally, until it starts to brown in spots, about 3–4 minutes. Add the peeled shrimp, garlic, jalapeño, paprika, salt, and pepper. Stir frequently until the shrimp turns pink and is halfway coiled. Add the sweet corn and butter. Cook 1–2 minutes more. Remove from the heat, stir in lemon juice to taste, and sprinkle with herbs.

Serve 3 johnnycakes per person, topped with the shrimp and vegetable mixture. Johnnycakes can be covered and stored in the refrigerator for 4–5 days. They can also be reheated in the toaster oven and eaten with whipped maple butter. The leftover shrimp mixture can be covered and stored in the refrigerator for 1–2 days and reheated in the microwave.

Summer

Herbed Heirloom Tomato Tart with Whipped Ricotta

Tomato season in New England is not to be missed. There are so many beautiful heirloom and hybrid varieties at the markets: Brandywine, Cherokee Purple, Black Krim, Green Zebra. This recipe makes two savory, free-form tarts featuring sun-ripened tomatoes, sweet ricotta, and fresh herbs in a crisp parmesan crust. For the best presentation, choose ripe tomatoes in assorted sizes and colors to showcase their variety and subtle differences in flavor. For herbs, you can use a generous scattering of chopped fresh basil or parsley, but my favorite is fresh marjoram leaves stripped from their woody stems. Serve alongside a vinegary summer bean salad, fresh fruit skewers, and a cold glass of white wine.

SERVINGS: 8–12

Crust

- 2 cups all-purpose flour
- ½ cup grated parmesan cheese
- ½ teaspoon table salt or fine sea salt
- ⅛ teaspoon freshly ground black pepper
- ¾ cup (1½ sticks) cold unsalted butter, cut into 12 pieces
- 5–6 tablespoons ice water

Filling

- 2 cups ricotta cheese
- ¼ cup Pecorino Romano cheese (or parmesan)
- Salt and black pepper, to taste
- 2 large ripe heirloom tomatoes, cored
- 2–3 ripe smaller tomatoes, cored, or a handful of cherry tomatoes

Preheat the oven to 425°F. Line a rimmed 12 × 17-inch baking sheet with parchment paper.

For the crust: Combine the flour, parmesan cheese, salt, and pepper in the bowl of a food processor. Add the cold butter and process 15–20 seconds, until the butter pieces stop jumping around like popcorn. With the motor running, add the ice water through the feed tube, 1 tablespoon at a time, until the dough starts to come together. Add only as much water as you need, and don't overprocess. The dough should hold together when gently squeezed. (If you don't have a food processor, you can work the butter into the flour mixture with a pastry blender, fork and knife, or your fingers.)

Gather the dough together, folding it over itself two or three times to make sure it holds together. Cut in half and form into two dough disks. Wrap them in wax paper, plastic wrap, or reusable wrap, and let them rest in the refrigerator for 30 minutes.

For the filling: Combine the ricotta, Pecorino Romano, salt, and pepper in a medium bowl. Set aside. Slice the tomatoes ¼ inch thick.

Flour your counter and rolling pin well. Roll out one of the disks of chilled pie dough about 12 inches wide and ¼ inch thick. It's okay if the edges are a little ragged. Transfer the

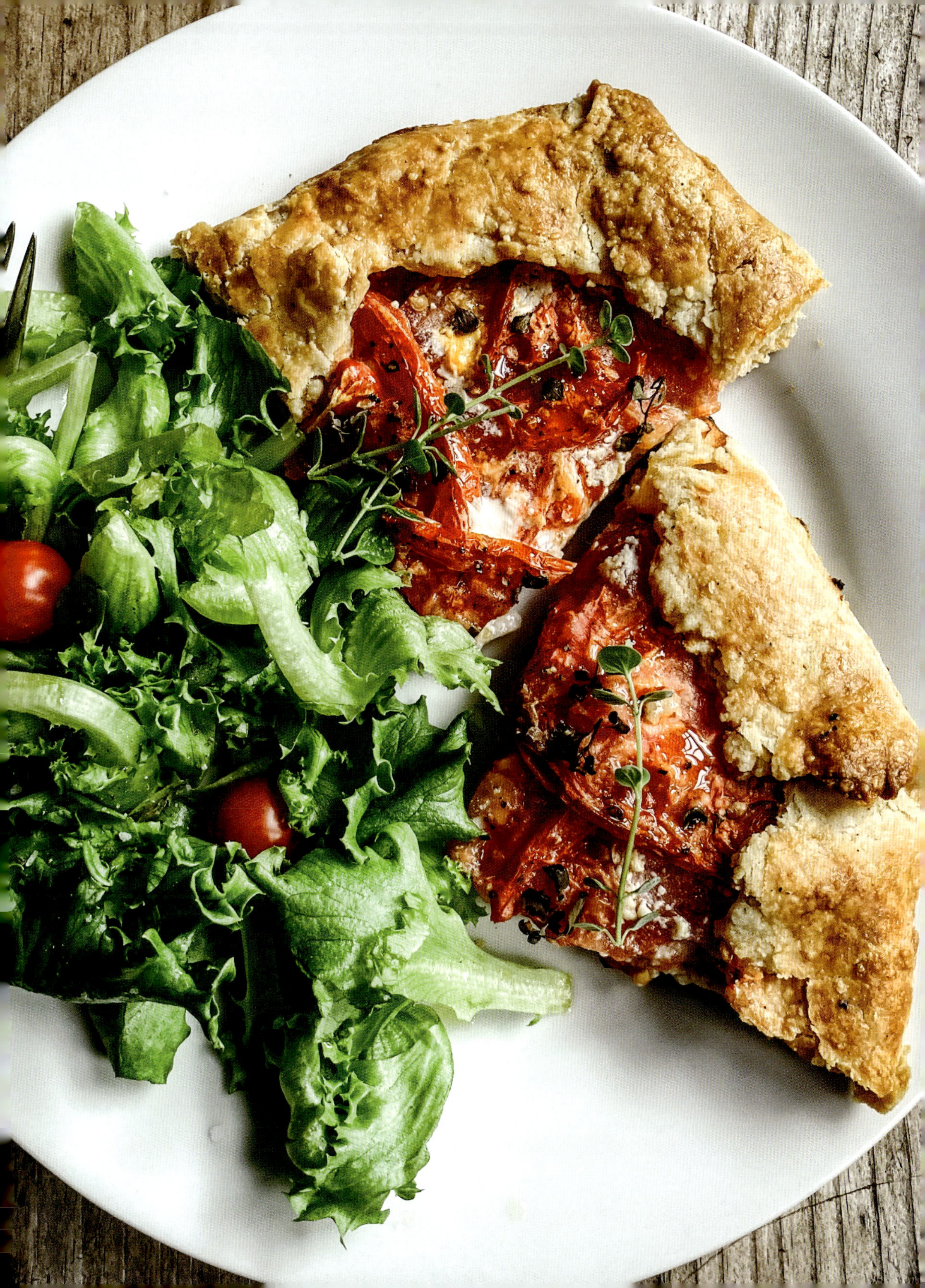

Assembly

Egg, beaten, for egg wash

Fresh herbs, like marjoram, parsley, or basil, roughly chopped

Grated parmesan cheese, for sprinkling

dough to the prepared pan by loosening it from the counter a little at a time with a bench scraper or spatula, and draping it over the rolling pin. Unroll it on one side of the prepared pan. With a spoon, spread half the ricotta mixture on top, leaving an inch or two of space around the edges of the dough. Arrange half the tomato slices over the top of the ricotta, overlapping them a little. Fold the edges of the crust up and over the edges of the tomatoes to contain their juices. Repeat the process for the second disk of dough. Beat an egg with 1 teaspoon water and brush it over the edges of the crust. Sprinkle the tops with more Pecorino Romano or parmesan cheese and freshly ground black pepper.

Bake 20 minutes, then reduce the heat to 375°F and bake 20–30 minutes more, until the crust is nicely browned. Remove from the oven and sprinkle the tomatoes with fresh chopped marjoram, parsley, or basil. Let cool 15–20 minutes before serving.

These tarts are best served warm the day they're made. Leftovers can be stored in the refrigerator, covered, for 2–3 days and reheated in the oven or toaster oven to help preserve the crispness of the crust.

Three Sisters Succotash

The Algonquin tribes of the Northeast Woodlands used corn, beans, and squash (known as the Three Sisters) as symbiotic gardening companions and complementary cooking ingredients. Succotash is an indigenous dish that combines the three beautifully. The name comes from the Narragansett word sohquttahhash, *which means "broken corn kernels." Lima beans (or butter beans) are traditional, but you can use any type of bean you want (navy, yellow-eye). The same goes for summer squash (zucchini, crookneck, pattypan). This is a great substitution for home fries if you're looking for something less carby that pairs well with runny eggs.*

SERVINGS: 8–10

- 4 tablespoons extra-virgin olive oil, divided
- 1 medium yellow onion, chopped
- 1 medium zucchini, ¾-inch dice
- 1 medium yellow squash or pattypan, ¾-inch dice
- ½ small red bell pepper, ¼-inch dice
- 2 cups fresh corn kernels (from about 4 cobs) or frozen (defrosted)
- 1 (15-ounce) can navy beans, rinsed
- ½ teaspoon freshly squeezed lemon juice
- ⅛ teaspoon ground cumin
- Handful of parsley or cilantro leaves, torn or roughly chopped
- Pinch of dried oregano
- Salt and freshly ground black pepper, to taste

In a large sauté pan, heat 2 tablespoons of the olive oil over medium-low heat. Cook the onion, stirring frequently so it doesn't brown, until softened, about 4 minutes. Add the squash and peppers. Increase the heat to medium-high. Season with ½ teaspoon salt and some black pepper. Cook, stirring occasionally, for 5–8 minutes, until the squash is tender and starting to brown. Transfer to a large bowl and cover to keep warm.

Add 1 tablespoon olive oil to the hot pan and reduce the heat to medium. Add the corn and ½ teaspoon salt. Cook, stirring frequently, for 1–2 minutes, until the corn is just starting to soften but still has a hint of crispness (frozen, defrosted corn only needs to be rewarmed). Add the beans to the pan and toss a minute or two until warm. Transfer them to the bowl of vegetables. Stir well.

To season, add the remaining 1 tablespoon olive oil, lemon juice, cumin, herbs, salt, and pepper. Stir well and add additional seasoning to taste. The succotash can be served warm or at room temperature.

Leftovers can be covered and stored in the refrigerator for 3–4 days and eaten as a side dish for any meal.

Cod Cakes with Preserved Lemon and Dill Sauce

Cod has been an important New England resource for hundreds of years. Vikings as well as Portuguese and Basque fishermen touched down on the shores of North America while in pursuit of the vast cod stocks of the region long before the British landed at Plymouth Rock. Cape Cod was named for the once-abundant fish. Unfortunately, decades of unregulated commercial fishing has decimated the cod population, and restrictions are now in place to help it rebound. For this reason, it's more sustainable at this time to substitute other types of white fish for cod, like haddock, pollock, or flounder, all of which are equally delicious.

SERVINGS: MAKES 6–8

Fish

1 pound cod, haddock, pollock, or flounder, cut into 3-inch pieces
½ medium yellow onion
1 stalk celery, cut in half
1 bay leaf
1 cup panko bread crumbs, divided
3 scallions, trimmed, thinly sliced
2 tablespoons capers, drained, chopped
2 teaspoons Dijon mustard
1 large egg, beaten
2–3 tablespoons mayonnaise
⅛ teaspoon Aleppo pepper (optional)
Salt and freshly ground black pepper, to taste
Canola or vegetable oil, for frying

Sauce

1 cup sour cream
1 tablespoon freshly squeezed lemon juice
1 small clove garlic, peeled, grated or pressed
¼ cup chopped fresh dill
2 tablespoons chopped preserved lemon (or the finely grated zest of 1 lemon)
Salt and freshly ground black pepper, to taste

Fill a medium saucepan halfway up with water and set it over high heat. Add the onion, celery, and bay leaf. When the water comes to a simmer, add the fish. Poach at a gentle simmer for 5–8 minutes, just until the fish flakes apart with a fork. Remove the fish from the water with a slotted spoon, transfer to a plate, and let cool.

While the fish cools, make the sauce. In a small bowl, stir together the sour cream, lemon juice, garlic, salt, and pepper. Add the dill and preserved lemon. Mix well. Refrigerate until ready to serve.

To a large bowl, add ⅓ cup of the panko bread crumbs. Crumble the fish with your hands into flakes. Add the scallions, capers, Dijon mustard, salt, and pepper. Beat the egg in a small bowl. Add the egg, 2 tablespoons mayonnaise, and the Aleppo pepper to the bowl. Mix everything together with your hands until well combined and it binds enough to form patties. If they fall apart, add up to 2 tablespoons more mayo. Take a handful of the mixture and press it into round patties about ¾ inch thick. Set them on a plate, cover with plastic wrap, and refrigerate at least 30 minutes (this helps them hold together).

Set a large, high-sided sauté pan over medium-high heat. Add enough vegetable or canola oil to come ½ inch up the side. While the oil heats up, pour the remaining ⅔ cup of panko bread crumbs into a shallow bowl. Season with salt and pepper, and mix. Carefully lift the patties from the plate with a spatula and dredge in bread crumbs. Flip gently to coat both sides. Set a paper towel–lined plate by the stovetop.

Shallow-fry the patties 3 or 4 at a time in the hot oil until golden brown, about 3 minutes per side. Drain on paper towels and season with salt. Serve immediately with the sauce.

Cherry Tomato Burrata Salad

This simple summer salad is perfect for the height of tomato season, when the cherry tomatoes are as sweet as actual cherries. The taste of the flavorful juices combined with the acidity of a light vinaigrette against the rich, creamy cheese and crisp lettuce is divine. Try to use a variety of cherry tomatoes for maximum visual appeal and flavor. In addition to red cherry or grape tomatoes, scan your local farmers' market for Sungolds and other similarly sweet orange hybrids, as well as the dark-red Black Cherry heirloom. Prevailing wisdom seems to be that fresh tomatoes should always be accompanied by fresh basil, and I do enjoy that combination. But what I love even more is chopped fresh marjoram, if you can find it, or a combination of the two. Serve with focaccia or Portuguese sweet rolls. Double or triple as needed.

SERVINGS: 4

- 1 pint mixed cherry tomatoes, halved
- 2 tablespoons extra-virgin olive oil
- 2 teaspoons red wine vinegar
- 1 medium garlic clove, pressed in a garlic press or finely grated with a fine-planed zester
- 1 head or 8 ounces crisp green and/or red leaf lettuce, torn or cut into bite-sized pieces
- 2 (4-ounce) burrata balls
- 1 teaspoon chopped fresh marjoram or 1 tablespoon chopped fresh basil (or both)
- Flaky sea salt and freshly ground black pepper

In a medium bowl combine the halved cherry tomatoes with the olive oil, red wine vinegar, garlic, and salt and pepper. Stir gently. Cover and let sit at room temperature for at least 1 hour and up to 4 hours.

Just before serving, arrange the lettuce on a serving plate or individual salad plates. Cut the burrata balls in half and arrange cut side up over the lettuce, letting some of the cheesy interior spill out. Spoon the tomatoes and the juices over the cheese and lettuce. Shower with chopped herbs, flaky sea salt, and freshly ground black pepper. Serve immediately.

Peach-Berry Sangria

At the peak of summer, the peaches are so juicy you almost have to drink them. That's the inspiration behind this lovely pitcher drink. A handful of raspberries or blackberries adds some color and tartness to this summery twist on the refreshing Spanish beverage.

SERVINGS: 6–8

- ¾ pound unpeeled peaches (about 3 medium), fuzz rubbed off under cold water
- ¼ cup triple sec
- ¼ cup fresh-squeezed lemon juice
- 2 tablespoons granulated sugar
- 6–8 fresh mint leaves, roughly torn
- 1 (750 milliliter) bottle Prosecco, chilled
- 1 (750 milliliter) bottle dry white wine like Sauvignon Blanc, chilled
- 2 tablespoons brandy
- 4 ounces raspberries or blackberries (about a handful)
- Ice cubes

Dice the peaches (¼- to ½-inch range) and add them to a medium pitcher. Add the triple sec, lemon juice, sugar, and mint leaves. Stir gently. Cover and refrigerate for 1–2 hours.

When ready to serve, add the chilled Prosecco, white wine, brandy, and berries to the pitcher. Fill wine glasses half full of ice, and pour the sangria over the top. Be sure to serve up some boozy fruit in each glass with a slotted spoon.

Blueberry Lemonade

This refreshing twist on a summertime favorite is the perfect New England thirst-quencher for kids and adults alike (those of age and inclination can feel free to splash a bit of vodka in their glass before tipping the pitcher). Making lemonade yourself is easier than you think, and bags of lemons are usually more cost-effective than buying them singly. I find store-bought lemonade is often too sweet and contains too many artificial ingredients. If you don't have a juicer, a handheld lemon squeezer will take care of business lickety-split, probably in less than five minutes. Go ahead and time yourself. Ready, set, go!

**SERVINGS: 6–8
(MAKES 1½ QUARTS)**

Finely grated zest of 3 lemons (about 1 tablespoon)

¾ cup granulated sugar

⅓ cup water

1½ cups blueberries, plus extra for garnish

1½ cups freshly squeezed lemon juice (from about 9 medium lemons)

4½ cups ice-cold water

Ice

Lemon slices, for garnish

Fresh mint, for garnish

In a small saucepan, gently rub the lemon zest into the sugar until moist and fragrant. Add the water and blueberries. Mash the berries with a potato masher. Stir over medium heat until the sugar dissolves. Bring to a simmer, cook for 1 minute, then remove from the heat and let cool.

Strain the freshly squeezed lemon juice through a fine-mesh sieve to remove the seeds and pulp. Add it to a 2-quart pitcher along with 4½ cups of ice-cold water. Strain the blueberry syrup through a fine-mesh sieve into a measuring cup (you should have ⅔–¾ cup of syrup). Add the blueberry syrup to the pitcher and stir. Cover and refrigerate.

When ready to serve, stir well. Add the ice to individual glasses instead of the pitcher to prevent dilution. Add extra blueberries to the pitcher or to the glasses. Garnish with lemon slices and mint.

Store leftover lemonade in a covered jar in the refrigerator. Shake well before serving over ice.

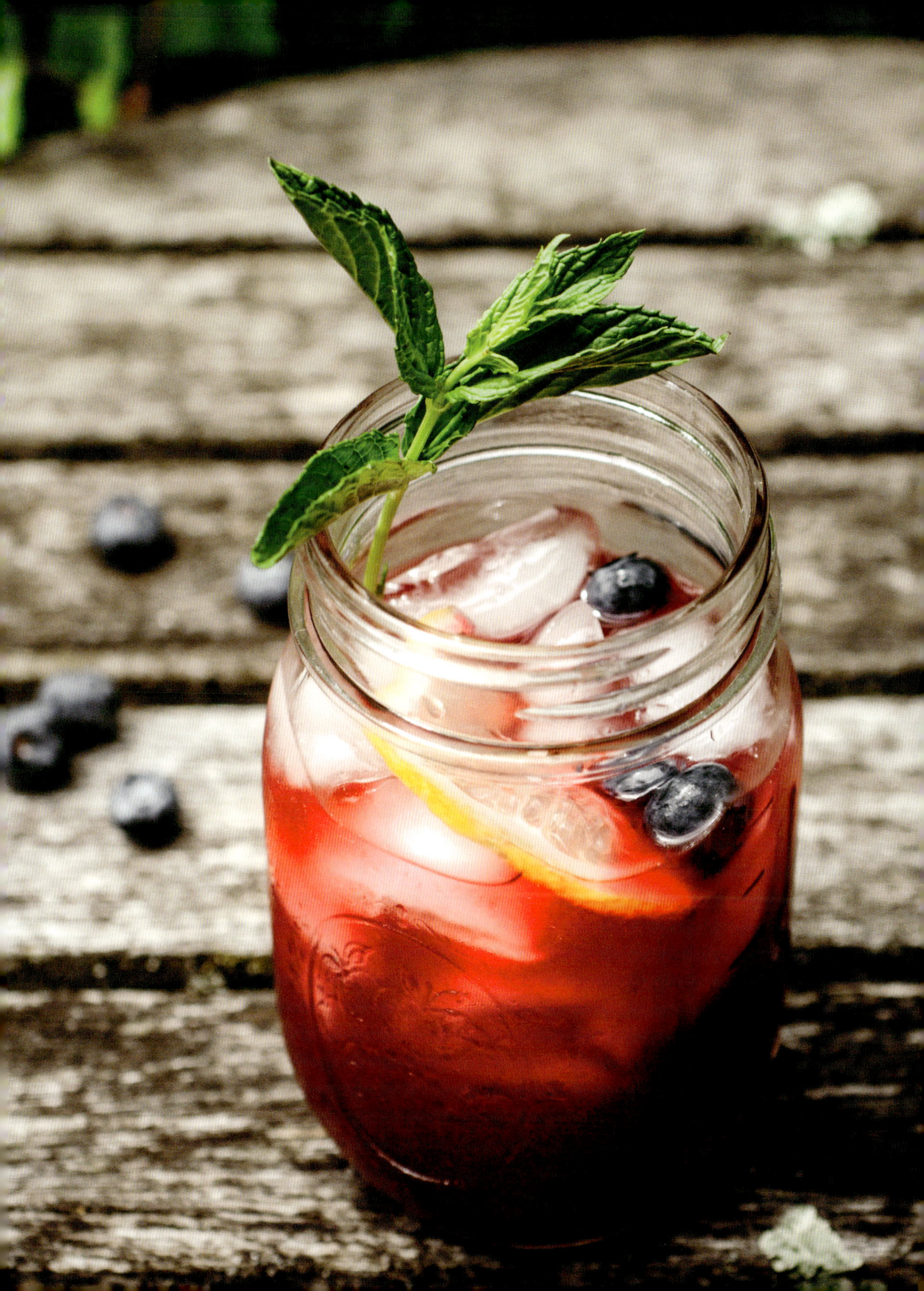

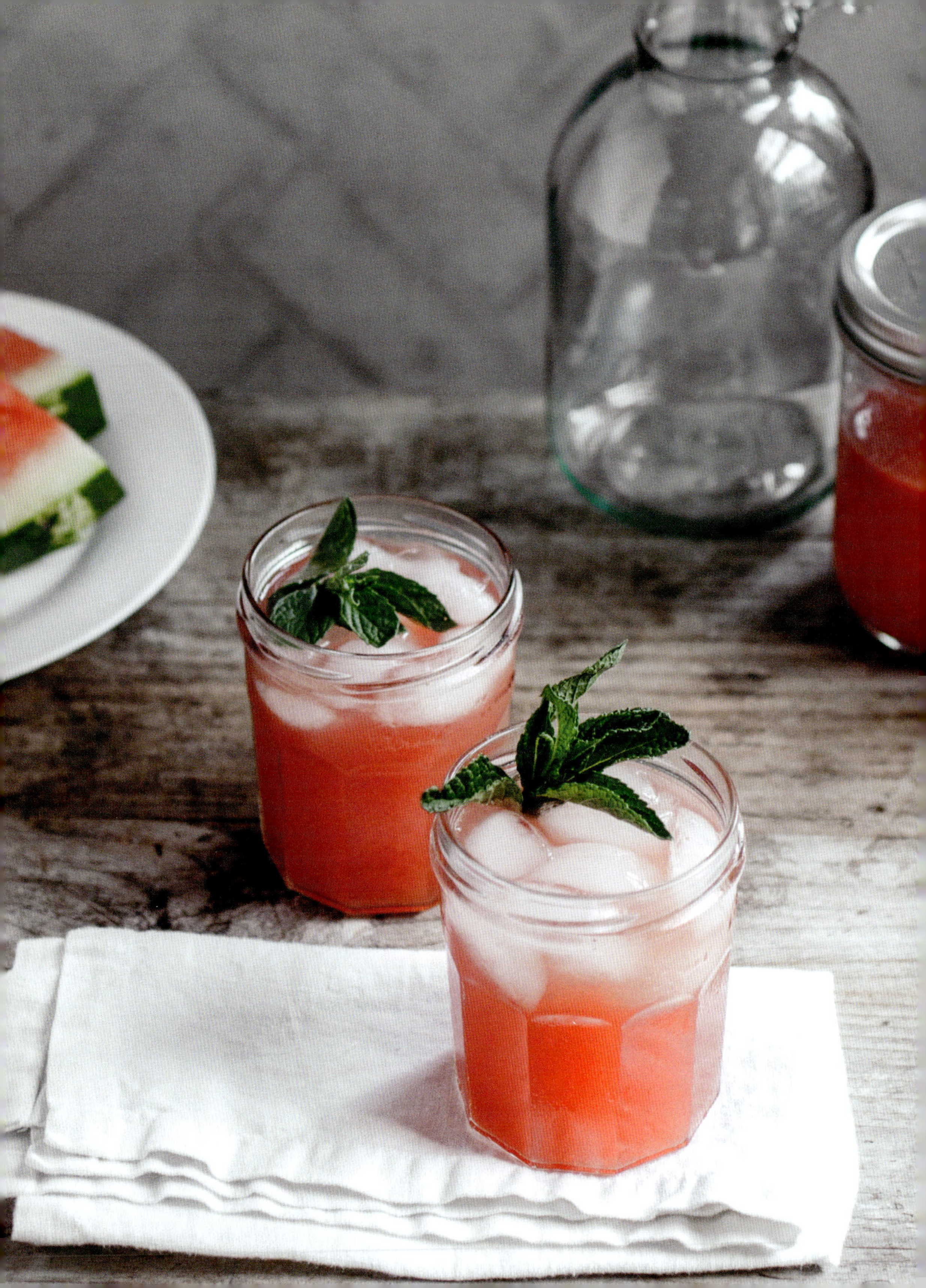

Mint Watermelon Gimlets

This refreshing beverage is summer in a glass. I recommend using Vermont's Barr Hill gin or Hendrick's. For a nonalcoholic version, replace the gin with club soda, tonic water, or seltzer, and then adjust the proportions to your taste. Instead of cooking a sugar syrup, I use a cold-steeped method, which creates a flavorful watermelon concentrate. Start the process the night before for best results. Don't throw away the leftover watermelon—it can still be eaten as is or in a fruit salad.

SERVINGS: 4–6

- 2½ pounds cubed watermelon (from a 4-pound watermelon)
- ¼ cup granulated sugar
- ¼ cup freshly squeezed lime juice (about 2 limes), plus more to taste
- Gin or vodka
- Ice
- Mint sprigs, for garnish
- Lime slices, for garnish

Combine the watermelon cubes and the sugar in a large bowl. Mash the watermelon with a potato masher until soupy. Cover and let sit in the refrigerator at least 4 hours or overnight.

Strain the watermelon juice through a fine-mesh sieve, pressing with the back of a spoon to extract more juice. The goal isn't to extract all the watermelon juice—only to get the sweetest, most-concentrated flavor. You should have about 2 cups of watermelon juice. Add the freshly squeezed lime juice. Cover and refrigerate until ready to serve.

Add a few mint leaves to the lowball glasses and fill them half-full of ice. Add a shot of gin or vodka (1.5 ounces). Then add the watermelon-lime juice (2.5 ounces), leaving some room at the top for adjustments. Stir well, adding more alcohol or lime juice to your taste. Garnish with mint sprigs and/or lime slices.

Lavender Lemon Martinis

My dear friend Shona is an excellent cook and makes the most wonderful cocktails: fresh, nuanced, and lovely. She served this Lavender Lemon Martini one New Year's Eve, and I swooned all night. Lavender can sometimes be overpowering, but that's not the case here. Don't be intimidated by the simple syrup. It takes less than five minutes to make. Dried lavender buds can sometimes be found in the spice aisle of the grocery store or sourced online (make sure the label says "food grade"). Try to find Dolin dry vermouth—it really makes a big difference. This cocktail—which can be served in a martini glass, champagne glass, or anything in between—is perfectly balanced and the most enticing brunch cocktail ever created as far as I'm concerned. The lavender syrup can also be added directly to Prosecco for a lighter brunch offering.

SERVINGS: 4

Lavender syrup

½ cup granulated sugar

½ cup water

1½ teaspoons dried lavender buds

Martini

1½ cups gin

¼ cup lavender simple syrup

¼ cup freshly squeezed lemon juice

¼ cup dry white vermouth (preferably Dolin)

For the lavender syrup: **Combine the sugar, water, and dried lavender buds in a small saucepan. Stir over medium heat until the sugar is fully dissolved. Remove from the heat and let steep until cool. Strain into a measuring cup; chill in the refrigerator until ready to use.**

For the martinis: **Combine the gin, ¼ cup of the lavender syrup, lemon juice, and dry vermouth in a large measuring cup with ice. Stir gently until ice cold, about 1 minute. Strain into cocktail classes. Garnish with a few dried lavender buds.**

The leftover syrup can be stored in a covered jar in the refrigerator for weeks.

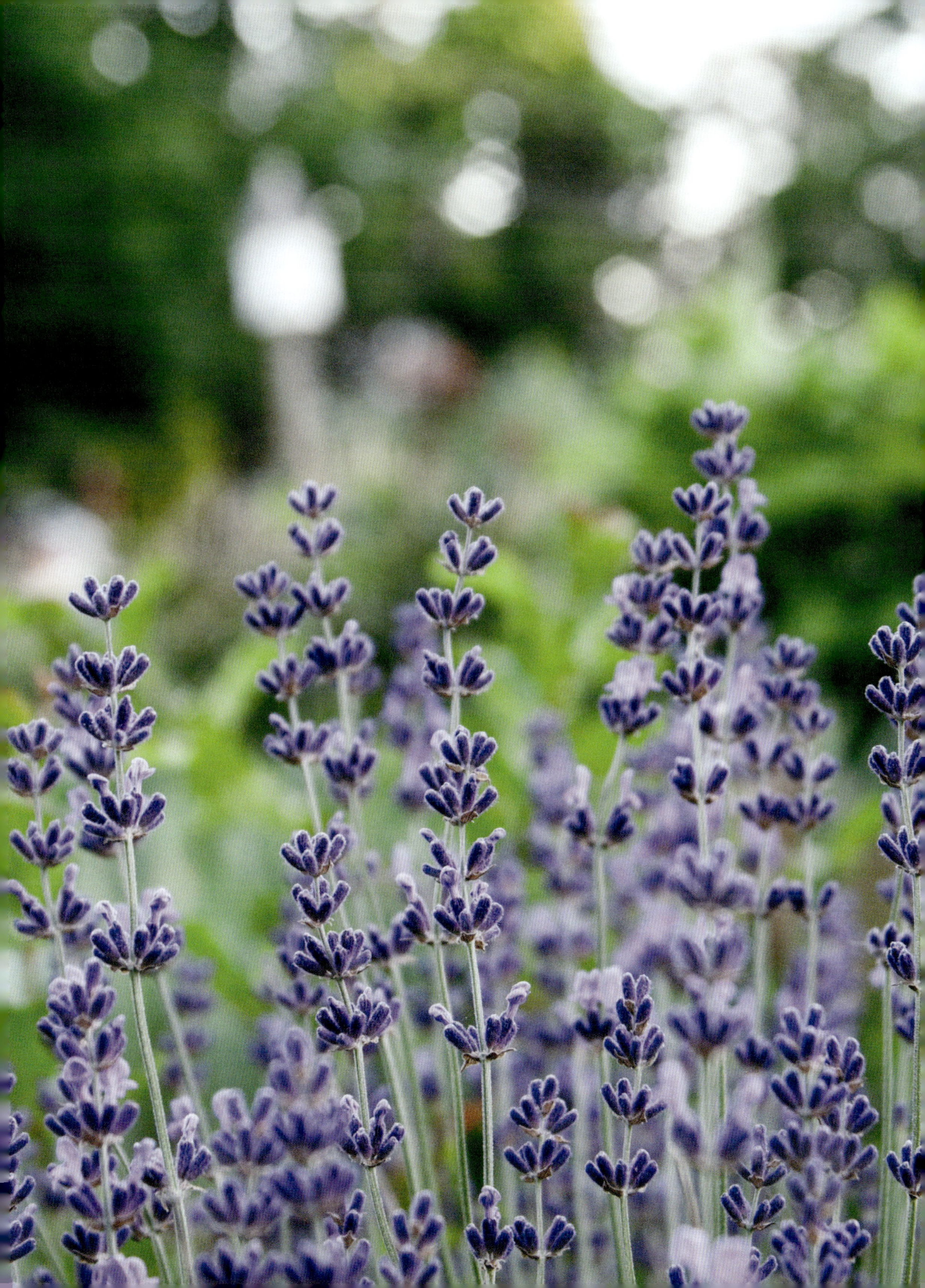

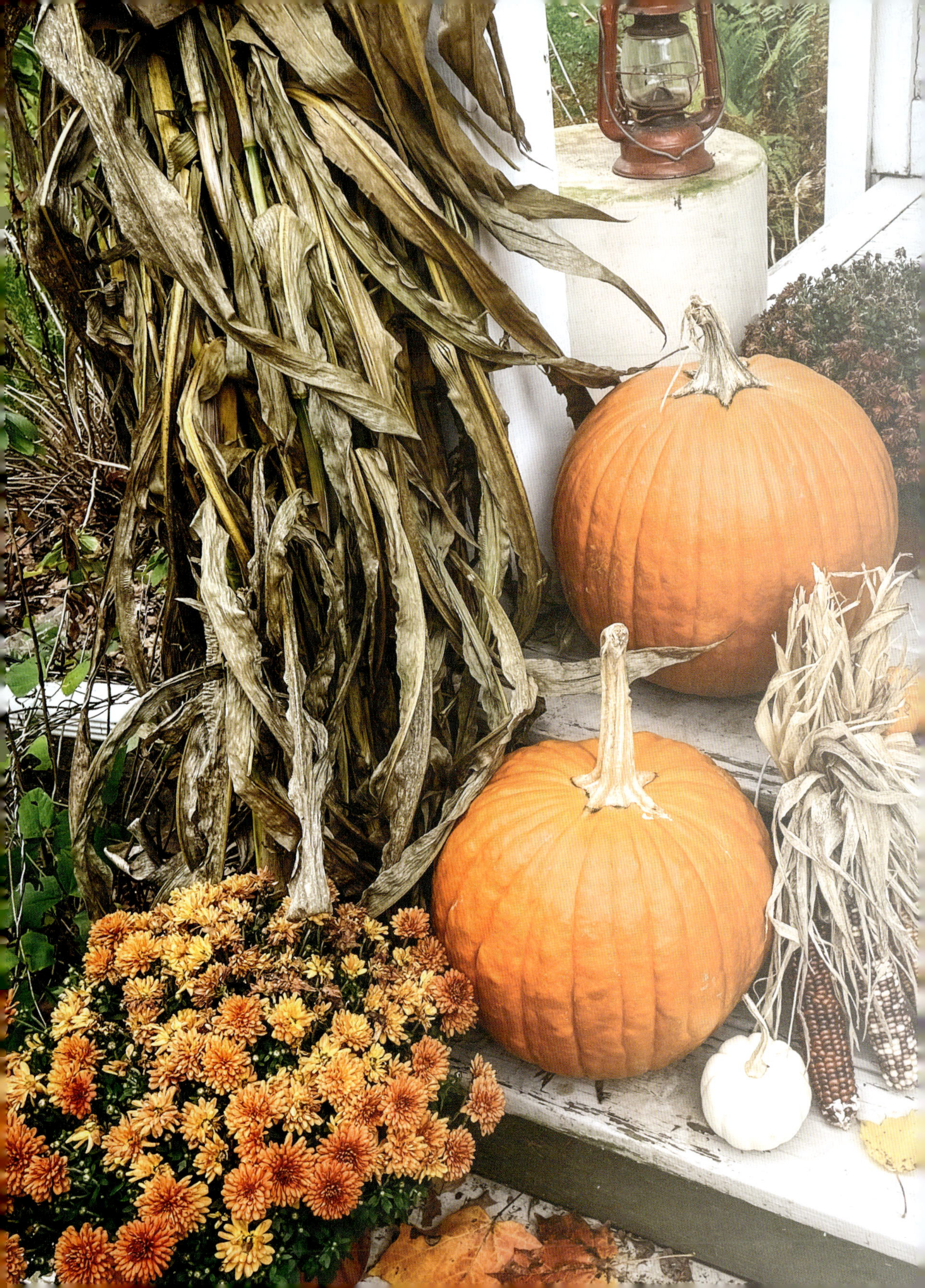

Fall

Pumpkin Whole Wheat Pancakes 106

Apple Fritters 109

Pumpkin Spice Granola 111

Cranberry Orange Coffee Cake 112

Caramel Apple Sticky Buns 115

Homemade Bagels 118

Cranberry Cornmeal Pancakes 121

Cinnamon Sugar Cannoli Popovers 123

Pear-Nutella Baked French Toast 125

Lobster, Corn, and Potato Pot Pie 127

Pumpkin Breakfast Bars 130

Squash and Sage Scones 132

Focaccia with Rosemary, Red Onion, and Olives 134

Acadian Buckwheat Crepes with Creamy Mushrooms 136

Brussels Sprouts and Pancetta Hash 138

Sausage and Stuffing Strata 140

Portuguese Kale Soup 142

Kale Caesar Salad with Squash Croutons and Pepitas 144

Smoked Bluefish 146

Warm Tomato Basil Bisque 147

Concord Grape Fizz 148

Spiced Pear Sangria 151

Mulled Pumpkin Cider 153

New England in the fall is a feast for the senses. Panoramic displays of spectacular foliage grace the skyline from the mountains of Maine to the coast of Connecticut. The local orchards open for apple picking—there's nothing quite like the juicy crunch of a fresh-picked apple. As the leaves start to fall, it's time to embrace all things spooky and pumpkin spice. Bright cranberries ripen, gathered from the flooded bogs of southeastern Massachusetts like shipwrecked jewels.

While we don't necessarily associate the autumn with brunch, I'm here to tell you that some of my favorite brunch dishes settle squarely into fall, when apples, cranberries, and pumpkins are at their peak. Combine them with various warming spices and rich batters and doughs to create homey and delicious dishes worth sharing, like Caramel Apple Sticky Buns, Pumpkin Breakfast Bars, and Cranberry Orange Coffee Cake.

Early autumn represents the best of summer and fall, produce-wise, including the last of the corn, tomatoes, and summer squash and the beginning of the heartier, more frost-tolerant fall crops, like kale, mushrooms, and winter squash. Don't miss the Lobster, Corn, and Potato Pot Pie. Also, it's officially soup season. Warm Tomato and Basil Bisque, inspired by my Italian roots, pairs wonderfully with the Focaccia with Rosemary, Red Onion, and Olives. Portuguese Kale Soup, made popular by the Portuguese Azorean community that settled along the southern coast of New England, is fantastic with Portuguese Sweet Rolls or Sweet and Spicy Cornbread. Afterward, serve up some warm apple fritters.

For festive fall beverages, try the Concord Grape Fizz, Spiced Pear Sangria, or Mulled Pumpkin Cider, the latter of which will warm you from the inside out. Keep it on repeat for the wintertime too—you'll wonder how you ever survived the chill without it.

Fall Brunch Menu Ideas:

Fall Birthday/Bridal/Baby Shower Brunch: Caramel Apple Sticky Buns or Cranberry Orange Coffee Cake. Kale Caesar Salad with Squash Croutons and Pepitas. Spiced Pear Sangria or Concord Grape Fizz.

Savory Fall Brunch: Lobster, Corn, and Potato Pot Pie. Brussels Sprouts and Pancetta Hash. Bloody Mary.

Fall Family Brunch: Pear-Nutella Baked French Toast, Pumpkin Whole Wheat Pancakes, or Cranberry Cornmeal Pancakes. Sheet Pan Bacon. Mulled Pumpkin Cider.

Indigenous Peoples' Day Brunch: Squash and Sage Scones or Pumpkin Breakfast Bars. Rhode Island Johnnycakes with Shrimp, Zucchini, and Sweet Corn or Smoked Bluefish. Three Sisters Succotash. Mulled Pumpkin Cider.

Vegan Fall Brunch: Focaccia with Rosemary, Red Onion, and Olives. Warm Tomato Basil Bisque. Kale Caesar Salad with Squash Croutons and Pepitas. Concord Grape Fizz.

Pumpkin Whole Wheat Pancakes

These pancakes are a pumpkin-lovers dream: fluffy, flavorful, and perfect for fall. Top with a dollop of whipped cream cheese, a drizzle of maple syrup, and a sprinkling of chopped walnuts to take them to next-level status. This pancake recipe can be halved for small families or doubled for a crowd. Any extra pumpkin puree can be used in the Pumpkin Breakfast Bars (page 130).

SERVINGS: MAKES ABOUT 20

- 2 cups all-purpose flour
- ⅔ cup whole wheat flour
- 2 tablespoons dark brown sugar, packed
- 2 tablespoons pumpkin spice (to make your own, see page xv)
- 1 tablespoon baking powder
- 1 teaspoon baking soda
- 1 teaspoon table salt or fine sea salt
- 2½ cups milk
- 2 tablespoons apple cider vinegar
- 2 large eggs
- 1 cup pumpkin puree (canned or fresh)
- ¼ cup vegetable oil
- Butter, for frying
- Maple syrup, for serving
- Chopped walnuts (optional)

For the pancakes: In a medium bowl, whisk together the all-purpose flour, whole wheat flour, dark brown sugar, pumpkin spice, baking powder, baking soda, and salt.

In a large measuring cup, combine the milk and apple cider vinegar.

In a large bowl, beat the eggs. Whisk in the pumpkin puree and vegetable oil until smooth. Gradually whisk in the milk. Add the dry ingredients and whisk until combined. The batter will be thick.

Heat a large nonstick skillet, cast iron pan, or griddle over medium heat until very hot (test by flicking some water into the pan; the water droplets should sizzle vigorously and disappear). Melt 1 tablespoon butter and swirl around the pan. Working in batches, use a ⅓-cup measuring cup to scoop the batter onto the pan. Cook 2 to 4 minutes per side, until bubbles start to pop on the top and the bottoms are beautifully brown. Repeat with the remaining batter, adding more butter to the pan as needed.

Stack on a large plate with thin slices of butter between them and cover with an inverted bowl or aluminum foil.

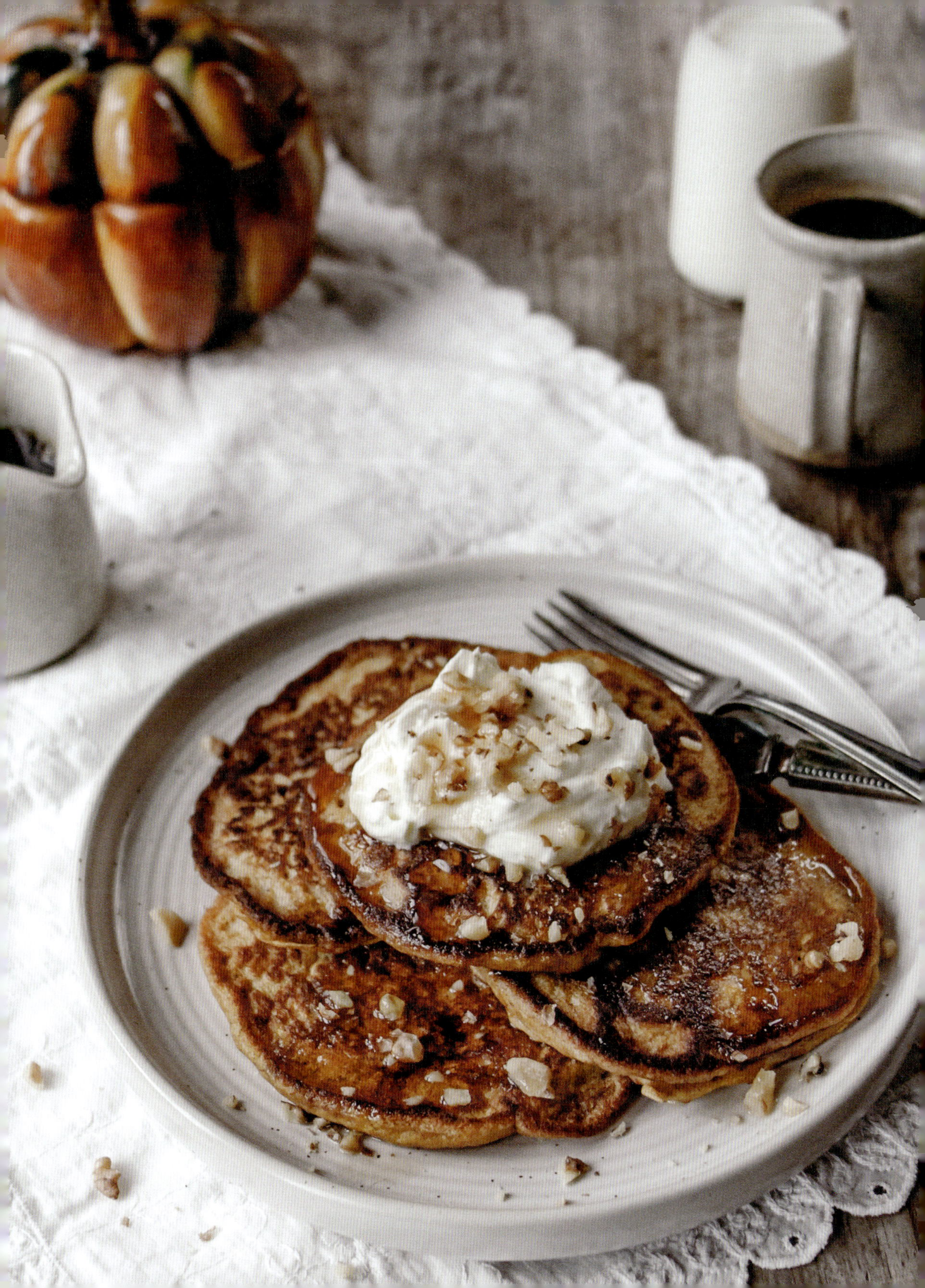

Whipped Cream Cheese

½ cup cream cheese, softened
¼ cup confectioners' sugar, sifted
Dash of vanilla
¾ cup heavy cream

For the whipped cream cheese: Combine the cream cheese, sugar, and vanilla in the bowl of an electric mixer fitted with the whisk attachment. Whip the mixture until smooth. Gradually add the cream down the side of the bowl while whipping on low speed. If the mixture gets too sloshy, hold off on adding more cream until the rest is fully incorporated. Once all the cream is added, continue to beat on medium-high until soft peaks form.

Serve the pancakes still warm with a dollop of whipped cream cheese, maple syrup, and chopped walnuts, if desired.

Leftover pancakes and whipped cream cheese can be covered and stored in the refrigerator for 4–5 days.

Apple Fritters

One highlight of apple season in New England are the apple fritters. If you've never had the pleasure, they're essentially chunky apple doughnuts minus the holes. These have a sweet apple cider glaze, but you could also toss the fritters with a mixture of ½ cup granulated sugar and ½ teaspoon ground cinnamon while they're still warm for more of an apple cider doughnut vibe. Sweet apples work best, especially fresh-picked, so hit up your local apple orchard for Honeycrisp, Jonagold, Gala, or Cortland apples.

SERVINGS: MAKES ABOUT 16

- 1⅔ cups all-purpose flour
- ¼ cup light brown sugar, firmly packed
- 1 teaspoon ground cinnamon
- ½ teaspoon baking powder
- ½ teaspoon fine sea salt
- ¼ teaspoon ground nutmeg
- 2 large eggs, separated
- 2 tablespoons unsalted butter, melted, cooled slightly
- ⅔ cup milk, at room temperature
- ½ teaspoon vanilla extract
- 2 medium sweet apples, peeled, cored, cut into ¼-inch slices, then into ⅓-inch pieces
- Vegetable oil, for frying

Heat 2 inches of vegetable oil in a heavy, wide saucepan or Dutch oven until the temperature reaches 375°F.

In a medium bowl, whisk together the flour, brown sugar, cinnamon, baking powder, salt, and nutmeg. In a large bowl, whisk the egg yolks with the melted butter. Slowly whisk in the milk and vanilla. Add the dry ingredients to the wet ingredients. Stir with a wooden spoon or rubber spatula just until combined. The batter will be very thick at this point.

In a separate, clean medium bowl, beat the egg whites with an electric mixer until they hold firm peaks (when you lift the beaters, the whipped whites form peaks that don't droop). Stir one-third of the beaten egg whites into the batter to loosen it. Stir in the apple chunks. Scrape the remaining beaten egg whites on top and gently fold them in with a rubber spatula.

You can drop the batter by heaping spoonfuls into the hot oil, but I prefer flatter fritters to ensure they cook through while also staying light and pillowy. To accomplish this, generously flour your work surface. Scoop a heaping tablespoon of batter (a 1½-ounce cookie scoop works well here) onto the floured surface. Generously sprinkle with flour and, with floured hands, press the mound into a flat, oval patty about ¾ inch thick. Use a spatula to transfer the fritter batter gently into the hot oil. Fry in small batches for 2–3 minutes on each side, until deeply golden. Remove the fritters from the oil with tongs or a slotted spoon, and let them drain on paper towels on a cooling rack set over a baking pan. Repeat for the rest of the batter.

Glaze

1½ cups confectioners' sugar, sifted

3 tablespoons apple cider (or milk)

Pinch of fine sea salt

For the glaze: Whisk together the confectioners' sugar and apple cider until smooth and thick enough to coat the back of a spoon. While the fritters are still warm, dip each fritter in the glaze on all sides and let the excess drip off. Let the glazed fitters cool on the cooling rack (remove the paper towels) until the glaze is set before serving, about 15–20 minutes.

Apple fritters are best served the day they're made. Leftovers can be stored at room temperature, loosely covered for a day or two (don't store in an airtight container or the glaze will lose its integrity).

Pumpkin Spice Granola

Pumpkin spice makes everything taste like magic. This crunchy, wholesome granola is the perfect way to bridge the transition between summer and fall. Sprinkle some over Greek yogurt with fresh raspberries, or take it with a splash of milk for a quick boost of whole grains, nuts, and seeds. Substitutions are allowed and encouraged. Swap out the grapeseed oil for coconut oil. Use honey instead of maple syrup. Add chopped figs or dates. I like to use egg whites to encourage the formation of crunchy little clusters, but if you're vegan, try this instead: Soak 1 tablespoon of the chia seed in 2 tablespoons of water and let sit five minutes. Stir well, then add to the mixture along with the wet ingredients.

SERVINGS: MAKES ABOUT 8 CUPS

3 cups rolled oats

1½ cups chopped pecans

1¼ cups pumpkin seeds (raw or roasted, salted or unsalted)

½ cup sunflower seeds

¼ cup brown sugar

1 tablespoon pumpkin spice (to make your own, see page xv)

2 tablespoons flaxseed or chia seeds

1½ teaspoons fine sea salt

1 teaspoon ground cinnamon

½ cup grapeseed, vegetable, or canola oil, plus 1 tablespoon for the pan

2 large egg whites

¼ cup maple syrup (amber or dark)

½ teaspoon vanilla extract

Preheat the oven to 300°F. Brush a rimmed 12 × 17-inch baking sheet with 1 tablespoon oil.

In a large bowl, stir together all the dry ingredients. In a medium bowl, whisk together the oil, unbeaten egg whites, maple syrup, and vanilla extract. Add the wet ingredients to the dry. Mix well with a wooden spoon. Spread evenly on the prepared pan and press flat with a spatula.

Bake 25–30 minutes, flipping the mixture every 10 minutes and re-flattening with a spatula. Remove from the oven and let the granola cool on the pan without stirring for 30 minutes to 1 hour. (It might seem slightly damp but will firm up on sitting.) Loosen the mixture from the pan with a spatula.

Once cool, transfer to jars or other airtight containers; the granola can be stored for up to 3 weeks.

Cranberry Orange Coffee Cake

The only thing that improves a traditional coffee cake is the addition of fresh, seasonal berries. In fall and winter, cranberries add a welcome zing of tartness and beautiful pop of color, making this coffee cake a great choice for holiday brunches. A festive sprinkling of seasonal spices in the crumbly topping and a hint of orange (or even lemon) zest in the batter adds even more dimension.

SERVINGS: 8–12

Cake

½ cup (1 stick) unsalted butter, at room temperature

1 cup granulated sugar

1 teaspoon vanilla extract

½ teaspoon finely grated orange zest (from ½ medium orange)

2 large eggs

1 cup all-purpose flour, divided, plus 1 tablespoon for the cranberries

1 teaspoon baking powder

¼ teaspoon fine sea salt

⅓ cup Greek yogurt

2 cups fresh or frozen cranberries, divided (no need to defrost)

Topping

¾ cup all-purpose flour

½ cup light brown sugar, firmly packed

1 teaspoon ground ginger

1 teaspoon ground cardamom

¼ teaspoon ground allspice

¼ teaspoon fine sea salt

4 tablespoons unsalted butter, melted

¼ teaspoon vanilla extract

Preheat the oven to 350°F. Grease or line an 8 × 8-inch baking dish with parchment paper.

For the cake: Cream the butter and sugar in the bowl of an electric mixer (preferably fitted with the paddle attachment) until creamy, 1–2 minutes. Scrape down the bottom and sides of the bowl as needed. Add the vanilla and orange zest. Mix on low until combined. Add the eggs, one at a time, beating well after each addition. Add ½ cup of the flour and all the baking powder and salt. Mix on low speed just until combined. Add the Greek yogurt and mix well. Scrape down the bottom and sides of the bowl, as needed. Add the remaining ½ cup flour and mix on low.

In a medium bowl, toss all but a handful of the washed cranberries with 1 tablespoon flour. Stir them into the batter by hand with a rubber spatula (reserve the remaining cranberries for the top). Spread the batter evenly in the prepared pan.

For the topping: Combine the flour, brown sugar, spices, and salt in a medium bowl. Add the melted butter and vanilla. Stir with a fork until clumps form. Break up the bigger clumps and keep stirring until you get a mixture of small and medium-sized clumps. Crumble the topping over the batter along with the remaining cranberries.

Bake 45–50 minutes until the top is golden brown, a toothpick inserted into the center comes out clean, and the cranberries on top are starting to burst. Remove from the oven and let cool completely.

Leftovers can be stored, loosely covered, at room temperature for 1–2 days.

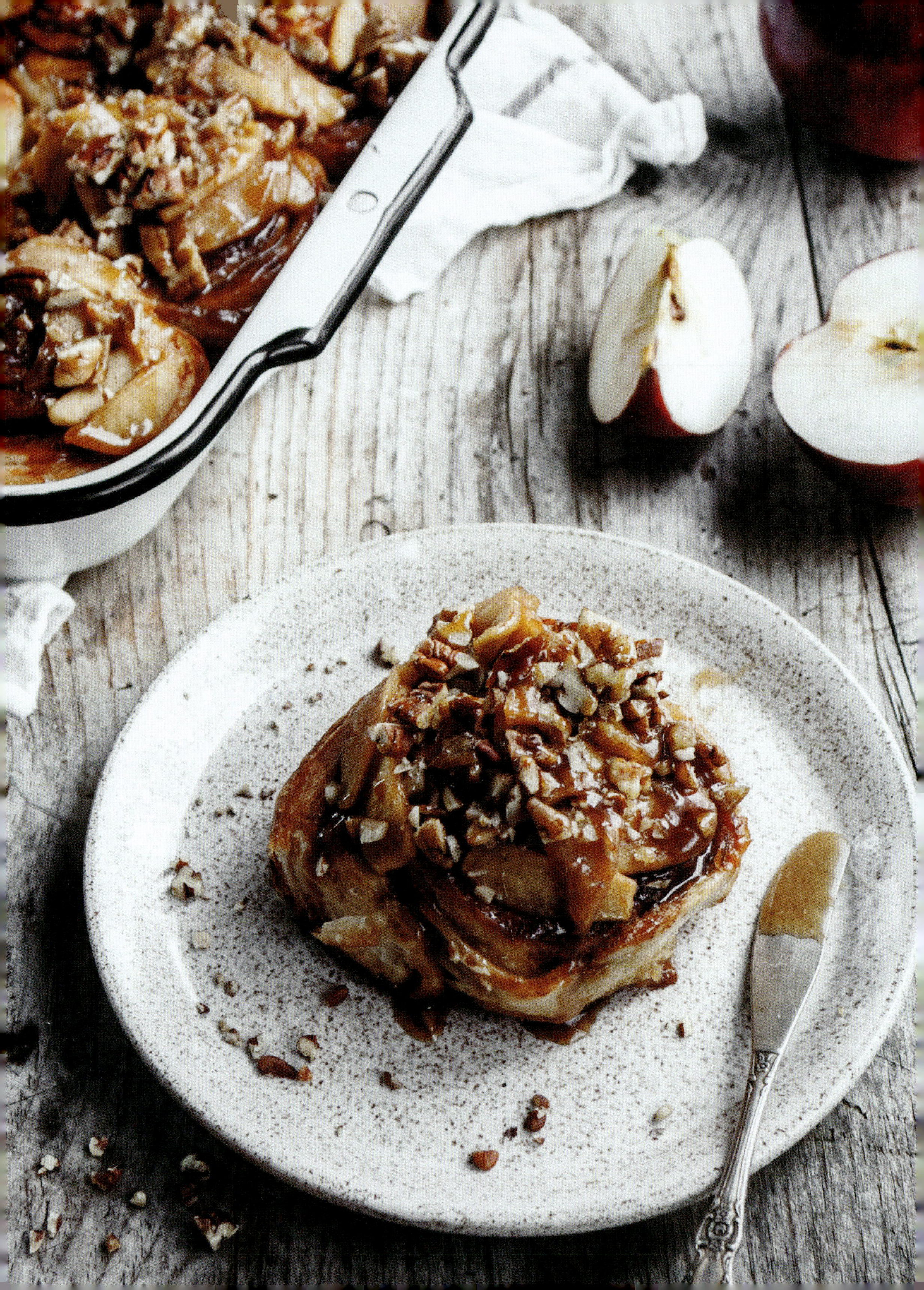

Caramel Apple Sticky Buns

I love the combination of sweet caramel and tart apples. Add some pecans and buttery pastry, and you've got the centerpiece for a fantastic brunch. These are not pillowy soft Cinnabon-style buns—for that, see the Maple Walnut Cinnamon Rolls on page 158. This dough, reminiscent of French laminated pastry, is made with bread flour and plenty of butter, so you get flaky, sturdy, not-overly-sweet layers of yeasted dough that can stand up to the sticky topping. Be advised: This recipe is a project. The apple topping and the dough should be started a day ahead of time so the dough gets a slow, overnight rise in the refrigerator. This advanced prep will also ensure you have plenty of time in the morning for the extra folding, resting, and proofing steps involved with laminated doughs (which take 4–5 hours total, but not much active work). The result will be well worth the effort, I assure you.

SERVINGS: MAKES 12

Dough

- 1½ teaspoons active dry yeast
- 1½ cups warm (not hot) water
- 1 tablespoon granulated sugar
- 3½–4 cups bread flour (or all-purpose flour), divided
- 1 teaspoon table salt or fine sea salt

For the dough: Combine the yeast, warm water, and sugar. Stir and let the mixture sit for 5 minutes until foamy. (If the mixture doesn't foam, the yeast may have expired.)

In the bowl of an electric mixer (preferably fitted with the paddle attachment), add 2 cups of the flour. Add the foamy yeast mixture and the salt. Mix on low speed until combined. Add the remaining flour, ½ cup at a time, mixing well after each addition. Stop adding flour once the dough comes together cleanly in the bowl but still feels a little tacky to the touch.

Turn the dough out onto a lightly floured surface and knead about 5 minutes until smooth (or use a dough hook with your mixer). Place the dough in an oiled bowl, turning to coat on all sides. Cover and let rise in the refrigerator overnight until doubled in size (or 1½ hours at warm room temperature).

Apples

- 2 tablespoons unsalted butter
- 1½ pounds cooking apples (about 4 medium), like Rhode Island Greening, Granny Smith, or Northern Spy, sliced thinly (about ⅛ inch thick)
- ⅓ cup apple cider
- 2 tablespoons granulated sugar
- 1 teaspoon ground cinnamon
- 1 teaspoon freshly squeezed lemon juice

Lamination

- ¾ cup (1½ sticks) unsalted butter, softened until spreadable

For the apples: Melt the butter in a large sauté pan over medium heat. Add the sliced apples and stir well, separating the slices. Stir in the apple cider, sugar, cinnamon, and lemon juice. Bring to a simmer and reduce the heat to medium-low. Continue cooking uncovered, 8–12 minutes, until the apple slices are translucent and bendy (tender, but not mushy) and the excess liquid has cooked off, leaving a loose, amber caramel sauce. Remove from the heat, transfer to a medium bowl, and let cool. If making ahead, cover and refrigerate overnight.

For the lamination: The next morning (once the dough has doubled in bulk), punch it down, turn it out onto a lightly floured surface, and let it rest for 10 minutes. Roll it out into a ⅛- to ¼-inch thick square (about 12 × 12 inches). Spread the softened butter on the right side of the dough, leaving a 1-inch border on the sides. Fold the left side of the dough over the butter, like a book, so you have a 12 × 6-inch rectangle. Press the edges closed. Fold the dough into thirds like a business letter (fold the bottom third up and the top third down to cover the bottom third). Turn the dough a quarter turn counterclockwise. Roll it up and down (not side to side) until it's 12 inches long. Fold the dough like a business letter again. If the dough isn't too stiff, you can repeat once more. Otherwise, wrap the dough in plastic wrap and let it rest in the refrigerator for 30 minutes to 1 hour first.

Filling

- ⅓ cup dark brown sugar, firmly packed
- 1 teaspoon ground cinnamon
- 1 teaspoon fine sea salt
- 2 tablespoons unsalted butter, melted

Caramel Topping

- 6 tablespoons unsalted butter
- 1½ cups light brown sugar, firmly packed
- ⅓ cup heavy cream
- 2 tablespoons honey
- 2 teaspoons vanilla extract
- ½ teaspoon apple cider vinegar
- ¼ teaspoon fine sea salt

Finishing

- 1 cup coarsely chopped pecans

Preheat the oven to 375°F.

For the filling: Stir together the dark brown sugar, cinnamon, and sea salt in a small bowl. Roll out the dough to an 18 × 12-inch rectangle. Brush the melted butter over the dough, leaving a ½-inch margin around the edges. Sprinkle the filling over the top of the dough, leaving a ½-inch margin around the edges. Roll up the dough into a log from the long side. Pinch the seams and the ends closed. Use a serrated knife (or unflavored dental floss wound around the log and pulled taut) to cut the log into 12 equal slices. Place them spiral side up in a 9 × 13-inch baking pan with about ½ inch of space between them. Cover with plastic wrap and proof in a warm place until doubled in bulk, about 30 minutes to 1 hour, or until the rolls are touching each other.

Remove the plastic wrap and bake the rolls 40–50 minutes, until deeply golden brown.

For the caramel topping: Melt the butter in a small saucepan over medium heat. Whisk in the brown sugar and cream. Add the honey, vanilla, apple cider vinegar, and salt. Whisk well over medium heat. Once the mixture comes to a simmer, cook 2–3 minutes more. Remove from the heat. If making ahead, cover and refrigerate overnight. Otherwise, add the cooked apples and stir to combine.

Remove the rolls from the oven. Let them cool about 20 minutes before serving. Top with caramel apples and sprinkle with chopped pecans. Serve warm or at room temperature.

Store, covered, in the refrigerator for 3–4 days. You can reheat the whole tray in a 300°F oven or gently warm individual rolls in the microwave for 10–20 seconds.

Homemade Bagels

These crisp, chewy bagels are a wonderful addition to—or centerpiece of—Sunday brunch. Bagels differ from other types of bread in that the circular rings of dough are boiled before baking, giving them their signature chew and a crackly crust. While there are multiple steps involved in making bagels, they are all relatively simple; the most important ingredient is time (okay, and yeast and high-gluten flour). The secret is to break up the process into manageable pieces over the course of two days. I recommend making the dough on Saturday night and letting it chill in the refrigerator overnight for a long, slow rise. By morning, they'll be ready to shape, boil, and bake, making your entire living space smell amazing. This recipe makes a base dough perfect for topping with sesame seeds, poppy seeds, sea salt, or Everything Bagel topping (which you can usually find in the spice aisle of the grocery store). You can also mince garlic and mix it into the dough. Serve these bagels with plain cream cheese, the vegetable schmear on page 120, smoked salmon, or the smoked bluefish on page 146.

SERVINGS: MAKES 8

- 1 teaspoon active dry yeast
- 4½ cups bread flour, divided
- 1½ cups warm water, plus 2 tablespoons warm water for the yeast
- 1 tablespoon kosher salt, plus more for boiling water
- 1½ tablespoons barley malt syrup (or molasses or honey), divided
- Optional toppings: poppy seeds, sesame seeds, coarse sea salt, Everything Bagel topping

In a small bowl, combine the yeast and 2 tablespoons warm water. Let sit until foamy while preparing the other ingredients.

In a large bowl (with or without the help of a stand mixer fitted with the paddle attachment), combine 3 cups of the bread flour with 1½ cups warm water. Add the yeast mixture and ½ tablespoon of the barley malt syrup. Blend until combined. Add 1 cup of the remaining bread flour along with all the salt. Mix well. Continue adding the remaining ½ cup bread flour just until the dough isn't sticky at all. (You may not need all the remaining flour, or you may need a bit more.) The dough will be very stiff.

At this point, turn the dough onto the counter and knead 10 minutes, until smooth; or switch out the paddle attachment for a dough hook and run on medium-low for the same amount of time. (Do not leave the mixer unattended—the motion tends to cause the machine to inch toward the counter's edge.)

Place the dough in a clean, oiled bowl and cover with plastic wrap or a damp towel. Let rise until nearly doubled in bulk, about 45 minutes to 1 hour at room temperature or overnight (8–10 hours) in the refrigerator.

Line a rimmed 12 x 17-inch baking sheet with parchment paper. Punch the dough down all over to degas it. Turn it out onto the counter in a round disk. Cut the dough into eighths, like a pizza. Shape the bagels by forming each piece of dough into a tight ball, pushing your thumb through the center to form a hole, and using both pointer fingers revolving around each other to gently stretch out the hole in the center. Set the bagels on the prepared pan and cut the parchment paper between the bagels with scissors until they're each resting on their own little mat. Cover with plastic wrap and let the bagels proof 15–20 minutes while the oven preheats and the water comes to a boil.

Preheat the oven to 425°F. Set a large pot of water to boil (cover for faster heating). Line a second pan with parchment paper. Arrange any toppings in separate shallow bowls.

When the water comes to a rolling boil, add a generous pinch of salt and the remaining 1 tablespoon of barley malt syrup. Stir to dissolve with a wooden spoon. In batches of 2 or 3, gently slip the bagels into the boiling water, peeling off the parchment paper as they fall. The bagels should float. Let the bagels boil for 30 seconds on one side, then flip them over and simmer 30 seconds more. Remove them with a slotted spoon and place them on the prepared pan to dry slightly. Repeat with the remaining dough. (You may need a second parchment-lined pan once the bagels have expanded in size.)

For the toppings: Place each bagel top side down while still damp and tacky into your topping of choice. Wiggle the bagel around until the coating sticks. Set the coated bagel back on the prepared pan, topping side up. Repeat for the others.

Bake the bagels for 24–28 minutes on the middle rack of the oven until golden brown. (If using Everything Bagel topping, you may need to cover the topping with a piece of foil during the last 5–10 minutes of baking to prevent the garlic from burning.) Remove from the oven and let cool before serving.

Leftovers can be stored in a sealed plastic bag at room temperature for a few days; or freeze, tightly wrapped, for longer storage.

Vegetable Schmear

While plain cream cheese is the way to go for purists, I can't get enough of this delicious vegetable schmear.

- ⅓ cup chopped, peeled carrot
- ¼ cup chopped celery and leaves
- 2 scallions, trimmed, sliced
- Leaves from a few sprigs of parsley and dill (stems removed)
- 1 pound cream cheese, at room temperature
- ⅛ teaspoon garlic powder
- Kosher salt and freshly ground black pepper, to taste
- Aleppo pepper, to taste (optional)

In a food processor, process the carrot, celery, scallions, and herbs until finely chopped but still chunky. Add the cream cheese, garlic powder, salt, black pepper, and Aleppo pepper, if desired. Process until combined. Taste and adjust the seasoning if necessary. Transfer to a bowl, cover, and chill in the refrigerator until ready to serve.

Cranberry Cornmeal Pancakes

These are a cross between traditional pancakes and Rhode Island johnnycakes, a Native American style of pan-fried corn cake. I use the cornmeal to boost the flavor and heartiness of the batter while keeping the fluffy interiors that one might expect in a pancake. The tartness of the cranberries balances the sweetness of the maple syrup. For me, these hybrid griddle cakes showcase native New England ingredients at their finest.

SERVINGS: 6–8

- 4 large eggs
- 2 cups milk, warmed
- 6 tablespoons unsalted butter, melted
- ¼ cup vegetable oil
- 2 cups all-purpose flour
- 1 cup yellow cornmeal
- 2 tablespoons baking powder
- 2 tablespoons granulated sugar
- 1 teaspoon table salt or fine sea salt
- 2 cups cranberries (defrosted, if frozen)
- 2 tablespoons confectioners' sugar
- Butter or canola oil, for frying
- Maple syrup, to serve

Whisk the eggs in a large bowl until light and foamy. Stir in the milk, melted butter, and oil. Sift the flour, cornmeal, baking powder, sugar, and salt into the wet ingredients. Whisk until combined.

In a separate medium bowl, toss the wet cranberries with the confectioners' sugar until coated.

Heat a 10- or 12-inch cast iron skillet, nonstick pan, or griddle over medium heat until hot (test by flicking some water into the pan; the water droplets should sizzle vigorously and disappear). Melt ½ tablespoon butter or oil in the pan and spread it around with a spatula. In batches of 2 or 3, add ¼ cup batter to the pan, spaced about 1 inch apart. Scatter cranberries on top. Cook until tiny bubbles start to pop on the surface of the batter and the bottoms are golden brown, 2–4 minutes per side (you may need to give them a half-turn to make sure they brown evenly). Repeat with the remaining batter, adding more butter or oil to the pan as needed. Transfer to a plate with a bit of butter in between each pancake; cover with foil or an inverted bowl to keep warm. Serve with extra butter and maple syrup.

Store leftovers well-wrapped in the refrigerator for 3–4 days.

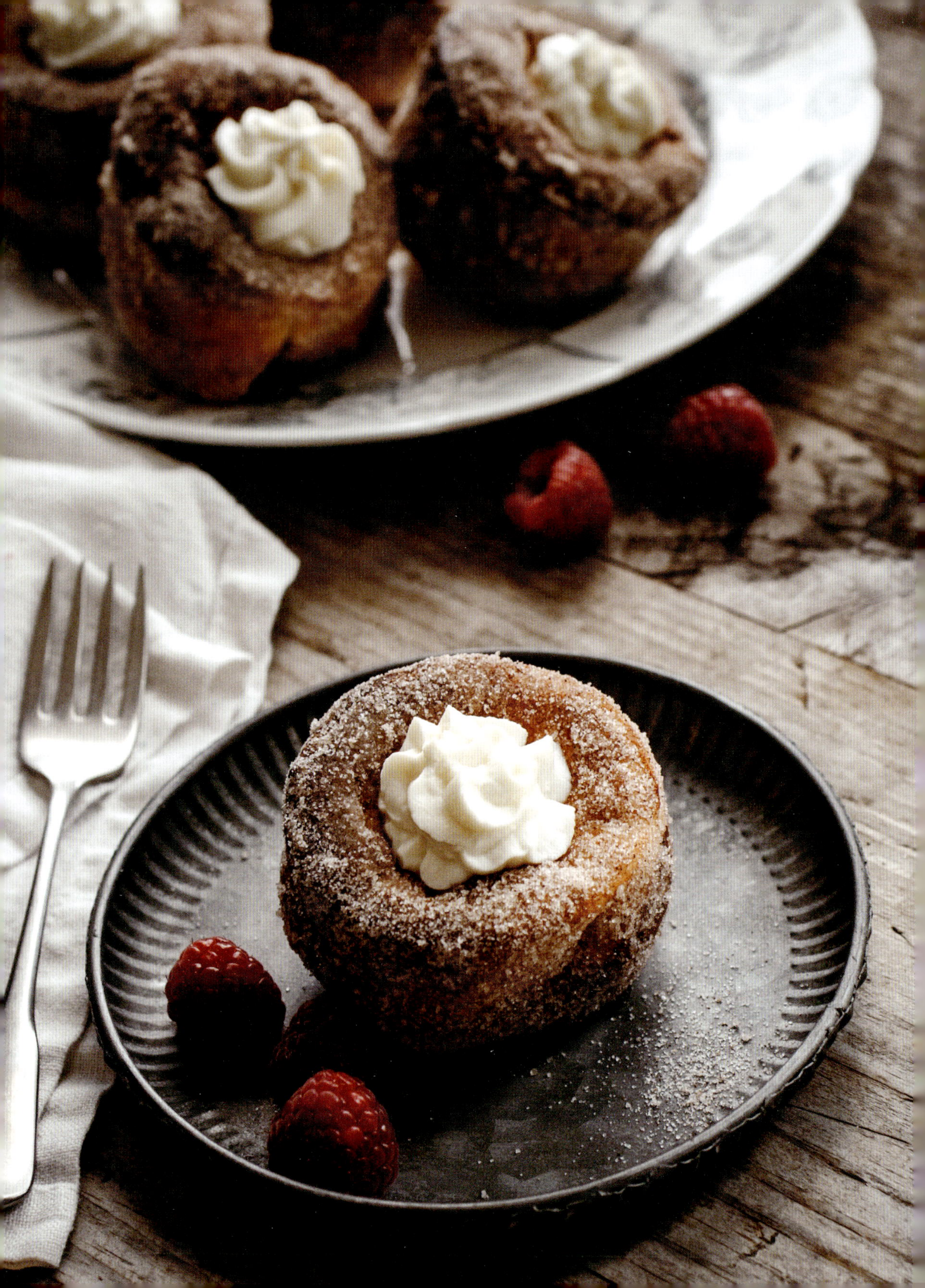

Cinnamon Sugar Cannoli Popovers

Popovers got their name because the hollow, steam-leavened pastries often pop up and over the edges of the pan when baked. They tend to run savory as an accompaniment to beef roasts, like the Rosemary Gruyère Popovers (page 191). But I also love the idea of lightly sweetened popovers. Here, I flavor mine with maple syrup, brush them with butter, and roll them in cinnamon sugar, apple cider–doughnut style. You could certainly eat them plain (or with a smear of fruit preserves), but I have a different proposition. Stuff them with pillowy, lemon-scented sweet ricotta filling and you'll end up with something like a Sicilian iris (a brioche bun stuffed with cannoli filling). You could also fill them with Greek yogurt swirled with jam. The instructions below are designed to yield somewhat subdued popovers with a well in the middle for filling, especially if using a standard-sized muffin pan instead of the deeper, narrower popover pans. But if yours puff all the way up in a loftier fashion (you overachiever, you), you can always poke a hole in the side and pipe the filling into the centers, jelly-doughnut style. To ensure the filling is thick enough, be sure to start the ricotta draining the night before. Serve the popovers with fresh fruit like fall raspberries.

SERVINGS: MAKES 12

Popovers
- 3 large eggs
- 2 tablespoons maple syrup
- 3 tablespoons unsalted butter, melted, divided
- 1½ cups milk, slightly warmed in the microwave
- 1½ cups all-purpose flour
- ½ teaspoon table salt or fine sea salt
- Dash of ground nutmeg

Preheat the oven to 425°F.

For the popovers: In a blender, combine the eggs and maple syrup. Mix on low speed just until combined. Stir 1 tablespoon of the melted butter into the warmed milk and add to the blender. Mix on low speed, briefly. Add the flour, salt, and nutmeg, and blend on high speed 10–15 seconds, until the batter is smooth and the consistency of heavy cream.

Set a standard 12-cup muffin tin in the preheated oven for 2 minutes to heat it up. Remove the pan from the oven and immediately brush the wells of the muffin tin with the remaining 2 tablespoons of melted butter. Fill the muffin wells three-fourths of the way up with batter (about ¼ cup). Bake 25–30 minutes. Remove the pan from the oven and let it cool slightly.

Filling

- 1½ cups ricotta, drained overnight in a sieve set over a bowl in the refrigerator
- ½ cup confectioners' sugar, sifted
- 1 teaspoon vanilla extract
- ¼ teaspoon finely grated lemon zest
- ⅛ teaspoon table salt or fine sea salt

Topping

- ⅓ cup granulated sugar
- ½ teaspoon ground cinnamon
- 2 tablespoons unsalted butter, melted

For the filling: Stir together the ricotta, confectioners' sugar, vanilla, lemon zest, and salt in a medium bowl. Refrigerate until just before serving.

For the topping: Combine the cinnamon and sugar in a small bowl. While the popovers are still slightly warm, remove each popover from the pan and brush all over with the remaining melted butter. Roll them all around in the bowl of cinnamon sugar.

When ready to serve, fill a pastry bag and pipe the filling into the wells of the popovers. If you don't have a pastry bag, you can approximate one by filling a zip-top bag, sealing it closed, and snipping off a bottom corner (about ½-inch) with scissors. Fill only as many as you plan to eat. These are best eaten as soon as possible after sugaring and filling.

Any leftover filling (or filled popovers) should be covered and stored in the refrigerator. Unfilled popovers can be stored at room temperature in a plastic bag and then warmed briefly in the microwave or toaster oven before filling.

Pear-Nutella Baked French Toast

Fresh pears, crunchy hazelnuts, and warm spices are a wonderful fall combination, and little pockets of melted Nutella add a luxurious richness. Still, this make-ahead brunch dish is a cinch to pull off. You can assemble it the night before and then pop it into the oven in the morning. You can use stale bread, fresh bread, or toasted bread. Fresh bread will give it a softer, bread pudding consistency. If you're not refrigerating it overnight, give it a good hour at room temperature (more for stale or toasted bread) so the bread has a chance to soak up the liquid. Be sure to use sweet, tender pears; you can tell the pear is ripe when you press the tapered neck and it gives with gentle pressure. It's best to buy pears four to five days in advance, store them at room temperature, and then, once they have ripened, place them in the refrigerator to hold them.

SERVINGS: 8–12

- 6 large eggs, beaten
- ½ cup light brown sugar, firmly packed
- 4 tablespoons unsalted butter, melted
- 2 tablespoons brandy (optional)
- 2 teaspoons vanilla extract
- ½ teaspoon fine sea salt
- 1 cup milk
- 1 cup heavy cream
- 1 loaf challah, Italian bread, or farmhouse white
- ⅓ cup Nutella, warmed in the microwave to loosen
- 1 pound ripe pears (2–3 medium), like Bosc or red pears

Butter a 9 × 13-inch baking dish.

In a large bowl, whisk together the eggs and brown sugar. Add the melted butter, brandy, vanilla, and salt. Mix well. Whisk in the milk. Slowly stir in the heavy cream until combined.

Trim any tough crusts from the bread and cut into 12 slices about ¾ inch thick. One at a time, dip both sides of each bread slice into the egg mixture and arrange in the prepared baking dish, overlapping like roof shingles (I do three columns of 4 slices, with the pan oriented horizontally). Add dollops of Nutella between the slices. Pour the remaining egg mixture over the top. With a spatula, press down on the bread firmly to encourage absorption.

Core and cut the pears into ½-inch dice (peeling is optional). Scatter the pears on top and in the gaps between the bread. Set aside.

In a small bowl, stir together the granulated sugar and cinnamon. Sprinkle with half the spiced sugar, reserving the rest to add just before baking. Cover with plastic wrap and refrigerate overnight.

1 tablespoon granulated sugar

½ teaspoon ground cinnamon

¼ cup hazelnuts (or walnuts), coarsely chopped (optional)

Preheat the oven to 375°F. Let the French toast come to room temperature while the oven is preheating.

Sprinkle the remaining spiced sugar over the top, along with the hazelnuts or walnuts, if using. Bake 25–30 minutes, until the French toast is golden brown and a toothpick inserted into the center comes out clean. Remove from the oven and let cool slightly. Serve with maple syrup.

Leftovers can be covered and stored in the refrigerator for 3–4 days.

Lobster, Corn, and Potato Pot Pie

Here's a decadent brunch idea that puts New England's favorite crustacean front and center. Lobster Pot Pie is essentially lobster chowder with a flaky crust on top. Homemade lobster stock is crucial to the success of this recipe—but don't worry, it's easy. Make the stock and the filling the day before, and all you have to do is reheat it and bake the store-bought puff pastry separately the next morning. (Be sure to leave it in the refrigerator overnight to defrost.) I prefer Dufour puff pastry, which is made with real butter. I've found buying one steamed lobster and supplementing with frozen lobster meat is the best way to save time and money while providing enough lobster shells for the stock. Serve the pot pie in a big cast iron pan, casserole dish, or individual ramekins.

SERVINGS: 6–8

Stock

- 1 (1½-pound) cooked lobster
- 2 medium yellow onions
- 2 celery stalks
- ½ bunch parsley stems
- 1 bay leaf

Filling

- 2 tablespoons unsalted butter
- 2 large leeks
- 3 medium celery stalks
- 12 ounces small red-skinned potatoes (about 10), cut into ¾-inch pieces
- 3 fresh thyme sprigs
- 2 teaspoons kosher salt
- ½ teaspoon paprika
- 12 ounces lobster meat (defrosted, if frozen), cut into ¾-inch pieces

For the stock: Remove the meat from the cooked lobster (see page 76) and set aside for the filling. Add the lobster shells and bodies to a large pot. Cover with water by 2 inches. Top with the lid and bring the water to a boil over high heat. Remove the lid and skim the foam off the top. Peel and halve the onions. Add them to the pot along with the celery, parsley stems, and bay leaf. Reduce the heat to maintain a gentle simmer. Cook uncovered for 1 hour.

Nest a strainer in a large bowl. Carefully pour the hot stock into the bowl. Remove the strainer and discard the shells and vegetables. Measure 3 cups of lobster stock back into the pot. Cover to keep warm (off heat) until ready to use. Any remaining stock can be frozen for future use.

For the filling: Trim the leeks, keeping the white and light green parts only. Quarter them lengthwise and slice them thinly. You should have about 4 cups. Halve the celery lengthwise and slice thinly. Melt the butter in a large sauté pan. Cook the leeks and celery over medium-low heat, stirring frequently, until softened, about 4 minutes. Stir in the potatoes. Add the 3 cups of reserved hot lobster stock, thyme sprigs, salt, and paprika. Cover the pan and bring to a simmer. Remove the lid and simmer 12–15 minutes, until the potatoes are tender.

Remove the thyme sprigs. Add the cooked lobster and corn to the pan. Stir in the cream.

Pumpkin Breakfast Bars

Like hermits, these delightfully spiced pumpkin bars get better with time, which means you can make them days ahead of when you plan to serve them. I tried to make this recipe as healthy as possible by stuffing them full of pumpkin, whole grains, nuts, and seeds—but they turned out so delicious, they don't seem healthy at all (sorry, not sorry). If nuts are a no-go, you can substitute rolled oats or white chocolate chips. This recipe can be doubled for a 9 × 13-inch pan. Freeze or use the leftover pumpkin puree for Pumpkin Whole Wheat Pancakes (page 106).

SERVINGS: 8–10

½ cup (1 stick) unsalted butter, melted

¾ cup light brown sugar, firmly packed

⅓ cup pumpkin puree

1 large egg

½ teaspoon vanilla extract

1 cup all-purpose flour

2 teaspoons pumpkin spice (to make your own, see page xv)

½ teaspoon table salt or fine sea salt

¼ teaspoon baking soda

1 cup walnut halves/pieces

½ cup rolled oats, plus more for sprinkling

2 tablespoons salted roasted pumpkin seeds, for sprinkling

Flaky sea salt, for sprinkling

Drizzle

1 ounce cream cheese, at room temperature

½ cup confectioners' sugar, sifted

1 tablespoon water

Preheat the oven to 350°F. Grease an 8 × 8-inch pan or line with parchment if desired.

Pour the melted butter into a large bowl and stir in the brown sugar. Add the pumpkin, egg, and vanilla; stir well. Add the flour, pumpkin spice, salt, and baking soda. Stir just until combined. Add the nuts and rolled oats; stir until well dispersed. Spread the batter evenly in the prepared pan (the batter will be thick). Sprinkle with roasted pumpkin seeds and flaky sea salt.

Bake 20–24 minutes, until a toothpick inserted into the center comes out with only moist crumbs attached (no raw batter). Let cool completely before icing.

Using an electric mixer or sturdy wooden spoon, beat the cream cheese until fluffy. Add the confectioners' sugar and half of the tablespoon of water; whip on low until combined. Increase the speed and continue to mix until there are no more lumps. Add the rest of the water, a few dribbles at a time, until the mixture reaches the desired consistency: thin enough to drizzle smoothly but thick enough to hold its shape. Scoop the mixture into a small zip-top bag and zip it shut. Snip off a bottom tip of the bag and drizzle the glaze over the tops of the bars. Let air-dry until the icing is set. Serve.

Bars can be stored in an airtight container at room temperature for 4–5 days.

Squash and Sage Scones

These scrumptious scones bridge the gap between sweet and savory. They're incredibly addictive—and a great use for pumpkins as well as all those beautiful winter squashes we like to collect this time of year. Don't let them go to waste. Butternut, kabocha, honeynut, buttercup, and Hubbard squash would all be delicious in these scones. Follow the instructions below to make your own squash puree (or use canned). Freeze any leftover squash to use in future scones and the Pumpkin Whole Wheat Pancakes (page 106) all winter long.

SERVINGS: 8

2 cups all-purpose flour

1 tablespoon baking powder

¼ cup granulated sugar

1 teaspoon ground sage

1 teaspoon table salt or fine sea salt

6 tablespoons cold unsalted butter, cut into 6 pieces

½ cup squash (or pumpkin) puree

½ cup heavy cream

1 tablespoon unsalted butter, melted

Fresh sage leaves, for garnish

Preheat the oven to 425°F. Grease a 12 × 17-inch baking sheet or line it with parchment paper.

In the bowl of a food processor, combine the flour, baking powder, sugar, sage, and salt. Process the mixture for a few seconds to blend. Add the cold butter and process 15–20 seconds, until the butter pieces are the size of small peas. (You can also cut the butter into the dry ingredients with a pastry blender or your fingers.)

Add the squash puree to a large bowl and gradually whisk in the cream. Dump the flour mixture from the food processor into the bowl. Fluff with a fork until it all comes together into a shaggy dough. Turn it out onto a floured surface and, with floured hands, fold the dough over itself several times until it holds together. Transfer the dough to the prepared pan. Gently pat the dough into a ¾-inch-thick disk. Cut it into 8 wedges like a pizza. Brush the tops of the scones with melted butter. Brush the fresh sage leaves with melted butter and press them on top of each scone. Pull out the scones slightly so they're about 1 inch apart.

Bake 15–20 minutes, until the tops brown and the centers of the scones are set. Remove the pan from the oven and let the scones cool on the pan. Serve warm or at room temperature.

The scones can be stored in an airtight container at room temperature for 2–3 days.

How to Prepare Fresh Pumpkin and Squash for Baking

Halve the gourds and set them cut-side-down on a large, lightly oiled, rimmed 12 × 17-inch baking sheet. Roast in a 375°F oven for 45 minutes to 1 hour, until soft. Let them cool slightly, then scoop out the seeds and discard. Scrape the flesh out of the skins and puree in a food processor until smooth. Drain in a colander set over a bowl for at least 1 hour, preferably overnight, to remove the excess liquid.

Focaccia with Rosemary, Red Onion, and Olives

I love focaccia. Not only is it a perennial crowd-pleaser, but you don't have to be a master bread baker to feel like one. You'll need an unreasonable amount of olive oil and a heavy hand with the salt. Just go with it. For best results, start the dough the night before with an overnight rise—in addition to better flavor, you'll find yourself in a better position time-wise to get the bread risen, proofed, and baked in time for the brunch crowd to arrive. But you can still pull it off without an overnight rise if you give yourself at least four hours in the morning.

SERVINGS: 12–16

2¼ teaspoons active dry yeast

Pinch granulated sugar

5 cups all-purpose flour, divided

2 cups warm water (not too hot)

2 tablespoons extra-virgin olive oil, plus ½ cup or more for assembly

2 teaspoons kosher salt

Flaky sea salt

Fresh rosemary leaves, coarsely chopped

Red onion, thinly sliced

Pitted olives, halved or quartered

Mix the yeast into the warm water with a pinch of sugar. Let it sit 10 minutes to activate.

Meanwhile, combine 2 cups of the flour with the warm water and 2 tablespoons olive oil in a large bowl. Mix well with a wooden spoon. Add the yeast mixture and stir to combine. Stir in the remaining 3 cups of flour and the salt until it forms a loose dough. Drizzle some olive oil over the top. Use your hands to loosen the dough from the bowl and flip it over so it's entirely coated in olive oil. Cover the bowl with plastic wrap and let the dough rise overnight in the refrigerator until doubled in bulk, 8–12 hours (or 2–4 hours at room temperature).

Grease a 9 × 13-inch baking pan with olive oil. Add enough oil that it puddles a bit. Sprinkle the oil with a few pinches of flaky sea salt. Give the risen dough a few kneads or turns so you have a nice smooth top. Set the dough in the pan and press or stretch it until it just about covers the bottom (it will fill in the corners as it proofs). Cover with plastic wrap and let it rise in a warm place for 2–4 hours until nearly doubled in bulk.

Preheat the oven to 450°F. When the dough is nice and puffy, remove the plastic wrap. Coat your hands in olive oil and use your fingers to dimple the surface deeply, holding each position for a second as if you were a tortured pianist. Drizzle more olive oil on top, sprinkle with flaky sea salt, and add your toppings, like fresh rosemary leaves, thinly sliced red onion, and olives.

Bake on the middle rack for 24–30 minutes, until the top is golden brown. Remove from the oven and let cool. Drizzle additional olive oil over the top if desired.

Once cool, leftovers can be stored in a sealed plastic bag at room temperature for 3–4 days.

Acadian Buckwheat Crepes with Creamy Mushrooms

Ployes are buckwheat crepes brought from Nova Scotia to Maine by the Acadians (French settlers who colonized the Canadian Maritimes). Ployes are more rustic than your typical Parisian-style crepes, notable for their "eyes" where the air bubbles pop. Here I've filled them with creamy, savory mushrooms topped with fried sage leaves, but you could err on the sweet side with Nutella, dulce de leche, or your favorite jam and top with fresh berries. Either way, they're hearty and delicious, with a slightly nuttiness from the buckwheat. Bouchard Family Farms in Fort Kent, Maine, makes their own ployes mix where you just add water. Below is a recipe to make them from scratch. Whenever possible, try to use Acadian light buckwheat flour from northern Maine or New Brunswick (also offered by Bouchard Family Farms) so the crepes have the right flavor and color (slightly golden instead of gray). See page 240 for mail-order info.

SERVINGS: 8–10

Crepes

- 1 cup Acadian light buckwheat flour
- 1 cup all-purpose flour
- 1½ tablespoons baking powder
- 1 teaspoon table salt or fine sea salt
- 2⅔ cups cold water

For the crepes: Combine the two flours, baking powder, salt, and water in a blender. Process until completely smooth, 30 seconds to 1 minute, scraping down the sides of the blender at least once. (If you don't have a blender, combine the dry ingredients in a large bowl. Whisk in half the water, then gradually whisk in the rest. Continue mixing until all the lumps are dissolved.) The mixture should be runny like cream. Let the batter rest at least 10 minutes.

Filling

2 tablespoons extra-virgin olive oil

2 medium yellow onions, chopped

4 cups sliced mixed mushrooms (hedgehogs, chanterelles, oysters, hen of the woods, shiitake caps, cremini, or button)

2 tablespoons all-purpose flour

1½ cups heavy cream

½ teaspoon chopped fresh thyme

Fresh sage sprig

2–3 tablespoons grated Pecorino Romano cheese

Salt and black pepper, to taste

Garnish

1 tablespoon extra-virgin olive oil

20 fresh sage leaves

For the filling: Heat the oil in a large sauté pan over medium-low heat. Add the chopped onions and cook for about 4 minutes until softened. Add the sliced mushrooms and stir well. Cover and let cook 5–10 minutes, stirring occasionally, until the mushrooms have released their moisture and reduced in size. Remove the lid and stir in the flour until no longer visible. Pour in the cream. Add the chopped thyme and a sprig of sage. Cook gently, uncovered, over low heat until the mushrooms have softened further and the cream sauce has reduced and thickened, 5–10 minutes. Remove the sage sprig. Stir in the cheese.

Heat a medium nonstick sauté pan or griddle over medium heat until very hot. Pour ¼–⅓ cup of batter onto the pan and swirl the batter around to thinly coat the bottom of the pan in a circle. Cook 1½ minutes on one side only until the crepe is covered in little eyes, the edges curl, and the center is dry and set. Transfer to a plate with a spatula and repeat for the rest of the batter. (If your nonstick pan doesn't live up to its name, you can brush some oil on the bottom of the pan. To cut the cooking time in half, use two sauté pans simultaneously.) Stack the crepes on top of each other and cover to keep warm.

For the garnish: Heat the olive oil in a small sauté pan and fry half the sage leaves over medium-low heat, 10–20 seconds, until they stop sizzling and before they brown. Let drain on a paper towel–lined plate. Repeat with the rest of the sage leaves.

To assemble: Set a warm crepe on a plate and spoon some warm mushroom filling down the center of the crepe. Fold the sides of the crepe over the mushroom filling. Top with fried sage leaves. If serving at the table, make sure the crepes are warm so they don't break when folded (cover warm crepes with a plate).

Keep leftover crepes well wrapped to prevent drying out and store in the refrigerator for 3–4 days. Extra mushroom filling can also be covered and stored in the refrigerator for 3–4 days.

Brussels Sprouts and Pancetta Hash

I'm a firm believer that there aren't nearly as many vegetables involved in brunch as there should be—and Brussels sprouts are one of my favorite vegetables. What's that, you say? Brussels sprouts are the devil's candy? Let's just agree to disagree. You can substitute fresh broccoli florets if you must. Pancetta is Italian-style salt-cured pork belly, but you can use thick-cut, New England–style smoked bacon instead. However you make it, I stand by my position that this hash is absolutely delicious with a fried egg on top. My favorite part: the crispy, caramelized, nearly burnt leaves scattered throughout.

SERVINGS: 4–6

1½ pounds Brussels sprouts, trimmed, quartered if big, halved if medium, whole if tiny

2 tablespoons extra-virgin olive oil

Kosher salt and freshly ground black pepper, to taste

4 ounces pancetta, cut into ¼-inch dice (or bacon)

1½ tablespoons red wine vinegar (or apple cider vinegar)

1 tablespoon maple syrup

1 teaspoon spicy brown mustard (or Dijon)

⅛ teaspoon Worcestershire sauce

Preheat the oven to 450°F. Place a rack in the bottom third of the oven.

Add the Brussels sprouts to a rimmed 12 × 17-inch baking sheet. Drizzle with olive oil, salt, and black pepper to taste. Toss until coated. Arrange on three-fourths of the baking sheet. Scatter the diced pancetta on the remaining one-fourth of the pan. Set the baking sheet on the bottom rack of the oven and roast 8–10 minutes, until the bottoms of the Brussels sprouts are well browned and the pancetta is cooked but not burnt.

Meanwhile, in a small bowl, whisk together the vinegar, maple syrup, mustard, and Worcestershire sauce until well blended.

Remove the pan from the oven. If the meat is starting to burn, transfer it to a plate. Otherwise, flip the Brussels sprouts and mix the pancetta in with the vegetables. Pour the rest of the sauce over the top and return to the oven. Roast 2–4 minutes more, until the liquid has been absorbed and the Brussels sprouts are cooked to your desired doneness. Remove the pan from the oven. Stir in the pancetta if it was removed earlier. Season with salt and pepper to taste, transfer to a bowl, and serve immediately.

Leftovers can be covered and stored in the refrigerator for 3–4 days.

Sausage and Stuffing Strata

This recipe is for the folks who wish they could eat Thanksgiving stuffing more than once a year. I've taken all the flavors of stuffing (substituting sweet Italian sausage for turkey) and made them into a breakfast casserole filled with root vegetables and herbs. I hope you love it as much as we do. For another delicious option, try the Spinach, Pancetta, and Tomato variation.

SERVINGS: 6–8

- 3 tablespoons olive oil, divided
- 1 medium red onion, peeled
- 1 medium celery root, peeled
- 2 medium carrots, peeled
- ½ pound sweet Italian sausage, casings removed
- 4 large eggs
- ¾ cup chicken broth
- ¼ cup heavy cream
- 1 teaspoon dried thyme, divided
- 1 teaspoon ground sage
- 1 teaspoon garlic powder
- ½ teaspoon ground mustard
- ¼ teaspoon dried rosemary
- ½ teaspoon fine sea salt or kosher salt
- Freshly ground black pepper, to taste

Preheat the oven to 375°F. Generously grease a deep-dish 9-inch pie plate or 8 × 8-inch casserole dish.

Cut the red onion, celery root, and carrots into ¾-inch pieces and add to a rimmed sheet pan. Add 1 tablespoon of the olive oil; season with salt, pepper, and some of the thyme. Toss the vegetables until coated. Roast on the middle rack of the oven for 20 minutes, flipping once halfway through the cooking time. Remove the vegetables from the oven and let cool slightly.

Meanwhile, heat 1 tablespoon of the olive oil in a large sauté pan. Cook the sausage over medium heat, breaking it up into bite-sized pieces. Continue cooking, stirring occasionally, until no pink color remains and the surface is browned in places, about 5–8 minutes. Remove from the heat and let cool.

In a large bowl, whisk the eggs with the chicken broth, heavy cream, the remaining thyme, sage, garlic powder, ground mustard, rosemary, salt, and pepper. Remove any tough crusts from the bread and cut it into 1-inch cubes. You should have about 6 cups. Add the bread cubes to the egg mixture and let them soak 10–15 minutes.

Flip the bread cubes over. Add the cooked sausage and vegetables. Stir to combine. Pour the mixture into the prepared baking dish. Top with shredded cheese and cover with foil.

8 ounces Italian or country-style bread

1 cup shredded Monterey Jack cheese (or half mozzarella, half cheddar)

Bake on the middle rack of the oven for 25 minutes. Remove the foil and continue baking uncovered for 25–30 minutes more, until nicely browned. Remove from the oven and let cool 5–10 minutes. Serve warm.

Leftovers can be covered and stored in the refrigerator for 3–4 days and reheated in the microwave.

Variation

Spinach, Pancetta, and Tomato Strata: In a large bowl, whisk 4 large eggs with ¾ cup milk and ¼ cup cream. Add ⅓ cup finely grated parmesan cheese, 1 teaspoon dried marjoram or oregano, 1 teaspoon garlic powder, ½ teaspoon fine sea salt, and freshly ground black pepper to taste. Add 6 cups of 1-inch bread cubes (about 8 ounces) to the bowl and press to submerge. Let soak while preparing the rest of the ingredients.

In a large sauté pan over medium heat, cook 4 ounces pancetta in 1 tablespoon olive oil for 5–6 minutes, until starting to crisp. Add 2 cloves minced garlic and cook 30 seconds. Add 5 ounces spinach with the water clinging to its leaves. Stir 2–3 minutes until wilted. Season with salt and pepper. Remove from the heat and let cool.

Cut a handful of cherry tomatoes in half (or dice 1 medium tomato). Flip the bread cubes. Add the spinach-pancetta mixture, tomatoes, and 4 ounces cherry-sized fresh mozzarella balls and mix. Transfer the mixture to the prepared baking dish. Top with 1 cup shredded mozzarella cheese and cover with foil. Bake as indicated above.

Portuguese Kale Soup

This warming autumn soup is perfect for sweater weather. Many European countries have a similar version using different meats, beans, and greens, but this one harkens back to the Portuguese immigrant community that settled along the southern New England coast of Massachusetts, Rhode Island, and Connecticut. I call for Portuguese smoked sausage like linguica or chouriço. My grocery store carries the local Gaspar's brand from North Dartmouth, Massachusetts, in the cured meat section, but if you can't find it, you can substitute Italian sausage and add 1 teaspoon smoked paprika. You can swap out the white beans for kidney beans. You can lose the kale and use collards or turnip greens instead. You can even add diced tomato. But this is my favorite way to make this soup, with the optional addition of leftover cheese rinds (like Manchego, Gruyère, or Gouda), which add big flavor to the soup and offer a soft, melty prize for whoever encounters them.

SERVINGS: 6–8

2 tablespoons extra-virgin olive oil

1 pound linguica or chouriço, sliced ¼ inch thick

1 large yellow onion, chopped

3 garlic cloves, peeled, crushed with the back of a knife

½ teaspoon smoked paprika (or regular paprika)

6 cups chicken stock (or water)

2 (15.5-ounce) cans cannellini or great northern beans

2 medium Yukon gold potatoes, peeled, cut into ½-inch cubes

5 cups shredded kale, from 1 large bunch, stems removed

Cheese rinds (optional)

Kosher salt and freshly ground black pepper, to taste

In a large, heavy-bottomed saucepan, heat the olive oil over medium-high heat. Cook the sausage slices, stirring occasionally, until cooked through and browned in spots, 5–7 minutes. Transfer the sausage to a bowl.

Reduce the heat to medium-low. Add the onions to the pot and cook, stirring frequently, until softened, about 4 minutes. If the onions start to brown, reduce the heat and stir. Add the garlic and paprika. Cook 1 minute more, stirring. Add about ¼ cup of the stock (or water), and deglaze the pan by scraping up the browned bits on the bottom of the pan with a wooden spoon. Add the rest of the stock to the pot, along with the beans, potatoes, kale, and cheese rinds, if using.

Cover, increase the heat to medium, and bring to a low boil. Reduce the heat to medium-low and simmer until the potatoes are cooked through and the flavors have melded, 20–30 minutes. Season to taste with salt and pepper (if using unsalted stock or water, you'll want to add at least 1 teaspoon of salt). Remove the pan from the heat and let cool slightly. Serve with Portuguese Sweet Rolls (page 17) or Anadama Bread (page 176).

Leftovers can be covered and stored in the refrigerator for 4–5 days. Reheat in the pot on the stove or in individual bowls in the microwave.

Kale Caesar Salad with Squash Croutons and Pepitas

This recipe was inspired by a kale salad I had at the farm-to-table restaurant Season to Taste in Cambridge, where I recently celebrated a milestone birthday. Their salad featured black garlic, pistachios, and Grana Padano, and it was incredibly satisfying. This is my simplified version, which I think works equally well for brunch. You can use any variety of kale, but I like the curlier types in salad so they don't lie flat. Gluten-free folks can omit the breading on the squash or use gluten-free bread crumbs. Vegans can replace the egg with a flax egg (mix 1 tablespoon flaxseed meal with 3 tablespoons hot water and let sit until thickened). The anchovies and Worcestershire sauce can be swapped out for miso and soy sauce. The dressing can be made a day or two ahead of time, but make the squash croutons fresh so they're still warm and crisp. Always dress the salad just before serving.

SERVINGS: 4–6

Squash Croutons

- 3 tablespoons extra-virgin olive oil, divided
- ½ pound winter squash (like butternut, kabocha, or buttercup), peeled
- 1 large egg
- 3 tablespoons plain bread crumbs
- 1 tablespoon panko bread crumbs (or another tablespoon of plain bread crumbs)
- ¼ teaspoon dried rosemary
- Kosher salt and freshly ground black pepper, to taste

For the squash croutons: Preheat the oven to 375°F. Drizzle a rimmed baking sheet with 2 tablespoons of the olive oil.

Cut the squash into 1 × ¾-inch dice. In a medium bowl, beat the egg well. Add the squash and toss to coat. In a small bowl, combine both types of bread crumbs, rosemary, and salt and pepper. In small batches, scoop up the squash pieces with a slotted spoon, let the excess egg drain back into the bowl, and toss them in the bread crumbs. Shake the excess coating from the squash and arrange on the oiled sheet pan. Repeat until all the squash is coated. Drizzle the squash with the remaining tablespoon of olive oil and roast for 10 minutes. Flip and roast for 10 minutes more, until the squash is easily pierced with a fork and the coating is golden brown. Let cool slightly.

Dressing

1 cup mayonnaise

2 small garlic cloves, peeled, pressed or grated with a fine-planed zester

2 tablespoons freshly squeezed lemon juice (about 1 lemon)

1 teaspoon anchovy paste (or 2 whole anchovies, mashed with a fork)

1 teaspoon Worcestershire sauce

1 teaspoon Dijon mustard

¼ cup grated parmesan cheese

¼ teaspoon kosher salt

¼ teaspoon freshly ground black pepper

Salad

1 medium bunch kale (6–8 cups)

Juice of ½ lemon

¼ teaspoon kosher salt

¼ cup roasted, salted pumpkin seeds (pepitas)

¼ cup shaved parmesan cheese

Freshly ground black pepper, to taste

For the dressing: Whisk together all the ingredients until combined. Add water as needed to thin it out to a pourable consistency. Taste for seasoning and adjust as desired. Refrigerate until ready to serve.

For the salad: Strip the kale leaves from the stems and tear or cut into bite-sized pieces. Wash and dry thoroughly. Add to a large serving bowl, squeeze a little lemon juice on top, and sprinkle with the kosher salt. Massage the leaves with your hands for 2–3 minutes until the leaves tenderize, turn a darker shade of green, and reduce substantially in volume. Sample a leaf—if it's still tough, keep massaging the kale until the mouthfeel softens to a pleasant al dente.

To serve: Lightly dress the greens right before serving. Scatter with pepitas, shaved parmesan cheese, squash croutons, and a generous grinding of black pepper. Serve more dressing at the table.

Smoked Bluefish

While smoked salmon is the more common fish to see on brunch spreads, smoked bluefish is another delicious and more sustainable option. Make this way ahead of when you want to serve it. I love it on bagels with goat cheese, capers, red onion, and dill. If you find the flavor too strong, you can temper it by turning it into pâté. Combine flaked smoked bluefish with an equal weight of softened cream cheese. Season with salt and pepper, lemon juice, and add minced red onion. Embellish with fresh dill or chives, capers, and a dash or two of Worcestershire sauce or hot sauce.

Brine

1 quart cold water
½ cup kosher salt
¼ cup granulated sugar
2 tablespoons freshly squeezed lemon juice
1 teaspoon black peppercorns
2 bay leaves

Fish

1-pound bluefish fillet
Freshly ground black pepper
4 cups wood chips (like alder, hickory, or apple), soaked in water

For the brine: In a large baking dish or gallon-size resealable storage bag, stir together all the brine ingredients until the salt dissolves. Rinse the fish well and submerge it in the brine. Refrigerate overnight. The brine adds flavor and keeps the fish moist during the smoking process, not to mention helping with preservation.

For the fish: Pat the fish dry and let it sit in the refrigerator for several hours while preparing the grill or smoker so the surface dries out further. This step enables the smoke to adhere to the outside of the fish, forming a flavorful pellicle (the shiny, dark, lacquer-like surface of properly smoked fish).

Prepare the smoker or grill according to the manufacturer's instructions. For a charcoal grill, you'll need to let the coals cool down to 200°F and monitor the temperature at all times to make sure it doesn't creep up.

Place the fish on the rack over indirect heat, skin-side-down. Smoke the fish (covered with the vents open) at 200°F for the first hour, then 150°F for the next 2–3 hours, until firm but not dried out like jerky (the internal temperature of the fish should reach 145°F). Add soaked wood chips to the coals every 20–30 minutes.

Remove from the grill or smoker and let cool. Smoked fish will last up to 2 weeks, covered, in the refrigerator.

Warm Tomato Basil Bisque

This beautiful bisque celebrates the last of the tomatoes and basil of late summer and early fall. It's warming, fresh, and flavorful. I opted for no garlic in this soup and don't miss it, but it wouldn't be out of place. The water content in tomatoes varies greatly, so be prepared to add water at the end, if needed, to adjust the consistency. Vegans can try replacing the cream with ½ cup cooked white beans or silken tofu blitzed with some soy milk or other nondairy milk to thin it out to the consistency of heavy cream. Serve with Focaccia with Rosemary, Red Onion, and Olives (page 134), Cheddar Thyme Biscuits (page 185), or Sweet and Spicy Skillet Cornbread (page 82).

SERVINGS: 4–6

- 3 tablespoons olive oil, divided
- 2 pounds fresh tomatoes (about 4 large)
- 2 medium yellow onions, chopped
- ½ teaspoon dried thyme
- Dash of dried oregano
- 1 (28-ounce) can crushed or whole plum tomatoes (preferably San Marzano)
- 4 cups chicken or vegetable broth
- 1 cup fresh basil leaves, loosely packed, plus extra for garnish
- 2 teaspoons kosher salt
- 1 teaspoon granulated sugar
- ½ cup heavy cream
- Salt and freshly ground black pepper, to taste

Preheat the oven to 400°F.

Add 2 tablespoons of the olive oil to a rimmed 12 × 17-inch baking sheet. Core the fresh tomatoes and cut them in half across the equator. Set them cut side up on the oiled pan. Sprinkle with salt and pepper. Roast for 20 minutes, then flip and roast for 15–20 minutes more, until very tender.

Meanwhile, in a large heavy-bottomed saucepan or Dutch oven, heat the remaining 1 tablespoon of olive oil over medium-low heat. Sauté the onions for 4–5 minutes, until tender but before they start to brown. Stir in the dried thyme and oregano. Add the canned tomatoes, broth, basil leaves, salt, and sugar.

When the roasted tomatoes come out of the oven, remove and discard the skins; add the tomatoes to the pot. Bring to a simmer over medium-high heat. Reduce the heat to medium-low and simmer uncovered for 25–30 minutes until reduced. Break up the whole tomatoes with a wooden spoon as they cook.

Remove the pot from the heat. Puree with a stick blender or in batches in a regular blender (for the latter, let cool for 15 minutes first, and don't fill the blender more than half full).

Add the heavy cream, and add more salt and pepper to taste. If the bisque seems a little thin, let it cook down a bit more. Too thick? Add some water. Reheat just before serving. Leftovers can be frozen or covered and stored in the refrigerator for 4–5 days.

Concord Grape Fizz

It is said that North America was once called Vinland by the Vikings who, in their pre-Columbian voyages, noticed the profusion of wild grapes growing along its shores. In 1849 Ephraim Wales Bull of Concord, Massachusetts, crossed some of these native grapes with European varieties on his farm and discovered a seedling that ripened before the killing frosts. Not only that, but the flavor was stellar. It won numerous awards at the 1853 Boston Horticultural Society Exhibition and later won over the world. This refreshing fizzy beverage tastes like fancy grape soda, with Cava and Angostura bitters to tamp down the sweetness. To make it nonalcoholic, replace the Cava with nonalcoholic sparkling apple cider, like Martinelli's.

SERVINGS: 4–6

3 cups Concord grape juice, chilled (preferably 100 percent juice)

3 cups Cava, chilled

Angostura bitters, to taste

In a standard-sized 64-ounce pitcher, combine the chilled grape juice and Cava. Fill wine glasses half-full of ice and pour the punch over the top. Add a dash or two of Angostura bitters to each glass. Garnish with fresh Concord grapes or a slice of lemon. For refills, combine the remaining grape juice and Cava in equal amounts.

How to Juice Concord Grapes

Buying Concord grape juice is undeniably faster, easier, and less messy, but if you're lucky enough to have productive Concord grape vines, here's how to make your own juice. For 3 cups of juice, you'll need at least 3 pounds of Concord grapes.

Remove the grapes from the vine and rinse well. Add to a large heavy-bottomed pot over low heat. Gently mash the grapes with a potato masher (wear an apron). Bring the mixture to a simmer and gently cook for about 15 minutes. Remove the pan from the heat and pour the mixture through a large strainer lined with a double layer of cheesecloth set over a large bowl. Discard the seeds and pulp. Let the juice cool and pour into a large jar. Cover and refrigerate overnight to allow the sediment to settle to the bottom. Pour off the juice, leaving the sediment behind.

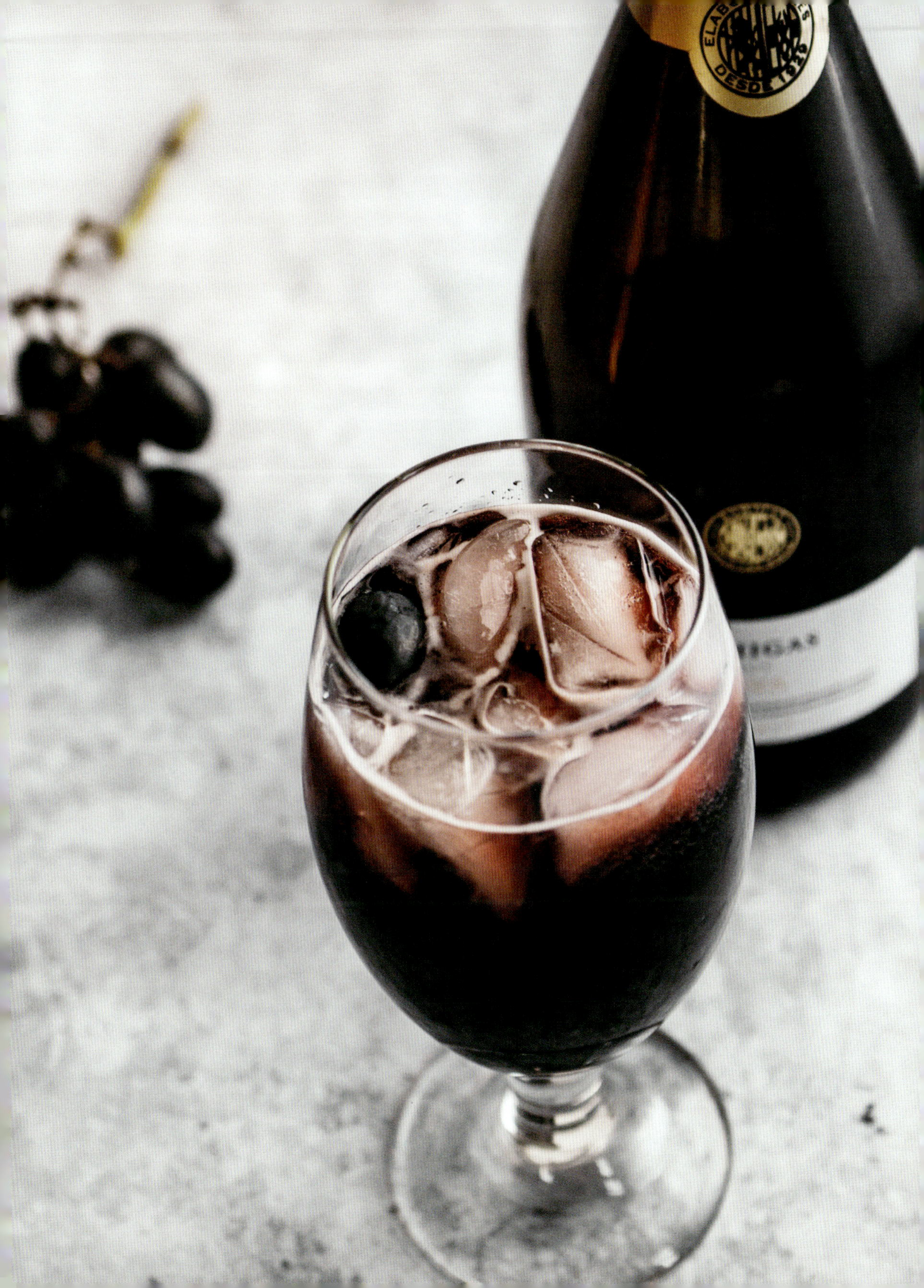

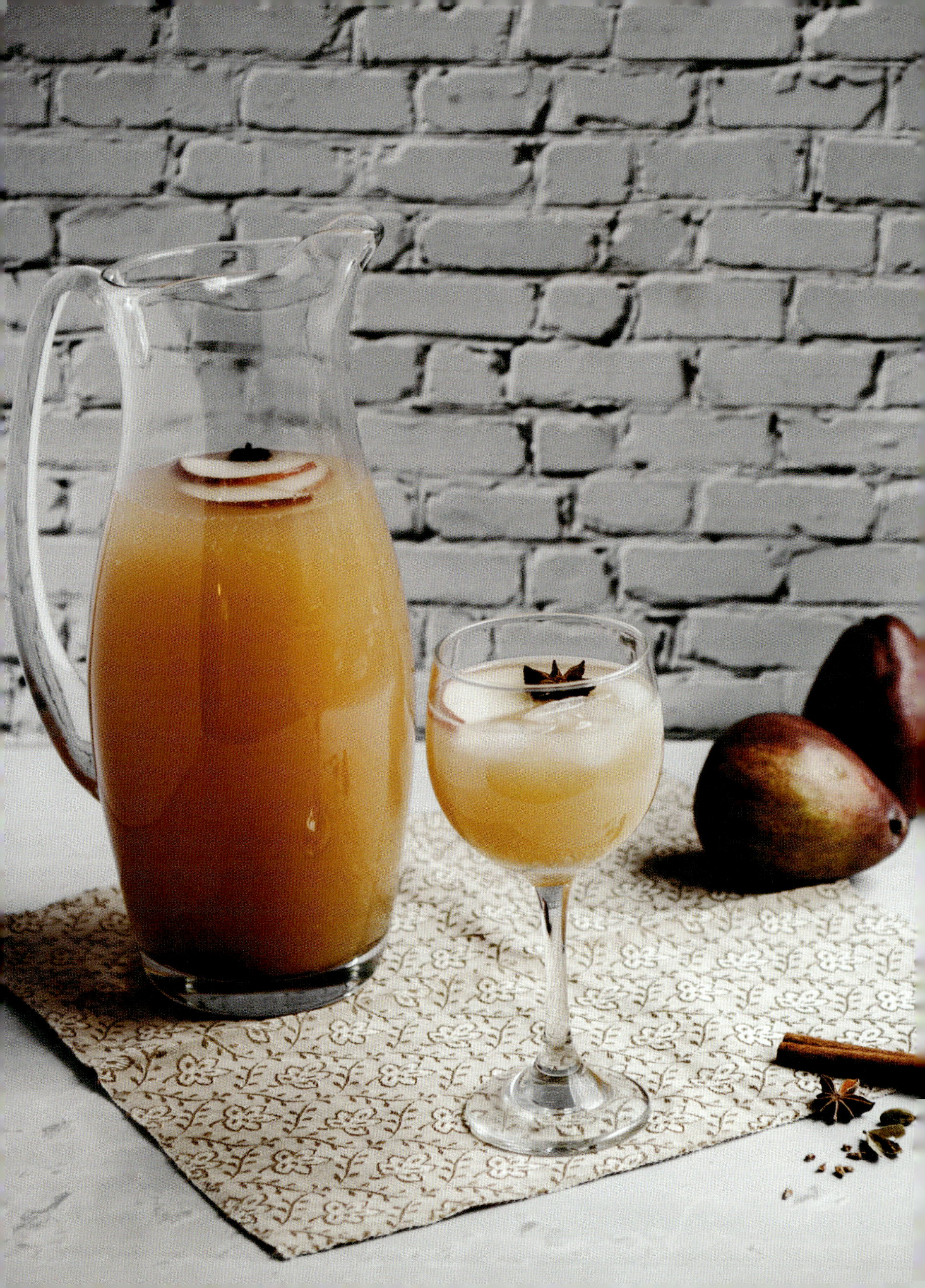

Spiced Pear Sangria

This festive punch highlights one of the more overlooked fruits of the colder season: pears. These sweet fruits pair wonderfully with dry Cava (Spanish bubbly), and I like to add a spiced sugar syrup that's cold-brewed overnight with cinnamon, ginger, star anise, and cardamom seed. For garnish, red pears are lovely when ripe. If they don't ripen in time, I recommend having an Asian pear on hand. Asian pears stay crisp and firm like apples even when ripe, and they'll add a welcome crispness and bright flavor that complements the spices.

SERVINGS: 4–6

Ginger-Cardamom Syrup

- ¼ cup granulated sugar
- ¼ cup water
- 1 cinnamon stick, plus more for garnish
- 1-inch sliver fresh ginger, unpeeled
- 2 green cardamom pods (not black) (or ¼ teaspoon ground cardamom)
- 1 small star anise, plus more for garnish
- Sliced ripe red pear or chopped Asian pear, for garnish

Sangria

- 1 bottle Cava, well chilled
- 2 cups pear nectar, well chilled
- ¼ cup freshly squeezed lemon juice (about 2 medium lemons)
- 2 tablespoons brandy
- 2 tablespoons ginger-cardamom syrup

For the syrup: Remove the cardamom seeds from the pods and grind with a mortar and pestle. Stir the sugar and water together in a small saucepan over medium heat until the sugar dissolves. Bring to a simmer. Add the cardamom seed, cinnamon stick, fresh ginger, cardamom seed, and star anise. Let cool. Transfer the syrup to a small jar, cover, and refrigerate until ready to serve.

Just before serving, combine the Cava, pear nectar, lemon juice, and brandy in a large pitcher. Strain the solids out of the sugar syrup and add 2 tablespoons syrup to the pitcher. Stir until combined. Taste and adjust to your liking. Add fresh pear slices and some of the whole spices for garnish (don't cut the pears too far ahead of time or they'll brown). Add some ice cubes to each glass instead of adding the ice cubes to the pitcher, which will dilute the sangria too much. Serve cold.

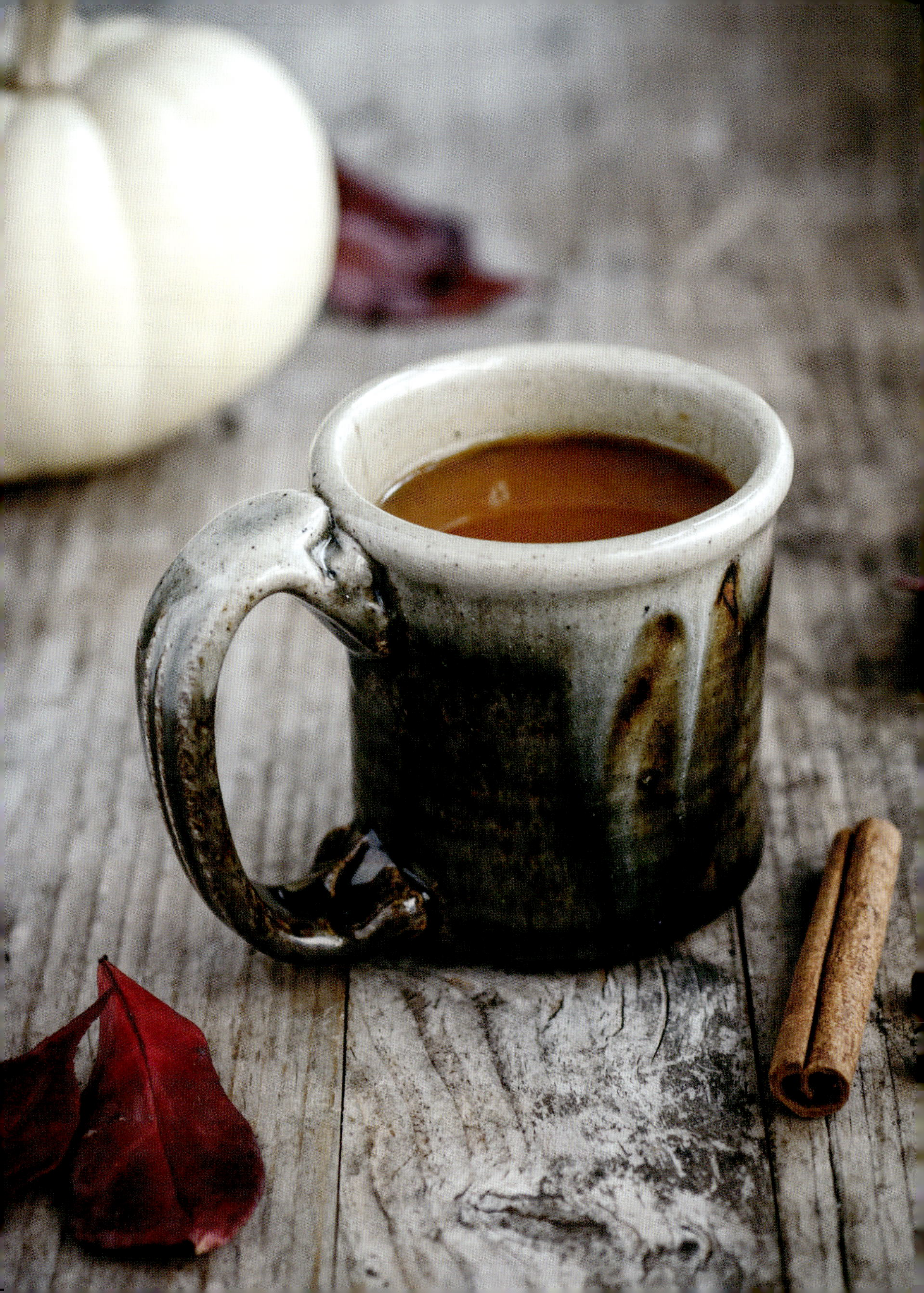

Mulled Pumpkin Cider

If you want your house to smell amazing, have this cider mulling on the stovetop—pure pumpkin spice nirvana. For an exceptional sipping experience, it's important to exercise a little restraint with the spicing. Having your house smell like a Yankee candle is one thing—drinking said candle is another. Less is more. Scale this recipe up as needed by doubling or tripling everything except the spices. Those can remain the same (spices are expensive, after all). Just steep a little longer if you want a stronger flavor. It's best to use whole spices to distribute the flavor better and avoid floating specks, but if you don't have them, you can substitute ground spices to your taste.

SERVINGS: 4

- 4 cups apple cider, divided
- 1 cup pumpkin puree
- 3–4 tablespoons light brown sugar
- ½ teaspoon vanilla extract
- 1 cinnamon stick
- ½-inch sliver whole nutmeg
- ½-inch sliver fresh gingerroot (unpeeled is fine)
- 2 allspice berries
- 1 whole clove
- Pinch of sea salt

In a blender, combine half the apple cider with the pumpkin puree, 3 tablespoons of brown sugar, and vanilla. Blend until completely smooth, about 1 minute on high (longer, if necessary). Pour into a medium saucepan and place over medium-low heat. Stir in the remaining 2 cups of apple cider. Add the whole spices and salt. Cover and bring to a simmer. Turn the heat to low and mull for 30 minutes. Remove from the heat, stir well, and taste. If you like it a little sweeter, stir in the last tablespoon of brown sugar until dissolved. Strain out the whole spices and serve immediately, or keep covered until ready to serve and reheating as necessary.

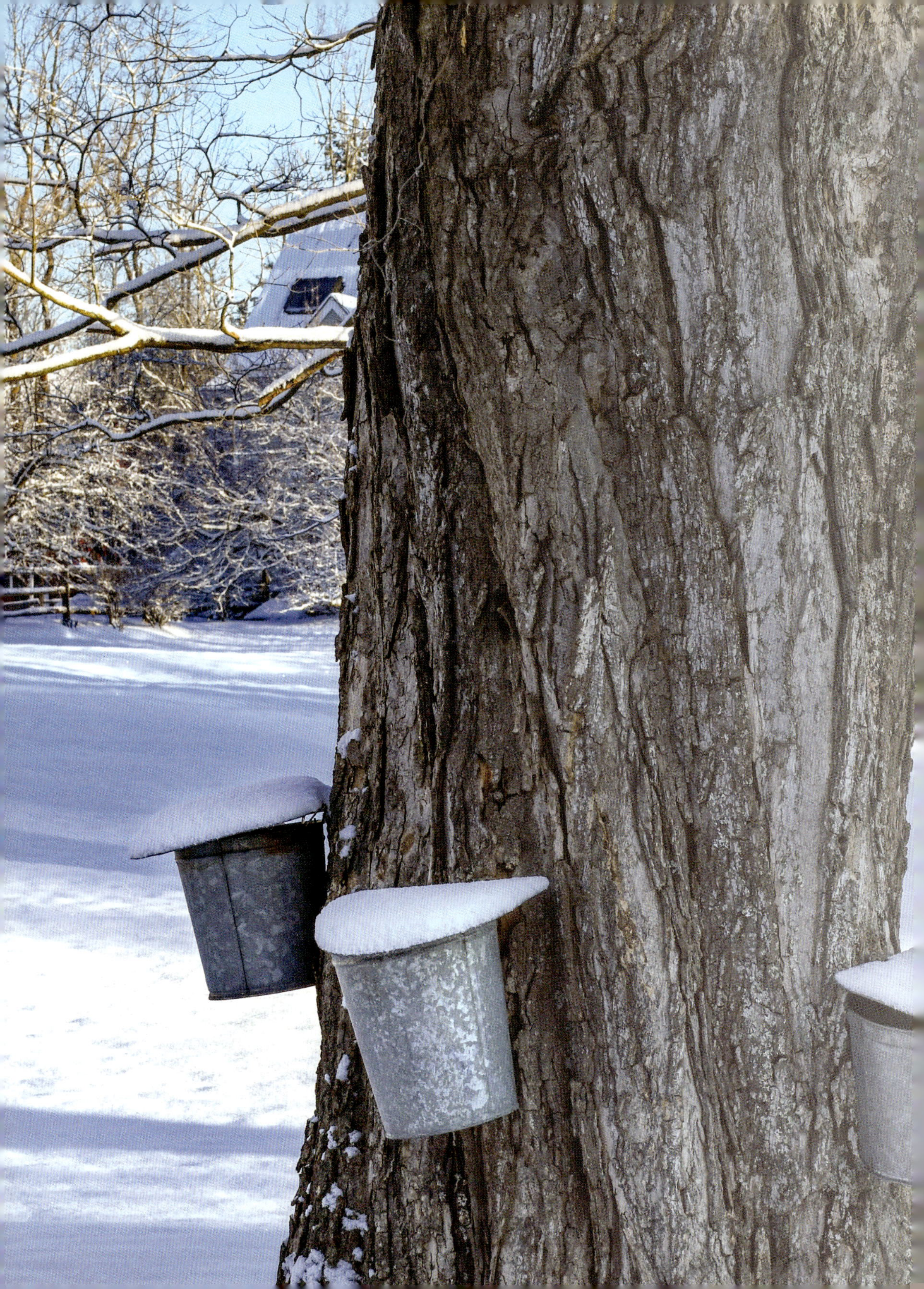

Winter

Maple Walnut Cinnamon Rolls 158

Cranberry Walnut Granola 161

New England Cornmeal Custard Cake 162

Cranberry Almond Scones 164

Cinnamon Raisin Bagels 166

**Cranberry Baked French Toast
with Maple Cream 169**

Apple Streusel Danish Pastry 172

Anadama Bread 176

Kabocha Butter 178

Brown Bread Muffins 180

Boston Baked Beans 182

Cheddar Thyme Biscuits 185

Maple Breakfast Sausage 186

**Red Flannel Hash with
Horseradish Cream 188**

Rosemary Gruyère Popovers 191

Parsnip and Juniper Latkes 192

Cranberry Applesauce 195

Home Fries 196

Cranberry Mimosas 198

Pumpkin Eggnog 199

Bailey's Irish Coffee 200

Maple Walnut Cinnamon Rolls

Maple walnut is a classic New England flavor pairing, and it works wonderfully in cinnamon rolls. Maple products can be expensive, so if you don't have maple sugar, you can substitute cheaper light brown sugar for a similar flavor profile in the filling. But do try to use an amber maple syrup in the glaze, where it really shines as a sweet, decadent counterpoint to the tangy cream cheese. Walnuts add a pleasant crunch to the pillowy buns, but you can omit them if you like. I prefer to give these rolls an overnight rest in the fridge for fantastic flavor. But if you're an early riser, you can make them from start to finish that very morning—they'll still be incredibly delicious. Give yourself at least five hours so you're not scrambling to get them done and they'll still be warm when your guests arrive. Finally, don't omit the sea salt in the glaze—it's just a pinch, but it's transformative, a bit of confectionary pixie dust.

SERVINGS: MAKES 12

Dough

- 2¼ teaspoons active dry yeast
- ¼ cup warm water (110°F)
- ⅓ cup granulated sugar
- ½ cup (1 stick) unsalted butter, melted, cooled slightly
- 2 large eggs, at room temperature
- ½ cup sour cream, at room temperature
- 3½–4 cups all-purpose flour, divided
- 1 teaspoon fine sea salt

For the dough: In a measuring cup, add the yeast to the warm water with a pinch of the sugar. Stir and let the mixture sit for 5 minutes until foamy. (If the mixture doesn't foam, check the expiration date on your yeast. It might have expired.)

In the bowl of an electric mixer (preferably fitted with the paddle attachment), mix the sugar and melted butter on medium speed. Add the foamy yeast mixture and mix until combined. Add the eggs, one at a time, followed by the sour cream, mixing well after each addition. Add 2 cups of the flour and the salt. Mix on medium speed for 1 minute. Add more flour, ½ cup at a time, on low speed until you get a soft dough that comes together cleanly in the bowl but still feels a little tacky to the touch.

Turn the dough onto a lightly floured surface and knead about 5 minutes, until smooth. Place the dough in an oiled bowl, turning to coat the dough on all sides. Cover and let rise in a warm place until doubled in size, about 1½ hours. (Alternatively, you can let it rise in the refrigerator overnight.)

When doubled in bulk, punch down the dough and let it rest for 10 minutes before shaping. (If it's coming straight from the refrigerator, give it a good 30–45 minutes to come to room temperature before rolling it out so it's not too stiff.)

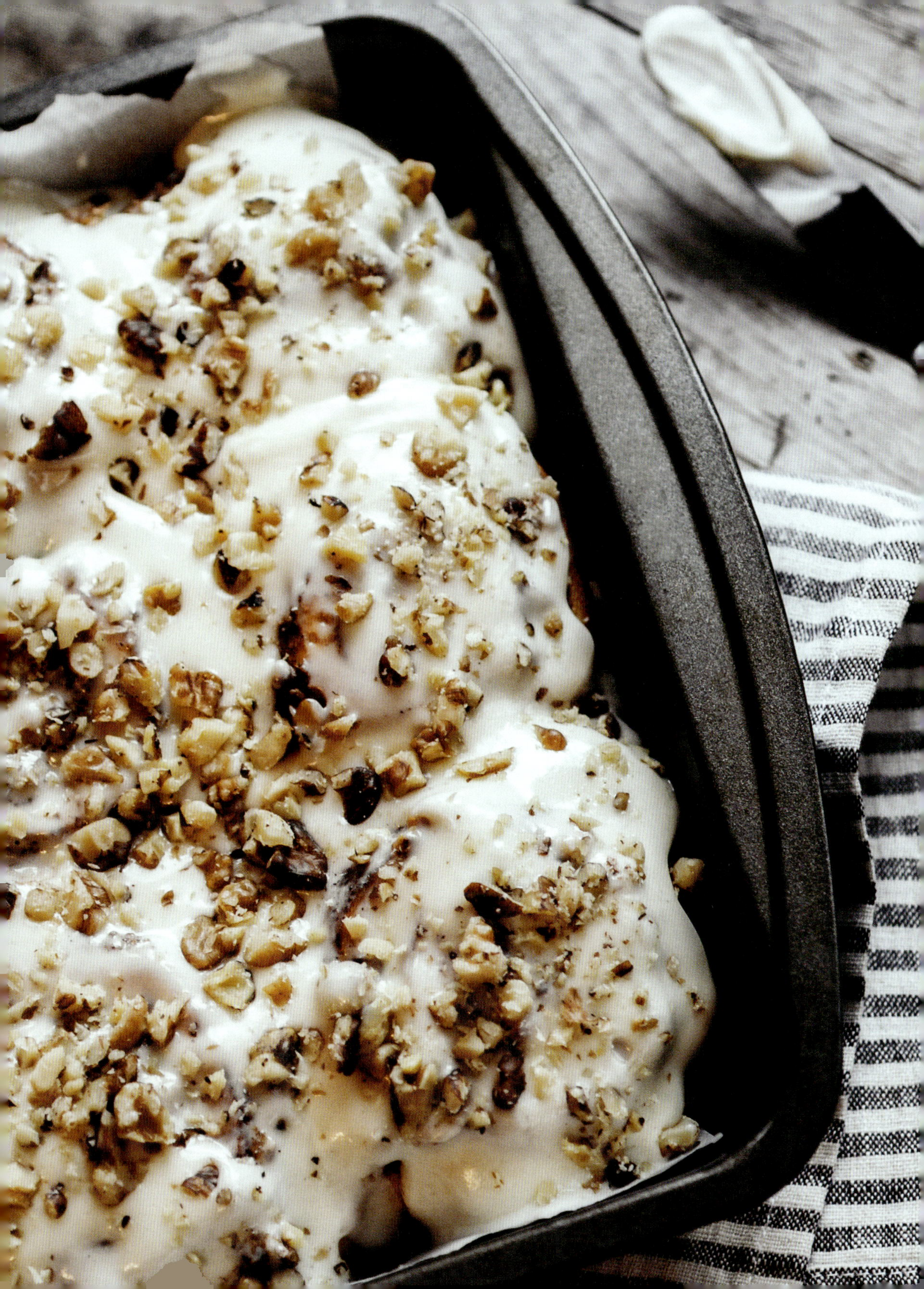

Filling

- 4 tablespoons unsalted butter, softened in the microwave
- 1 cup finely ground maple sugar or light brown sugar, firmly packed
- 2 tablespoons ground cinnamon
- 1 tablespoon ground cardamom
- 1 cup coarsely chopped walnuts, plus more for the topping if desired
- Dash of fine sea salt

Glaze

- 4 ounces cream cheese, at room temperature
- 4 tablespoons unsalted butter, at room temperature
- 1 cup confectioners' sugar, sifted
- 1 tablespoon maple syrup
- Pinch of fine sea salt (or table salt)

Generously butter a 9 × 13-inch baking pan or line it with parchment paper hanging over the sides. On a lightly floured surface, roll out the dough to a 12 × 24-inch rectangle.

For the filling: Spread the softened butter over the top of the dough with an offset spatula or your hands, leaving a ½-inch margin around the edges. Sprinkle the maple sugar, cinnamon, cardamom, walnuts, and salt on top. Roll up the dough from the long side and pinch the ends closed. Use a serrated knife (or unflavored dental floss wound around the log and pulled taut) to cut the log into 12 equal slices. Place them spiral side up in the prepared pan. Cover and let proof in a warm place until doubled in bulk, about 1 hour.

Preheat the oven to 350°F.

Bake the rolls 25–30 minutes, until golden brown.

For the glaze: Combine the cream cheese and butter in the bowl of an electric mixer. Mix on medium-high speed until smooth. Add the confectioners' sugar and mix on low until incorporated, then increase to medium-high and whip until smooth. Mix in the maple syrup and salt.

Remove the rolls from the oven. Let cool about 10 minutes. Spread the glaze on top of the rolls while still warm. Sprinkle additional chopped walnuts on top. Serve the rolls warm or at room temperature.

Cover and store any leftovers in the refrigerator for 3–4 days. If desired, gently warm individual rolls in the microwave for 10–20 seconds.

Cranberry Walnut Granola

This granola can be made any time of year, but I particularly love dried cranberries in the fall and winter with walnuts and maple syrup. I cook my granola at a low temperature to give me half a chance of not burning it. I also like to use egg whites to encourage the formation of crunchy little clusters, but if you're vegan you can leave them out. Or try this trick: Soak 1 tablespoon of the chia seeds in 2 tablespoons water and let sit five minutes. Stir well, then add to the mixture along with the wet ingredients. You can also add ¼ cup chopped crystallized ginger along with the cranberries at the end for a gingery punch.

SERVINGS: MAKES ABOUT 6 CUPS

- 3 cups rolled oats
- 2 cups chopped walnuts
- ¼ cup light brown sugar, packed
- 2 tablespoons flaxseed or chia seeds
- 2 tablespoons hemp hearts (optional)
- 2 teaspoons ground cinnamon
- ½ teaspoon ground ginger
- 1½ teaspoons fine sea salt
- ½ cup grapeseed, vegetable, or canola oil, plus 1 tablespoon for the pan
- ⅓ cup maple syrup
- 2 large egg whites
- ½ teaspoon vanilla extract
- 1 cup dried cranberries

Preheat oven to 300°F. Brush a rimmed 12 × 17-inch baking sheet with 1 tablespoon oil.

In a large bowl, stir together all the dry ingredients except the cranberries (they get added after baking). In a medium bowl, whisk together the oil, maple syrup, unbeaten egg whites, and vanilla. Add the wet ingredients to the dry. Mix well with a wooden spoon. Spread the mixture evenly on the prepared pan and press it flat with a spatula.

Bake 25–30 minutes, flipping the mixture once halfway through and re-flattening with a spatula. Remove from the oven and let cool on the pan without stirring for 30 minutes to 1 hour. (It might still seem slightly damp, but it will firm up on sitting. Don't brown the granola too much or the walnuts will taste bitter.) Loosen the mixture from the pan with a spatula and let it cool completely.

When fully cool, add the dried cranberries. Store in sealed jars for up to 3 weeks.

New England Cornmeal Custard Cake

This old-fashioned recipe was originally called New England Spider Cake, not because of any unusual eight-legged ingredients, but because of the type of pot it was cooked in—a footed cast iron vessel called a spider with a lid and looped handle that can sit over the embers of the fire. I own one; it's great for cooking over the coals of a campfire, so consider this recipe for your next car-camping trip. The rest of the time, however, this cake is much more practical to make in the oven in a cast iron skillet. The unusual step of pouring cream right into the middle of the batter before baking causes a custardy filling to form between two layers of corn cake. Serve warm with maple syrup and a small pitcher of cream. You may be shocked at how delicious a simple, one-bowl recipe can be.

SERVINGS: 8–12

2 cups milk

1 tablespoon apple cider vinegar (or white vinegar)

1 cup all-purpose flour

¾ cup yellow cornmeal

½ cup granulated sugar

1 teaspoon baking powder

½ teaspoon baking soda

¾ teaspoon fine sea salt

2 large eggs

2 tablespoons unsalted butter

1 cup heavy cream, plus more for serving

Maple syrup, for serving

Preheat the oven to 350°F. Place a 10-inch cast iron skillet (or casserole dish) in the oven for 5 minutes while it preheats.

Combine the milk and vinegar in a measuring cup and let sit 5–10 minutes to thicken.

In a large mixing bowl, combine the flour, cornmeal, sugar, baking powder, baking soda, and salt. Add the eggs and the milk mixture. Whisk until it forms a smooth, loose batter.

With an oven mitt, remove the hot skillet from the oven. Add the butter and return the pan to the oven for a few minutes until the butter melts. Swirl the butter around the bottom and halfway up the sides of the pan until coated. Pour the excess into the batter and whisk. Pour the batter into the hot skillet, scraping the bottom and sides of the bowl. Pour the heavy cream directly into the center of the batter without stirring. Carefully place the skillet back into the oven. Bake 40–45 minutes, until the cake is golden on top and starting to crack, but still a little jiggly in the middle.

Remove the pan from the oven and let cool about 20 minutes, until sliceable but still warm. Serve with maple syrup and heavy cream.

Leftovers should be removed from the cast iron pan promptly to preserve the pan's seasoning. The cake can be covered and stored in the refrigerator for 2–3 days. Gently warm in the oven or microwave.

Cranberry Almond Scones

I love the tart pop of cranberries in these buttery, almond-scented scones. And they're just as beautiful as they are delicious, lovely for a Christmas brunch, bake sale, or winter tea. Not a fan of cranberries? Try these scones with frozen blueberries or raspberries instead.

SERVINGS: MAKES 8

- 2 cups all-purpose flour
- ⅓ cup granulated sugar, plus extra for the top
- 1 tablespoon baking powder
- ½ teaspoon sea salt
- 6 tablespoons cold unsalted butter, cut into 6 pieces
- ½ teaspoon vanilla extract
- ½ teaspoon almond extract
- 1 cup heavy cream, plus extra for the top
- 1 cup cranberries (thawed, if frozen)
- ¼ cup sliced almonds (optional)

Preheat the oven to 425°F. Grease a 12 × 17-inch baking sheet or line it with parchment paper.

In the bowl of a food processor, combine the flour, sugar, baking powder, and salt. Process the mixture for a few seconds to blend. Add the cold butter and process 15–20 seconds, until the butter pieces are the size of small peas. (You can also cut the butter into the dry ingredients with a pastry blender or your fingers.)

Dump the mixture into a large bowl. Add the vanilla and almond extracts to the cream. Drizzle half of the cream mixture over the dry ingredients and fluff with a fork. Scatter the cranberries and almonds on top, along with the rest of the cream mixture, and toss with the fork until it all comes together into a shaggy dough. Gently bring the dough together on a floured surface and, with floured hands, fold the dough over itself several times until it holds together. Gently pat the dough into a ¾-inch-thick disk. Cut it into 8 wedges like a pizza. Transfer the scones to the prepared pan and space them out at least 2 inches apart. Brush the tops with cream and sprinkle with sugar.

Bake 15–20 minutes, until the tops are golden and the centers of the scones are set. Remove the pan from the oven and transfer the scones to a rack to cool.

These are best eaten the day they're made, but they can be stored in an airtight container for 3–4 days at room temperature and reheated in a toaster oven.

Cinnamon Raisin Bagels

I know people have strong feelings about cinnamon raisin bagels, which is why I was careful to keep this recipe well apart from the traditional bagel recipe on page 118, as if it were a different animal entirely. Among the haters are the bagel purists (whom I respect), as well as the staunch raisin-loathing contingent (hello, Husband). But I happen to love cinnamon raisin bagels for their chewy cinnamon toast vibes. For fun, I conducted an unscientific social media poll; the results surprised me, with 65 percent of the vote in favor of cinnamon raisin bagels and 35 considering them an abomination. I expected it to go the other way. Granted, my sample was pulled mostly from New England, not New York City, which might explain the results. After all, New England is where the cinnamon raisin bagel was born. It was the brainchild of the late Moe Eagerman of the Original King Bagel in Natick and Eagerman's in Brookline, which used to supply the local Stop & Shop and Star Markets with freshly baked bagels. That's how I came to know them. I breakfast-binged on cinnamon raisin bagels all through high school, toasted, with butter or cream cheese. This recipe gives me all the cozy, cold-weather feels. I've spread the work out over two days so you can have fresh bagels on the morning of Day 2 instead of the evening of Day 1.

SERVINGS: MAKES 8

- 1 cup raisins
- 2 cups hot water, plus ¼ cup warm water for the yeast
- 1 tablespoon active dry yeast
- ½ teaspoon light brown sugar, packed
- 4½ cups bread flour, plus 1–2 tablespoons more for the raisins
- 3 tablespoons barley malt syrup (or molasses, but not blackstrap), divided
- 1 tablespoon kosher salt, plus more for boiling water
- 1 teaspoon ground cinnamon

Soak the raisins in 2 cups hot water and set aside for 10–15 minutes to soften.

In a small bowl, combine the yeast, brown sugar, and ¼ cup warm (not hot) water. Let sit until foamy while preparing the other ingredients.

To a large bowl (with or without the help of a stand mixer fitted with the paddle attachment), add 4 cups bread flour. Drain the raisins and reserve the soaking water, which should still be warm. Measure out 1⅓ cups of the warm water and add to the flour; mix well. Add the yeast mixture and 2 tablespoons barley malt syrup (or molasses) to the bowl. Mix until combined. Add 1 tablespoon kosher salt to the bowl. Continue adding up to ½ cup additional bread flour until you have a stiff dough that isn't sticky at all.

In a small bowl, dredge the raisins in 1–2 tablespoons bread flour to coat. Set aside along with the cinnamon.

At this point, turn the dough onto the counter and knead 10–15 minutes, until smooth. Or switch out the paddle attachment for a dough hook and run on medium-low for the same amount of time. (Do not leave the mixer unattended, as the

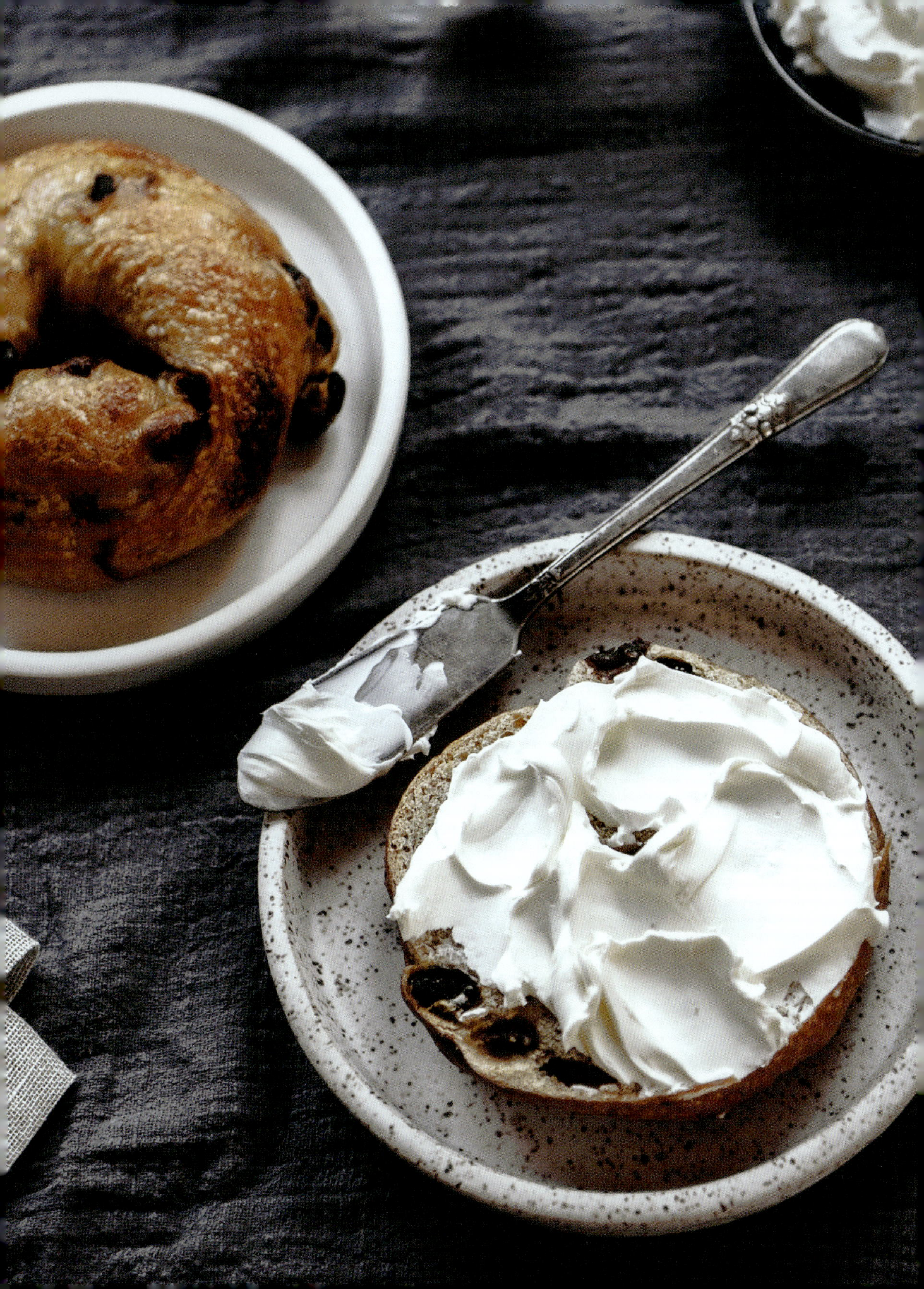

motion causes the machine to inch dangerously close to the counter's edge.) Gradually add the raisins and 1 teaspoon ground cinnamon to the dough during the last 2 minutes of kneading. I like to do this by hand, topping the dough with a little of each, folding the dough in half and in half again, kneading a few times, then repeating until all the raisins and cinnamon are incorporated. The dough will be very stiff. Place the dough in a clean, oiled bowl and cover with plastic wrap or a damp towel. Let rise at room temperature until nearly doubled in bulk, 1½–2 hours.

Line a 12 × 17-inch rimmed baking sheet with parchment paper. Punch down the dough all over to degas it, and turn it out onto the counter in a round disk. Cut the dough into eighths, like a pizza. Shape the bagels by forming each piece of dough into a tight ball, pushing your thumb through the center to form a hole, and using both pointer fingers revolving around each other to gently stretch out the hole in the center. Set the bagels on the prepared pan with at least 1 inch of space between them. Cover the baking sheet with plastic wrap and refrigerate overnight, 12–18 hours, until puffed but not quite doubled in bulk.

Preheat the oven to 425°F. Line a second 12 × 17-inch sheet pan with parchment paper. Set a large pot of water to boil (cover for faster heating). With scissors, cut the parchment paper between the bagels until they're each resting on their own little mat of parchment paper. (Try not to jostle them too much so they don't lose air.)

When the water comes to a rolling boil, add a generous pinch of salt and the remaining tablespoon malt syrup (or molasses). Stir to dissolve with a wooden spoon. Gently slip the bagels into the boiling water, 2 or 3 at a time, peeling off the parchment paper as they fall. Boil for 30 seconds. Flip the bagels and simmer 30 seconds more. Remove them with a slotted spoon, and place them on the prepared pan to dry slightly. Repeat with the remaining dough.

Bake the bagels on the middle rack of the oven for 18–22 minutes, until golden brown. Remove from the oven and let cool. Serve warm or at room temperature.

Leftovers can be stored in a sealed plastic bag at room temperature for a few days; or freeze, tightly wrapped, for longer storage.

Cranberry Baked French Toast with Maple Cream

I love a dish I can throw together the night before, stagger out of bed the next morning, and throw it in the oven. You can use stale bread, fresh bread, or toasted bread. Fresh bread will give it a softer, bread pudding consistency. If you're not refrigerating it overnight, give it a good hour at room temperature (more for stale or toasted bread) to give the bread a chance to soak up the liquid. Serve with maple cream, which is good enough to drink, and a side of bacon or breakfast sausage.

SERVINGS: 8–12

- 1 cup fresh or frozen cranberries (defrosted)
- 1 tablespoon granulated sugar, plus 2 tablespoons for the topping
- 6 large eggs, beaten
- ½ cup light brown sugar, firmly packed
- 4 tablespoons unsalted butter, melted
- 2 teaspoons vanilla extract
- ½ teaspoon table salt or fine sea salt
- 1 cup apple cider
- 1 cup heavy cream
- ½ teaspoon ground allspice
- ¼ teaspoon ground cinnamon
- ⅛ teaspoon ground nutmeg
- 1 loaf challah, Italian, or farmhouse white bread
- ½ cup walnuts, coarsely chopped (optional)

Butter a 9 × 13-inch baking dish.

In a small bowl, toss the washed cranberries with 1 tablespoon of the granulated sugar to coat.

In a large bowl, whisk together the eggs and brown sugar. Add the melted butter, vanilla, and salt. Mix well. Whisk in the apple cider. Slowly stir in the heavy cream until combined.

In a small bowl, stir together the remaining 2 tablespoons granulated sugar, allspice, cinnamon, and nutmeg.

Remove any tough crusts from the bread. Cut into 12 slices about ¾ inch thick. One at a time, dip both sides of each bread slice into the egg mixture and arrange in the prepared baking dish, overlapping like roof shingles (I do three columns of 4 slices, with the pan oriented horizontally). Pour the remaining egg mixture over the top. Press down on the bread firmly with a spatula to encourage absorption. Scatter the cranberries on top. Sprinkle with half the spiced sugar, reserving the rest to add just before baking. Cover with plastic wrap and refrigerate overnight.

Winter 169

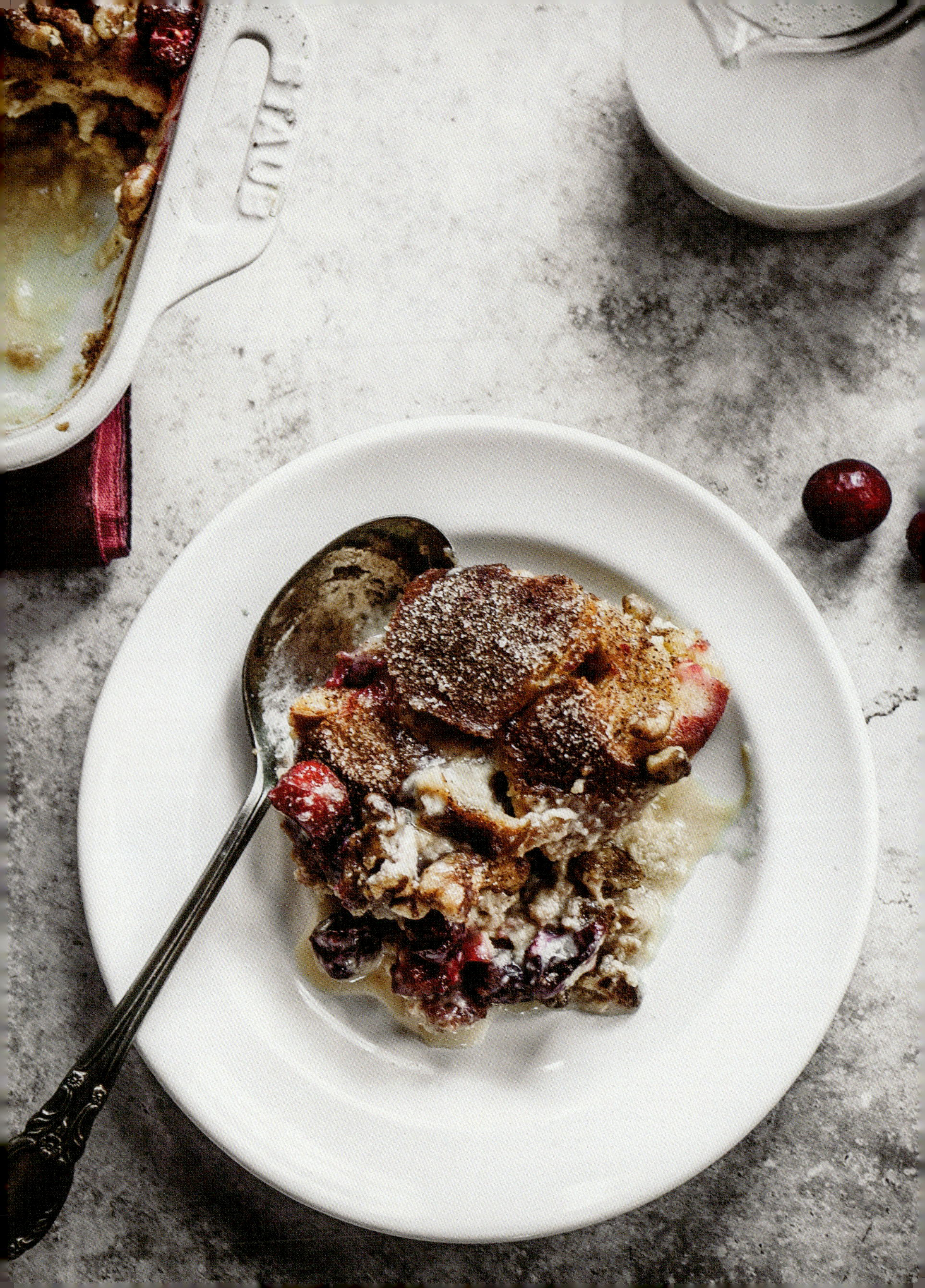

Maple Cream

⅓ cup dark maple syrup

⅓ cup heavy cream

Preheat the oven to 375°F. Let the French toast come to room temperature while the oven is preheating.

Sprinkle the remaining spiced sugar over the top, along with the walnuts, if using. Bake 25–30 minutes, until the French toast is golden brown and a toothpick inserted into the center comes out clean. Remove from the oven and let cool slightly.

For the maple cream: Whisk together the maple syrup and heavy cream just until combined (it will be a liquid sauce). Transfer to a creamer or other serving vessel with a spout. Keep refrigerated until ready to serve.

Leftovers can be covered and stored in the refrigerator for 3–4 days.

Apple Streusel Danish Pastry

This recipe is a project—a fun, stunningly delicious project—but not something I'd recommend for Christmas brunch unless you're extremely organized and/or don't have children expecting presents on Christmas morning. Pick a chill weekend in January or February instead. Make it the day before you want to serve it, refrigerate it overnight, then ice it in the morning. To add some variety, you can add a handful of cranberries or swap out the spiced apple filling for any number of fruit preserves (blackberry is one of my favorites). Or put different flavors in different quadrants to offer your guests some variety. You don't need a lot of jam, just a thin layer to lend color and a sweet counterpart to the tangy cheese filling. Once chilled, this crumbly-topped pastry is to die for.

SERVINGS: 12–16

Dough

- 1 teaspoon active dry yeast
- 1 tablespoon warm water
- 2 cups all-purpose flour, plus more for the counter
- 2 tablespoons granulated sugar, plus a pinch for the yeast
- ½ teaspoon fine sea salt
- ¼ teaspoon ground cardamom (optional)
- 1 large egg
- ½ cup milk (preferably whole), slightly warmed
- ½ cup (1 stick) unsalted butter, soft enough to spread

For the dough: Stir together the yeast, warm water, and a pinch of sugar in a small bowl or ramekin. Let it sit for 5 minutes to activate while preparing the rest of the dough.

In a large bowl, whisk together the flour, sugar, salt, and cardamom. Make a well in the center. Add the egg, milk, and the yeast mixture. Whisk together the wet ingredients in the center, gradually incorporating the surrounding dry ingredients, a little at a time. When the mixture gets too thick, trade in the whisk for a sturdy wooden spoon. Work in all the flour until you have a shaggy dough. Turn it out onto a well-floured surface and knead until smooth with floured hands, about 1 minute. (The dough will start out sticky, and you'll likely need to work in several more tablespoons of flour as you knead so it comes together smoothly.)

Grease a 9 × 13-inch pan. Flour the counter and rolling pin well. Roll out the dough to a 12-inch square. To turn a circle of dough into a square, build up some corners by rolling the left third of the dough with the right side of the rolling pin (start where the dough is widest and roll up or down from there) and rolling the right third of the dough with the left side of the rolling pin. You can also pull on the corners gently, if necessary. Spread the softened butter over the right half of the dough with the back of a spoon or your hands, leaving a 1-inch margin around the edges. Fold the left side of the dough over the buttered side, like you're closing a book. Press

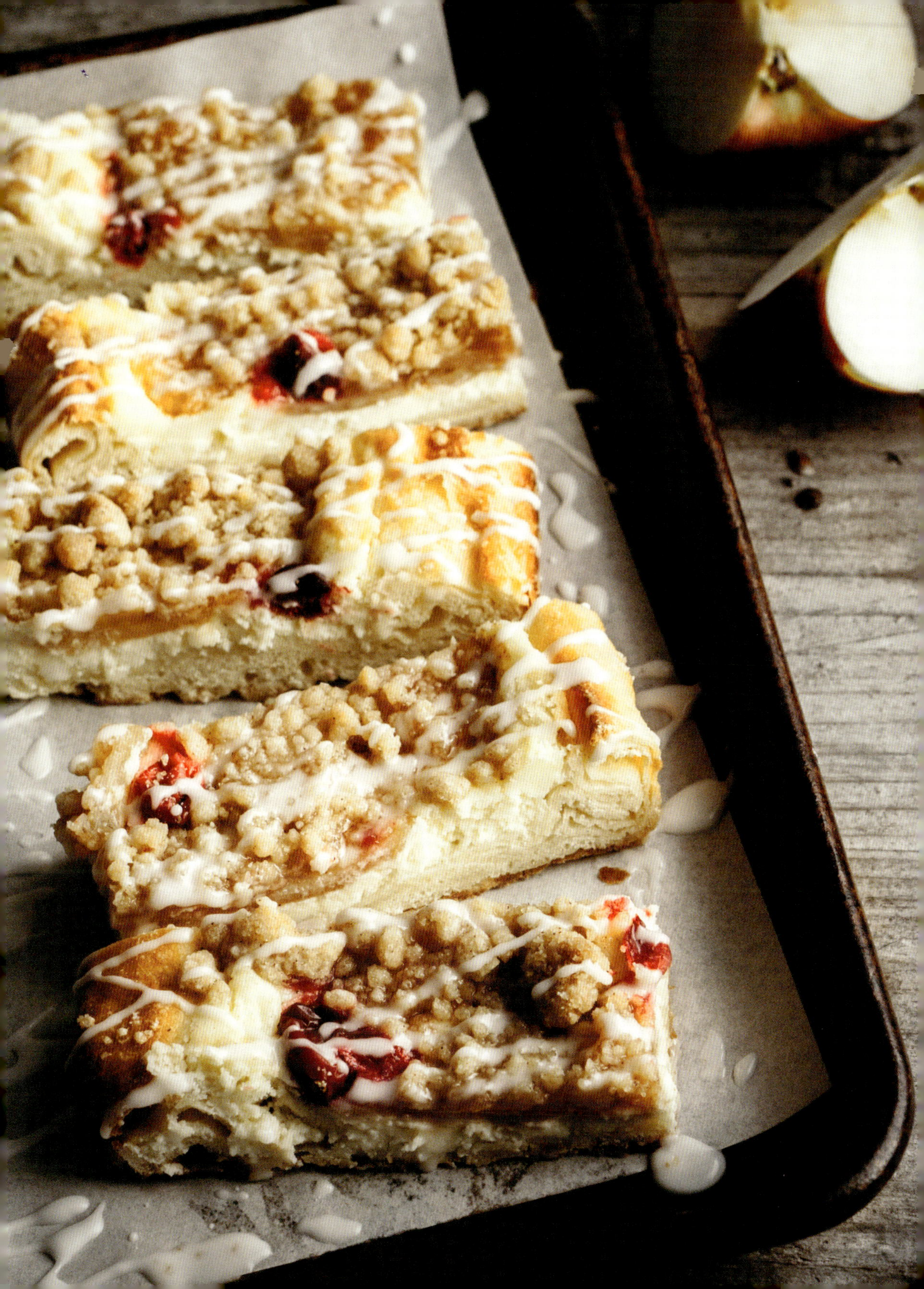

Apple Filling

1 tablespoon unsalted butter

2 large, sweet apples (like Honeycrisp, Jonagold, or Gala), peeled, cored, cut into ¼-inch slices

½ cup apple cider

¼ cup granulated sugar

1 teaspoon freshly squeezed lemon juice

½ teaspoon ground cinnamon

⅛ teaspoon ground nutmeg

Pinch of ground allspice

Pinch of table salt or fine sea salt

1 tablespoon cornstarch

1 tablespoon cold water

Handful of cranberries (optional)

Cheese Filling

12 ounces cream cheese (not light or whipped), at room temperature

½ cup granulated sugar

1 large egg (reserve ⅛ teaspoon yolk for the egg wash)

⅛ teaspoon table salt or fine sea salt

the edges to seal shut. Fold the dough into thirds like a business letter; then fold it in half the other way. Now that you've sealed the butter into the dough in multiple layers, you can either wrap the dough in plastic wrap for a rest in the refrigerator for 30 minutes to 1 hour or proceed with the next step.

Roll out the dough on a floured surface to a 12- to 13-inch square. Again, build up those corners. Transfer the dough to the prepared pan by loosening one side of the dough with a bench scraper or spatula, flipping it over the top of the rolling pin. Loosen the other side of the dough and it should drape right over the rolling pin. Center and unfurl the dough over the pan. The dough should reach almost to the edge of the short side of the pan and hang over the edges of the long sides equally. For the excess dough on one side, fold it over an inch and then back over itself to build up an edge that's higher than the middle. Repeat for the other side. Cover the pan tightly with plastic wrap and set in a warm place to rise, about 1 hour.

For the apple filling: Melt the butter over medium heat in a large sauté pan. Add the sliced apples, cider, sugar, lemon juice, cinnamon, nutmeg, allspice, and salt. Bring to a simmer and cook, uncovered, over medium-low heat, stirring occasionally, for 8–10 minutes, until the apples are tender but not mushy. In a small bowl or ramekin, whisk together the cornstarch and water. Add to the apple mixture and continue cooking, stirring frequently, until thickened, 1–2 minutes. Remove from the heat and let cool. Save the cranberries for assembly.

For the cheese filling: Whip the cream cheese and sugar in a large bowl with an electric mixer until fluffy. Add the egg and salt. Whip the mixture until fully incorporated and no lumps remain. Set aside.

Streusel

- ⅓ cup all-purpose flour
- ¼ cup light brown sugar, firmly packed
- ¼ teaspoon ground cinnamon
- ⅛ teaspoon fine sea salt
- 2 tablespoons unsalted butter, melted

Icing

- 1 cup confectioners' sugar, sifted
- 2 tablespoons milk
- A few drops of almond or vanilla extract

Preheat the oven to 375°F.

Once the dough looks puffy, spread the cheese filling over the dough, leaving the raised edges clear. Dot the apple filling (or jam) over the cheese filling until mostly covered in a thin layer. Scatter with cranberries, if desired. Make an egg wash with the reserved ⅛ teaspoon of yolk, the whites left in the eggshells, and a splash of water (or beat a new egg with a splash of water). Brush the exposed edges of the dough with the egg wash.

For the streusel: Stir together the flour, brown sugar, cinnamon, and salt. Add the melted butter and stir with a fork until a crumbly mixture forms. Crumble up the streusel mixture and scatter over the fruit and cheese filling.

Bake 30–34 minutes until the pastry is nicely browned and the streusel is starting to turn golden brown. The center of the cheese filling may still be slightly jiggly, but it will set as it cools. Remove from the oven to a rack and let cool to room temperature. Cover and chill overnight.

In the morning, mix up the icing. Stir together the confectioners' sugar, milk, and extract. Stir well, until there are no lumps and the consistency is thick enough to drizzle. If needed, add a teaspoon or two more sugar to thicken. To thin, add a few drops of milk. Using a fork or a zip-top bag with a corner snipped, drizzle the icing all over the cold Danish pastry. Chill, uncovered, to set the icing.

To serve, slice straight down the middle of the pan the long way, then cut into 1-inch-thick slices. Transfer to a serving platter.

Cover and store leftovers in the refrigerator for 3 to 4 days.

Anadama Bread

This rustic, caramel-colored bread is said to have originated in Rockport, Massachusetts. Legend has it that a salty fisherman grew fed up with his wife's standard supper of cornmeal porridge sweetened with molasses, so he threw in some flour and yeast and shoved it in the oven while muttering, "Anna, damn her." The bread turned out so well that the neighbors started making it. In truth, breads made with cornmeal were not all that uncommon in colonial times, since corn was native to the land and wheat was scarce. Still, who can resist fishermen's folklore? This version of anadama bread is adapted from the bygone Blacksmith Shop restaurant in Rockport. The cornmeal is soaked beforehand, so there's none of the grit associated with traditional cornbread. It's delicious toasted with salted butter and jam, and resists staling.

SERVINGS: MAKES 2 LOAVES

- ½ cup fine yellow cornmeal
- 1 teaspoon fine sea salt
- 2 cups boiling water
- 2 tablespoons unsalted butter
- 2¼ teaspoons active dry yeast
- ¼ cup warm water
- ½ cup molasses (not blackstrap)
- 5 cups all-purpose or bread flour, divided

Add the cornmeal and salt to a large mixing bowl. Gradually pour in the boiling water, whisking all the while to prevent lumps. Add the butter and let the cornmeal soak for 1 hour. (If you have a coarser cornmeal, you should soak it longer—up to overnight.)

Once the cornmeal is soft, whisk the mixture to loosen it and incorporate the butter. Add the yeast to a measuring cup with ¼ cup warm water and let it sit 5 minutes to activate. Stir the molasses, 3 cups of the flour, and the yeast mixture into the bowl of cornmeal. Keeping adding the flour until the mixture is too thick to be stirred, then start kneading in the rest of the flour with floured hands until the full 5 cups are used. Knead for 10 minutes, until the bread is cohesive, smooth, and no longer sticks to clean hands.

Lightly oil a large, clean bowl. Transfer the dough to the bowl, turning it around to coat with oil. Cover and let rise in a warm place until doubled in bulk, 1–1½ hours.

Preheat the oven to 400°F. Grease two standard-sized loaf pans and line each with a sheet of parchment paper folded in half and tucked across the wide side of the pan like a sling. Fold the edges down or clip them with binder clips to get them out of the way.

Once doubled, nudge the dough out of the bowl onto the counter. Cut it in half with a floured knife or bench scraper. While lifting the dough, tuck the pointy ends underneath to form a football shape; place each half cut side down in the loaf pans. Cover and let rise until doubled in bulk again, about 1 hour.

Bake 25–30 minutes, until the tops are brown, the bread sounds hollow when you tap it, and a thermometer inserted into the center reaches 200°F. Let cool completely; otherwise the escaping steam will cause gummy crumbles to form, making it seem underbaked when it's not.

To serve, slice with a serrated knife, not too thin. Great as toast with salted butter or rewarmed in the microwave.

Leftovers can be stored at room temperature, well wrapped in plastic wrap or in an airtight bag, for 3–4 days.

Kabocha Butter

We all love pumpkin butter, but did you know that it can also be made with all manner of winter squash? Kabocha is a particular favorite of mine, but you can use butternut, blue Hubbard, buttercup, or red kuri, thus extending the pumpkin butter season well into the winter. Canned pumpkin and squash, which are undeniably convenient, work well too. Traditional pumpkin butter doesn't contain actual butter (and I've stuck to that tradition, if only to keep the recipe vegan), but there are no rules against adding a tablespoon or two to the final product if you wish.

SERVINGS: MAKES ABOUT 1 PINT

- 1 6-pound kabocha squash
- ½ cup light brown sugar, firmly packed
- ¼ cup water or apple cider
- 1–2 tablespoons freshly squeezed lemon juice
- ¾ teaspoon ground ginger
- ½ teaspoon ground cinnamon
- ½ teaspoon ground nutmeg
- ¼ teaspoon ground allspice
- ⅛ teaspoon ground cloves
- ½ teaspoon table salt or fine sea salt

Preheat the oven to 375°F. Lightly oil a rimmed 12 × 17-inch baking sheet with vegetable, canola, or grapeseed oil.

Halve the squash and set the halves cut-side-down on the prepared baking sheet. Roast for 45 minutes to 1 hour, until the squash is soft and scoopable. Remove the pan from the oven, flip the squash halves over with tongs, and let cool until they can be handled.

Scoop out and discard the seeds and strings. Scrape out the orange flesh and puree in a food processor until completely smooth, about 1 minute, scraping down the sides and bottom as needed. Discard the skins. Measure out the squash puree— you should have about 2 cups.

To a small saucepan, add the squash puree, brown sugar, water or apple cider, 1 tablespoon of the lemon juice, and all the spices and salt. Cook on medium-low heat, stirring frequently, until the color darkens and a wooden spoon leaves a thick trail in the mixture when swept across the bottom, 10–15 minutes. If the mixture gets too thick too soon, or if you want to cook it longer to deepen the flavor, just add more water as needed and continue cooking, stirring often.

Remove the pan from the heat and let cool slightly. Taste for flavor and add more lemon juice or salt if desired. Transfer to small jars and keep in the refrigerator, covered, for 1–2 weeks.

Brown Bread Muffins

Steamed brown bread was one of those old Yankee recipes served all over New England as an accompaniment to Boston baked beans. The dense, moist loaf was more like a firm steamed pudding, dark with molasses and cooked in a coffee can knee-deep in water in a covered pot to trap the steam. Sometimes it was studded with raisins; sometimes it was plain. Once unmolded from the can, the cylindrical loaves were sliced with a string wrapped around the circumference, crossed, and pulled taut. These muffins have the essential character of brown bread without having to be steamed for hours. They're lighter than the original, but still have that big molasses flavor. Raisins can be omitted, if desired, though I like them. I serve these muffins warm, halved, with big pats of butter; or you can fry the halves in butter to get them extra brown and toasty. They're also great slathered with cream cheese. Short on time? You can still find cans of premade brown bread (like B&M) alongside cans of baked beans at many New England supermarkets.

SERVINGS: MAKES 12

- 1 cup all-purpose flour
- 1 cup rye flour
- 1 cup cornmeal (finely ground)
- 1 teaspoon fine sea salt
- ¾ teaspoon baking soda
- 2 large eggs
- ⅓ cup dark brown sugar, firmly packed
- ¾ cup molasses (not blackstrap)
- 2 teaspoons vanilla extract
- ½ cup (1 stick) unsalted butter, melted
- ½ cup buttermilk, shaken, warmed
- 1 cup raisins

Preheat the oven to 350°F. Grease or line a standard 12-cup muffin tin with liners.

In a medium bowl, whisk together the all-purpose flour, rye flour, cornmeal, salt, and baking soda. Set aside.

In a large bowl, whisk the eggs with the brown sugar. Slowly whisk in the molasses; once it's all incorporated, whisk 1 minute more. Add the vanilla. Slowly whisk in the melted butter and buttermilk.

Add the dry ingredients to the wet, and whisk until smooth. Fold in the raisins with a rubber spatula. Fill the muffin wells to the top (I use a heaping 1½-ounce cookie scoop).

Bake 22–25 minutes, until the tops crack and spring back when gently pressed. Remove from the oven and let cool.

Leftovers can be stored in an airtight container at room temperature for up to 1 week.

Variation

Gingerbread Muffins: Omit the raisins and add 1 teaspoon ground ginger, ½ teaspoon ground cinnamon, and ¼ teaspoon ground cloves.

The Great Molasses Flood

A tidal wave of molasses bearing down on the city of Boston may sound like an absurd urban legend, but the Great Molasses Flood is as true as it is tragic. In January 1919, a fifty-foot steel tank full of molasses on Commercial Street in the North End collapsed, causing more than 2 million gallons of molasses (13,000 tons) to inundate the heavily populated neighborhood. In a massive deluge that started out forty feet high and traveled thirty-five miles per hour, the wall of molasses demolished buildings, submerged streets, flooded basements, and toppled one section of the elevated railway. Twenty-one people were killed (along with dozens of horses) and 150 injured. After the disaster, residents brought one of the first class-action lawsuits in Massachusetts, which paved the way for future corporate regulation. A plaque marks the site where the tank once stood, near the baseball diamond at Langone Park. Some say that on a hot day, a faint whiff of molasses can still be detected in the air.

Boston Baked Beans

Perhaps New England's most famous contribution to the culinary canon is baked beans, which were so popular that Boston came to be known as Beantown. When I was growing up in New England, Saturday nights were beans and franks night, perhaps with a side of brown bread. Despite the undeniable convenience of canned beans, homemade, slow-cooked baked beans are something of a religious experience: creamy, deeply flavored, and immensely satisfying. I recommend starting your beans a day ahead of time so they can be soaked, parboiled, and have plenty of hands-off cooking time that will translate into exceptional flavor and texture. You can make them in an old-fashioned clay beanpot with excellent results, or you can use a Dutch oven, covered casserole dish, or slow-cooker. I don't like my beans too sweet, but molasses is an essential ingredient that gives the beans their distinctive flavor and richness. If you can't find salt pork, you can substitute thick-cut bacon. Some folks in Connecticut prefer their beans with a tomato base. In that case, serve with ketchup on the side. Warm Brown Bread Muffins (page 180) slathered with butter or cream cheese complete this traditional brunchtime meal.

SERVINGS: 8

- 1 pound dried navy, yellow eye, or Marfax beans, soaked overnight
- ½ pound salt pork, cut into ¾-inch pieces
- 1 medium yellow onion, chopped
- ⅓ cup molasses (not blackstrap)
- 1 tablespoon Dijon mustard (or 1 teaspoon dried mustard)
- 1 tablespoon apple cider vinegar
- 1 teaspoon kosher salt
- Freshly ground black pepper, to taste
- 3–4 cups water

Soak the beans in cold water 8–12 hours or overnight.

Bring a large pot of water to a boil. Parboil the soaked beans 20–25 minutes, stirring occasionally and skimming the foam as needed, until the skins start to split. Drain the beans.

For a beanpot, Dutch oven, or casserole dish: Preheat the oven to 300°F. Layer the pork, onion, and parboiled beans in a pot or dish. Add the molasses, mustard, vinegar, salt, pepper, and enough water to cover the top of the beans. Cover the pot and place in the center of the oven. Bake 4–6 hours, checking the water level every 2 hours and adding more as necessary to keep the beans covered. The beans are done when they're perfectly tender and the cooking liquid has reduced to a sauce. Remove from the oven and let cool slightly.

For a slow-cooker: Layer the pork, onion, and parboiled beans in the crock. Add the molasses, mustard, vinegar, salt, pepper, and enough water to cover the top of the beans. Cover the pot and cook overnight on low (6–8 hours) or set to high first thing in the morning (4–6 hours). Check the water level before you go to bed or first thing in the morning and add more to cover if necessary. The beans are done when they're perfectly tender and the cooking liquid has reduced to a sauce. Keep warm until ready to serve.

Beans can be served directly from the hot crock with a ladle.

Leftovers can be stored in the refrigerator, covered. Reheat in the microwave, adding a bit of water as needed.

A Brief History of Baked Beans

Boston baked beans are typically attributed to the Puritans who settled in the Massachusetts Bay Colony (the area surrounding modern-day Boston and Salem). Religiously observing the Sabbath meant no work on Sundays, so the dried beans were started on Saturday evenings and left to cook in a crock of water in the embers of the hearth or baked in a communal oven all night long. Come Sunday, the slow-cooked beans were especially tender and tasty. While it's true that the particular flavor profile of Boston baked beans, seasoned with salt pork and molasses, reflected the commodities that were traded at the colonial ports at that time, baked beans have been around much longer than that. The Indigenous peoples of the region had been cooking beans in their own traditional ways for thousands of years before, using heirloom varieties they developed, like yellow eye, red eye (soldier), and trout (Jacob's cattle). Maple syrup was the predominant flavoring, and venison or bear fat could be added. The Penobscot people of the Wabanaki Confederacy in Maine introduced the bean hole. They cooked their beans in earthenware pots in a stone-lined pit in the ground, complete with burning embers, and covered it with soil so the beans could cook slowly and undisturbed overnight. In short, baked beans are an authentic Native American dish that adapted well to colonial life.

Cheddar Thyme Biscuits

New England is lucky to have many excellent locally made cheeses. Here I've incorporated cheddar into buttery, flaky biscuits scented with thyme. Serve these biscuits with eggs and Maple Breakfast Sausage (page 186) to make killer breakfast sandwiches, or as an accompaniment to Portuguese Kale Soup (page 142).

SERVINGS: MAKES 10–12

- 2 cups all-purpose flour
- 2 tablespoons baking powder
- 1 tablespoon chopped fresh thyme (or 1 teaspoon dried), plus extra for topping
- 1 teaspoon table salt or fine sea salt
- ¾ cup shredded sharp white cheddar
- ½ cup (1 stick) cold unsalted butter, cut into 8 pieces
- ¾ cup milk, plus extra for brushing

Preheat the oven to 425°F. Grease a 12 × 17-inch baking sheet or line it with parchment paper.

Add the flour, baking powder, thyme, salt, and cheddar to the bowl of a food processor. Process briefly to combine. Add the butter and process 15–20 seconds, until the butter pieces are the size of small peas. (You can also work the butter into the dry ingredients with a pastry blender or your fingers.)

Dump the mixture into a medium bowl. Add the milk and fluff the mixture with a fork until all the liquid is absorbed and it comes together into a shaggy dough. Turn the dough onto a floured counter. Bring the dough together and fold it over itself several times to create layers. Gently pat the dough into a disk about ¾ inch thick. Using a 3-inch biscuit cutter or jelly jar, cut out as many rounds as possible, cutting straight down without twisting (or you can cut into 3½-inch squares with a bench scraper or sharp knife). Dip the cutter or knife into the flour to prevent sticking. The scraps can be rerolled and cut. Set the biscuits on the prepared pan about 1 inch apart. Brush the tops with milk.

Bake the biscuits for 14–18 minutes, until they're golden brown and crusty on top. Remove from the oven and transfer the biscuits to a rack to cool slightly. For best results, serve the biscuits warm with butter.

Cooled biscuits can be stored in an airtight container at room temperature for 3–4 days. Rewarm in a toaster oven or microwave if desired.

Maple Breakfast Sausage

We get delicious ground pork in our meat CSA from Chestnut Farm in Hardwick, Massachusetts, and this is an excellent way to use it. If you're a fan of biscuits and gravy, I've included an optional gravy recipe to serve with the biscuits on page 185. For a vegan option with a similar flavor profile, sauté 1–2 pounds sliced shiitake mushroom caps (or other mushrooms) in 2 tablespoons of olive oil with all the spices for about 5 minutes, until lightly browned and no longer releasing any liquid. Serve with a drizzle of maple syrup.

SERVINGS: MAKES ABOUT 12 SMALL PATTIES

- 2 pounds ground pork
- 1½ teaspoons fine sea salt
- 1 teaspoon ground sage
- 1 teaspoon ground thyme
- 1 teaspoon ground black pepper
- ¼ teaspoon red pepper flakes
- ¼ cup maple syrup (the darker, the better)
- Grapeseed, canola, or vegetable oil, for frying

Break up the pork into pieces and add to a large bowl. Add the salt, sage, thyme, black pepper, and red pepper flakes to the pork. Toss the pork with your hands to coat with the herb mixture. Add the maple syrup and gently work it into the pork mixture until combined.

On a sheet pan, form the pork into 12 small, round patties, about ½ inch thick. Press a shallow dip in the centers of the patties to help the middle cook faster and keep them from puffing up too much.

Heat 1 tablespoon of oil in a large sauté pan over medium-low heat. When hot, cook the patties in two or three batches for about 3–4 minutes per side. They will brown very quickly as the maple syrup caramelizes. (Make sure your kitchen fan is on, or open a window slightly to keep the smoke under control.) Serve with eggs and Home Fries (page 196) or alongside your favorite pancakes.

How to Make Sausage Gravy

Wipe out any blackened bits of caramelized maple syrup from the inside of the pan with a paper towel. Melt 3 tablespoons unsalted butter in the skillet over medium-low heat, scraping up any residual sausage bits. Add 3 tablespoons all-purpose flour and cook 1–2 minutes, stirring constantly with a wooden spoon, until bubbly and foamy. Gradually whisk in 3 cups warm milk. Turn the heat up to medium-high, add a sprig of fresh thyme, and bring to a simmer, whisking occasionally. Reduce the heat to medium-low to maintain a simmer and cook, whisking occasionally, until the gravy reaches your desired thickness, 3–5 minutes. Remove from the heat. Stir in 1 teaspoon soy sauce and 1 teaspoon apple cider vinegar. Remove the thyme sprig. Season with salt and pepper to taste. Serve over biscuits.

Red Flannel Hash with Horseradish Cream

If you find yourself with leftovers from an Irish boiled dinner, take a page from our thrifty New England ancestors and make red flannel hash for brunch the next day. While straight-up corned beef hash is typically made with corned beef and potatoes only, red flannel hash features the addition of beets. I like adding other root vegetables too: carrots, parsnips, rutabagas, and turnips. The term "hash" comes from the French word hacher, *which means "to chop." Early lumberjacks, hunters, and trappers who spent weeks at a time deep in the northeastern wilderness found hash to be a convenient and hearty meal to make over the campfire. The creamy horseradish sauce adds a delightful kick. If you're starting with uncooked corned beef, allow yourself several hours of cooking time either in the morning or the night before to ensure enough time to precook the meat and vegetables before chopping into hash. Serve this hearty, rib-sticking dish with eggs (poached, fried, or steamed in the wells of the hash) with apple cider vinegar on the side.*

SERVINGS: 6–8

- 2 pounds corned beef
- 1 pound Yukon gold or other starchy potatoes (about 2 large potatoes)
- ½ pound carrots and/or parsnips, peeled (about 4 medium)
- ½ pound turnips, peeled (about 1 large)
- 1 pound beets, peeled (about 2 medium)
- 2 large yellow onions, chopped
- Salt and black pepper to taste

In a large pot, cover the corned beef by 2 inches with cold water. Cover and bring to a boil over high heat. Turn down the heat to medium and continue simmering for 5 minutes, skimming the foam from the top. Stir in the contents of the spice packet. Adjust the heat, if needed, and continue simmering for about 2 hours or until tender. Remove the meat and let cool slightly.

Return the water to a boil. Cut the potatoes, carrots, turnips, and beets into 1-inch pieces. Add the potatoes, carrots, and turnips to the pot of boiling water, but not the beets (the beets will discolor the other vegetables). Cook 6–8 minutes, until the vegetables can be pierced with a fork. Remove the vegetables with a slotted spoon to a large plate to cool. Add the beets to the boiling water. Cook until tender, about 10–12 minutes. Remove the beets to a separate plate to cool.

Before shredding the meat, trim the fatty layer off the corned beef and dice the fat very finely. Melt about 2 tablespoons of the fat in a large 12-inch cast iron skillet or other heavy nonstick skillet over medium-low heat. (If there's no fat to trim,

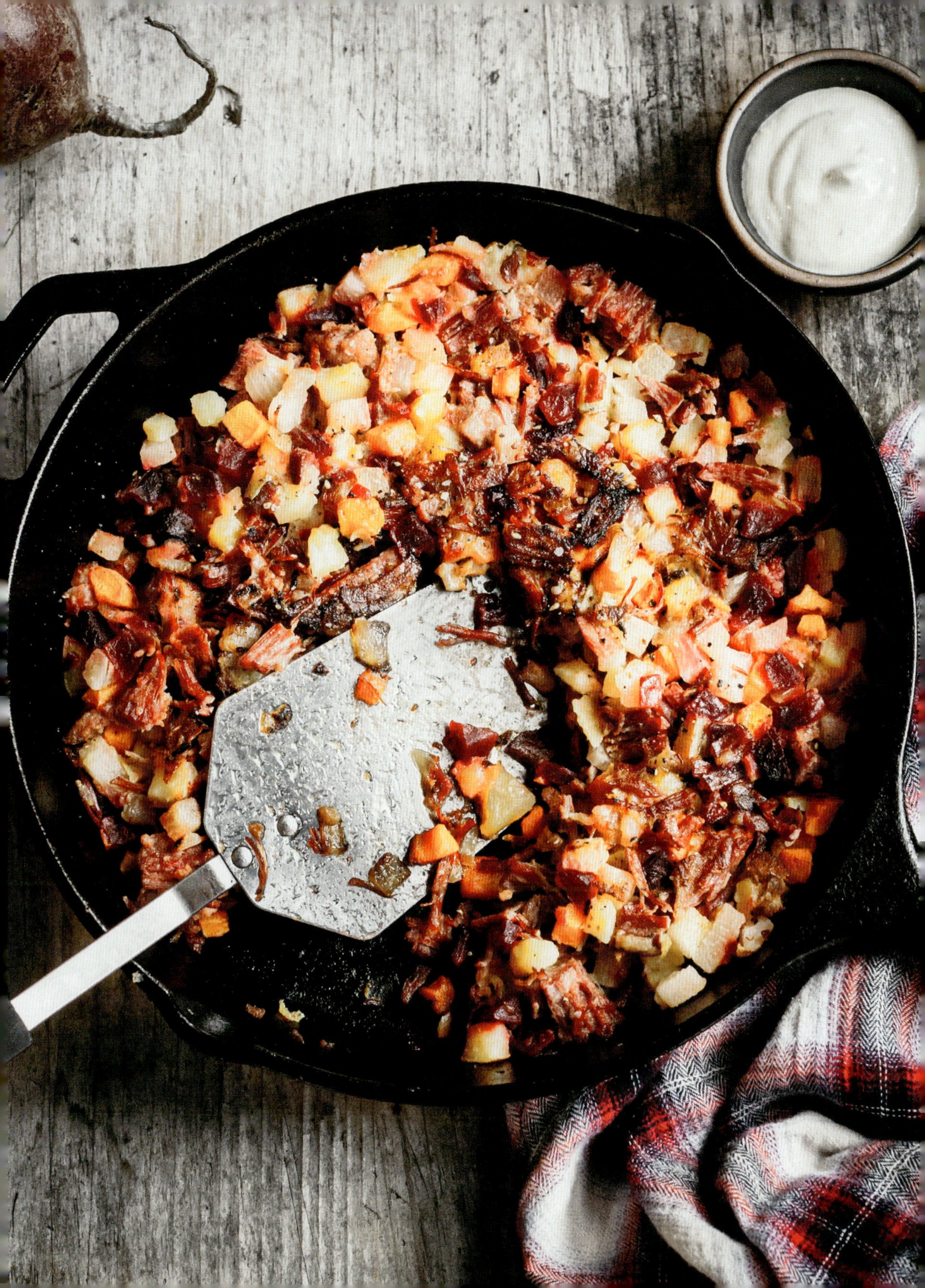

1 tablespoon unsalted butter

⅓ cup heavy cream (optional)

Horseradish Sauce

1 cup sour cream

2 tablespoons prepared horseradish

2 teaspoons Dijon mustard

1 teaspoon white wine vinegar

Salt and freshly ground black pepper to taste

you can substitute bacon fat, butter, or olive oil.) Add the chopped onions and gently cook 3-4 minutes, until softened.

If the meat is cold, submerge it in the boiling water and turn off the heat. Let it sit for 5–10 minutes. Remove the meat with tongs and shred it with a fork and knife. Cut the shredded strips into small bite-sized pieces. Add to a large bowl.

Once the potatoes, carrots, turnips, and beets are cool enough to handle, dice them into small pieces (again, saving the beets for last). The fastest way to do this is to lay out the pieces in batches on the cutting board so they're touching each other. Make vertical cuts through all of them, then horizontal cuts. Add the vegetables to the bowl of meat along with the onions. Season with salt and pepper. Stir everything until well combined.

Melt 1 tablespoon butter in the same pan you cooked the onions in over medium-high heat. Add the corned beef hash, distributing evenly in the pan and flattening with a spatula. Fry undisturbed for 3–5 minutes, until you hear popping sounds and the bottom has browned. Flip the mash in batches to brown the other side. Pour ⅓ cup of the boiling liquid (my first choice) or heavy cream evenly over the top, but do not stir. Cook for 3 more minutes or so until browned.

If cooking eggs in the hash, add them at this point. Make wells in the mixture with a large spoon, crack an egg into each one, season with salt and pepper, and cover until the eggs are done to your liking. If the bottom of the hash is getting too brown, just add a tablespoon or two of water to the pan and cover.

Remove the pan from the heat and uncover.

For the horseradish sauce: Stir the sour cream, horseradish, mustard, and vinegar together in a small bowl. Season with salt and pepper to taste. Serve at the table with the red flannel hash.

Leftovers can be covered and stored in the refrigerator for 3–4 days. Hash can be reheated in the pan by adding a bit of water and a lid over medium-low heat for 5–10 minutes until warmed.

Rosemary Gruyère Popovers

Popovers are puffy, egg-leavened pastries that are baked until deeply golden brown on the outside and hollow on the inside. They're the American version of British Yorkshire puddings. In New England, popovers are traditionally served with Yankee pot roasts, but I think they're a great savory alternative to sweet muffins or rolls for brunch. I've taken inspiration from French gougères and flavored these with rosemary and Gruyère cheese, but they're equally good with sharp cheddar and thyme.

SERVINGS: MAKES 12

- 3 large eggs
- 1½ cups milk, slightly warmed in the microwave
- 3 tablespoons unsalted butter, melted, divided
- 1½ cups all-purpose flour
- ½ teaspoon dried rosemary
- ½ teaspoon table salt or fine sea salt
- ½ cup shredded Gruyère cheese

Preheat the oven to 425°F. Set a standard 12-cup muffin tin (no liners) in the oven to preheat.

In a large bowl, whisk the eggs well. Slowly whisk in the milk and 1 tablespoon of the melted butter (reserve the remaining 2 tablespoons of melted butter for the pan). Add the flour, rosemary, and salt. Whisk well. Stir in the shredded cheese with a rubber spatula.

Carefully remove the muffin tin from the oven with mitts. Quickly brush the wells of the muffin tin with the remaining melted butter. Fill each well three-fourths of the way up with the batter (about ¼ cup).

Bake 25–30 minutes, until deeply golden brown (err on the side of longer baking to ensure the popovers don't collapse when they cool). It's important not to open the oven during the first half of the baking time; otherwise the steam will escape and your popovers won't puff up as much as they should. Remove from the oven and let cool slightly.

While these are best eaten warm as soon as possible, leftovers can be covered and stored at room temperature for 2–3 days and gently warmed in the microwave.

Parsnip and Juniper Latkes

Latkes are delicious Hanukkah fare and so brunch-like in nature that I propose they be added to the New England brunch repertoire year-round. Not only that, but they don't have to be limited to potatoes—root vegetables like turnips, carrots, and parsnips or sweet potatoes can be paired or substituted. I use parsnips here for their earthy sweetness. Remove the tough inner core by cutting each parsnip into quarters lengthwise and shaving off the sharp corner edge along the tannish demarcation line. You can shred the potatoes and parsnips using the grating disk on your food processor or with a box grater. If you don't have matzo meal, you can substitute water crackers—or, even better, crisp rosemary crackers—ground into crumbs (this is a good use of leftover crackers from holiday cheese plates). Juniper berries add the occasional festive pop of flavor, but they can be omitted. Serve with sour cream and the Cranberry Applesauce on page 195.

SERVINGS: MAKES 10–12

- ½ pound Yukon gold potatoes (or other starchy potato), peeled, grated
- ¾ pound parsnips, peeled, tough inner cores removed, grated
- 1½ teaspoons kosher salt, divided
- 1 large egg
- 1 teaspoon juniper berries, coarsely cracked using a mortar and pestle
- Freshly ground black pepper, to taste
- 1 small yellow onion, peeled, diced small
- 1 scant cup matzo meal
- Canola oil, for frying
- Applesauce and sour cream, for serving

Line a colander set over a bowl with two layers of cheesecloth or a lint-free dish towel. Add the grated potato and parsnip. Sprinkle with 1 teaspoon of the salt and mix with your hands. Let sit for 30 minutes to draw the water out of the vegetables.

Meanwhile, beat the egg in a large bowl. Add the remaining ½ teaspoon of salt, juniper berries, and black pepper. Stir in the diced onions.

Set a large cast iron skillet or other heavy-bottomed skillet on the stove. Add the canola oil to a depth of about ½ inch. Line a plate with a double layer of paper towels and set on the counter nearby.

Gather up the ends of the cheesecloth or dish towel and twist until the grated potato and parsnips are in a tight ball. Keep squeezing until the excess liquid drips out. Continue twisting and squeezing to get out as much liquid as you can. Then add the shredded potato and parsnips to the bowl with the egg. Stir the mixture with a wooden spoon until the egg is well dispersed. Add the matzo meal or crackers crumbs to the mixture about ¼ cup at a time, mixing before adding more. Add only as much as you need so the mixture holds together in your hand when gently squeezed.

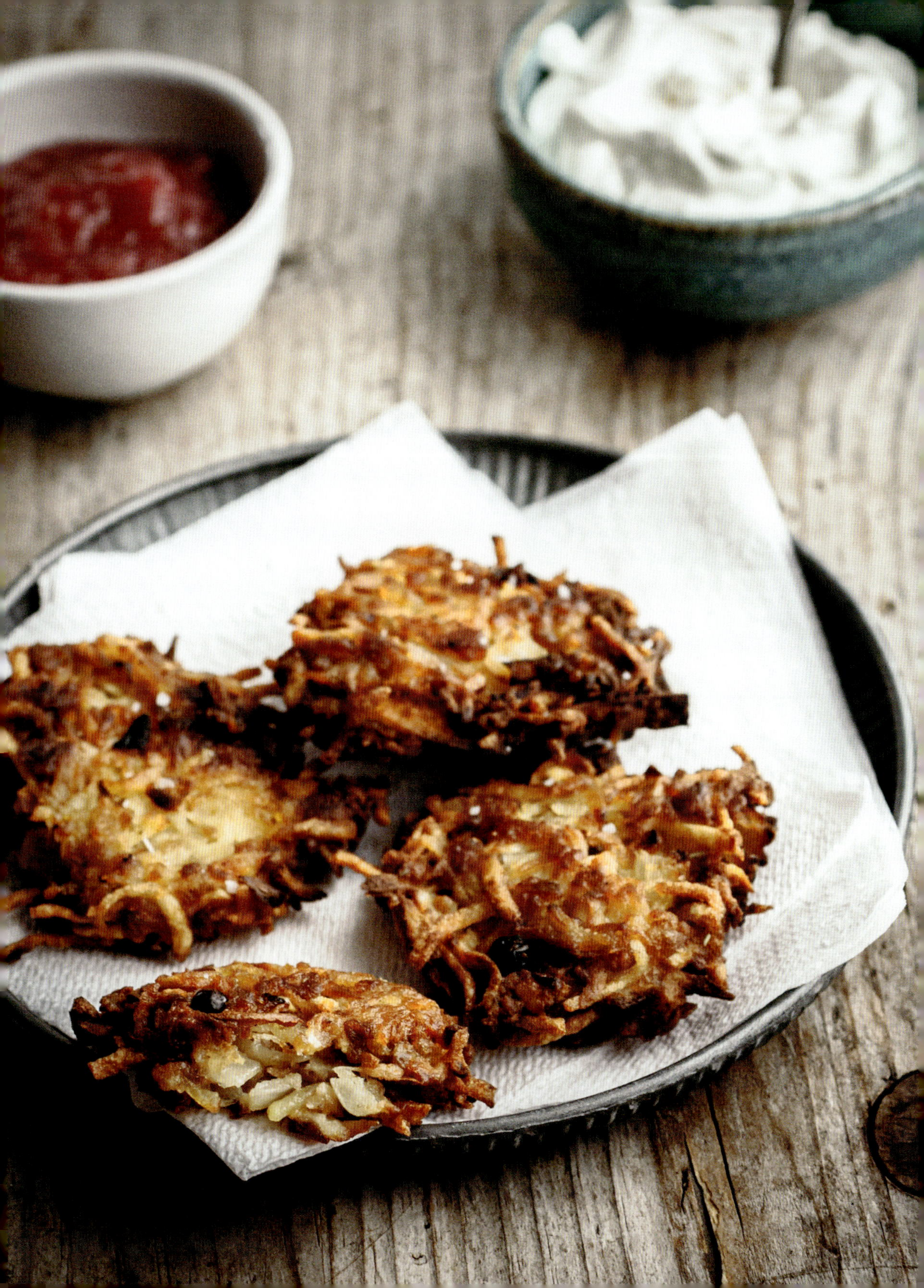

Heat the oil over medium heat until hot (a bit of the potato mixture should sizzle immediately when dropped into the oil). Form patties 3–4 inches wide and ½ inch thick and add to the oil (make sure the hot oil splashes *away* from you). In batches of 3 or 4 at a time, fry them for 3–5 minutes on each side until golden brown. Transfer the latkes to the paper towel–lined plate and sprinkle with salt. Between batches, strain out the crispy bits from the oil with a slotted spoon or spider strainer—they are the cook's reward. Continue frying the rest.

Serve latkes warm with sour cream and applesauce.

Latkes are best eaten fresh as soon as possible, but they can be covered and refrigerated for 1–2 days and reheated in a toaster oven to retain their crispness.

Cranberry Applesauce

This sweet-tart applesauce has a beautiful deep rosy hue that's sure to brighten your fall or winter table. It works equally well with fresh or frozen cranberries. It can be served with a dusting of cinnamon as part of a larger buffet-style brunch, stirred into oatmeal, or eaten alongside the Parsnip and Juniper Latkes (page 192). A food mill makes short work of pureeing the mixture while removing the skins and seeds, but if you don't have one, you can accomplish the same result with a metal sieve, sturdy wooden spoon, and some muscle.

SERVINGS: 4–6

- 2 pounds McIntosh apples (6–7 medium), quartered
- 1 cup frozen cranberries
- ½ cup granulated sugar
- ¼ cup water
- 1 teaspoon freshly squeezed lemon juice
- Pinch of salt

Add the apple quarters to a heavy-bottomed medium pot (no need to peel or core the apples). Add the cranberries, sugar, water, lemon juice, and salt. Cover the pot with the lid and bring to a simmer over medium-low heat. Cook 20–25 minutes, stirring occasionally, until the apples are soft and the cranberries are starting to burst. Remove the pot from the heat and let it sit with the lid on for 5 minutes. Remove the lid and let the applesauce cool slightly.

Set a food mill fitted with the disk with medium holes over a large bowl. Add the apple mixture and crank the food mill until a puree comes out the bottom into the bowl. (Or you can press the mixture through a metal sieve with a wooden spoon, scraping the mixture against the metal grate. Discard the seeds and skins.) Taste and add more sugar if desired. Transfer to a large jar and chill in the refrigerator. Serve plain or with ground cinnamon.

Home Fries

I like my home fries to be assertively spiced, with crispy browned bits mixed in with tender, well-salted chunks of potato. Here's a version of savory home fries that leans Italian in its flavor profile, with garlic, red pepper, and rosemary, among other spices. But you could change up the spicing in myriad other ways (see variations). Serve them alongside other brunch favorites or by themselves with a fried egg on top, runny yolk cascading down to create the perfect sauce.

SERVINGS: 8–10

- 2 pounds Yukon gold or other starchy potato (about 5 large)
- 1 large yellow onion, peeled, cut into ½-inch dice
- ½ medium red bell pepper, cut into ½-inch dice
- 1½ tablespoons dried rosemary
- 1½ teaspoons paprika
- 1 teaspoon garlic powder
- 1½ teaspoons kosher salt, plus more for the boil
- ½ teaspoon ground black pepper
- Dash of dried marjoram or thyme
- Dash of dried sage
- ¼ cup olive oil

Preheat the oven 425°F. Brush a rimmed 12 x 17-inch baking sheet with olive oil.

Set a large pot of water to boil over high heat. Meanwhile, cut the potatoes (no need to peel) into cubes no bigger than 1 inch square. When the water comes to a boil, add a big pinch of salt and the potatoes to the water. Bring back to a boil and, lowering the heat slightly to maintain a low boil, cook for 5 minutes. Drain the potatoes and place in a large bowl.

Add the diced onions and peppers to the potatoes. Sprinkle with the spices, salt, and pepper. Add the olive oil and mix. Arrange in a single layer on the prepared baking sheet.

Roast the potatoes on the middle rack of the oven for 10–15 minutes, until the bottoms are golden brown. Flip with a spatula and roast for another 10–15 minutes, until crisp, browning, sizzling, and whistling. Serve immediately.

Leftovers can be covered and stored in the refrigerator for 4–5 days and reheated in the microwave.

Variations

Spanish: Substitute ½ diced green bell pepper or 1 minced jalapeño for the red bell pepper. For the spicing, keep the salt and black pepper the same, but replace the other spices with 1 tablespoon chili powder, 1 teaspoon smoked paprika, 1 teaspoon garlic powder, ½ teaspoon ground cumin, and a dash of dried oregano.

Indian: Omit the bell pepper or add 1 small hot chili, minced. For the spicing, keep the salt and black pepper the same, but replace the other spices with 2 teaspoons ground cumin, 1 teaspoon cumin seed, 1 teaspoon ground coriander, ½ teaspoon ground turmeric, and a dash of ground cayenne. Bake on the lowest rack in the oven to encourage the onions to brown deeply.

Cranberry Mimosas

This beautiful crimson beverage is perfect for a holiday brunch. A dose of orange-flavored liquor is a nod to the classic mimosa, which happens to pair very well with cranberry. A splash of almond extract adds a bit of mai tai intrigue and helps soften the tart edges. This recipe can be scaled up as needed for a crowd. To preserve its effervescence, add the chilled Prosecco to the batch just before serving, or fill each glass halfway with the cranberry mixture and top off with Prosecco.

SERVINGS: 4–6

- 2 cups cranberry juice cocktail, chilled
- ¼ cup Cointreau, triple sec, or other orange liqueur
- ⅛ teaspoon almond extract
- 2 cups Prosecco, chilled
- Frozen cranberries, for garnish

Combine the cranberry juice cocktail, orange liqueur, and almond extract in a pitcher. Stir to combine. Chill overnight. Just before serving, stir in the Prosecco and a handful of frozen cranberries. Pour into champagne flutes or other elegant glasses, adding a few cranberries to each glass.

Pumpkin Eggnog

Is there a more polarizing drink than eggnog? Love it or hate it (my family splits right down the middle), it's a long-standing Christmas tradition. This version has less egg and more pumpkin, which I think is an improvement conceptually over a purely egg-based beverage. It's true to the natural sweetness of the pumpkin but keeps the fresh nutmeg flavor of traditional eggnog—however, you're welcome to infuse it with more of a pumpkin spice profile. Add a tablespoon or two of rum to each glass or enjoy it without.

SERVINGS: 4–6

- 3 large egg yolks
- ⅔ cup granulated sugar, divided
- 2 cups milk
- 1 cup heavy cream
- 1 cup canned or cooked, pureed pumpkin (page 133)
- ½ teaspoon vanilla extract
- ½ teaspoon ground nutmeg (preferably freshly grated)
- ¼ teaspoon fine sea salt
- Dark or spiced rum
- Cinnamon sticks, for garnish

In a large bowl, whisk the egg yolks with ⅓ cup of the sugar. Continue whisking until the mixture turns pale yellow and thickens enough to form a thick ribbon as it falls off the whisk.

In a medium, heavy-bottomed saucepan, add the milk and cream. Whisk in the remaining ⅓ cup of sugar over medium heat. Continue cooking, whisking frequently, until it reaches a bare simmer. Remove the pan from the heat. Slowly whisk 1 cup of the hot cream mixture into the yolk mixture. Slowly whisk the yolk mixture into the pot. Set back on medium heat, whisking constantly, for 2–3 minutes, until slightly thickened. Do not let simmer. Remove from the heat and pour into a blender bowl. Let cool slightly.

Add the pumpkin, vanilla, nutmeg, and salt to the blender bowl. Puree until smooth, about 30 seconds. Taste and adjust the spicing if necessary. Chill in the refrigerator overnight. To serve, pour into lowball glasses, stir in 1–2 tablespoons of rum if desired, and sprinkle with additional grated nutmeg.

Bailey's Irish Coffee

Irish coffee, which originated in Limerick, Ireland, in the 1950s, is typically spiked with Irish whiskey, topped with cream, and served as an after-dinner drink with dessert. But I hope the Irish don't mind if I borrow it for brunch in New England, where the descendants of Irish immigrants are plenty. I'm partial to using Bailey's because it's sweet enough to forgo the sugar (if using straight Irish whiskey, you may want to stir in some maple syrup to taste). Top with fresh, lightly whipped cream and perhaps a sprinkling of cinnamon or cardamom for good measure. Special Irish coffee glasses exist and can be found in thrift stores. They're typically glass pedestal goblets with a handle on the side or a thick, knobby stem at the base so you don't burn your fingers, but regular mugs work too. Scale this recipe up or down as needed.

SERVINGS: 4

- 4 cups good strong coffee
- ⅓ cup heavy cream
- ¼–½ cup Bailey's Irish Cream (or Irish whiskey like Jameson), plus more for the whipped cream
- Maple syrup (optional)
- Ground cinnamon or cardamom, for garnish (optional)

While the coffee is brewing, whip the cream with a splash or two of Bailey's in a medium bowl with an electric mixer. You can whip it as fluffy as you'd like, but I prefer it very lightly whipped so it barely holds its shape.

Divide the coffee among four glasses. Stir in 1–2 tablespoons Bailey's into each glass (or the same amount of Irish whiskey plus a bit of maple syrup to taste). Top with the whipped cream and a shake of cinnamon or cardamom if desired. Serve immediately.

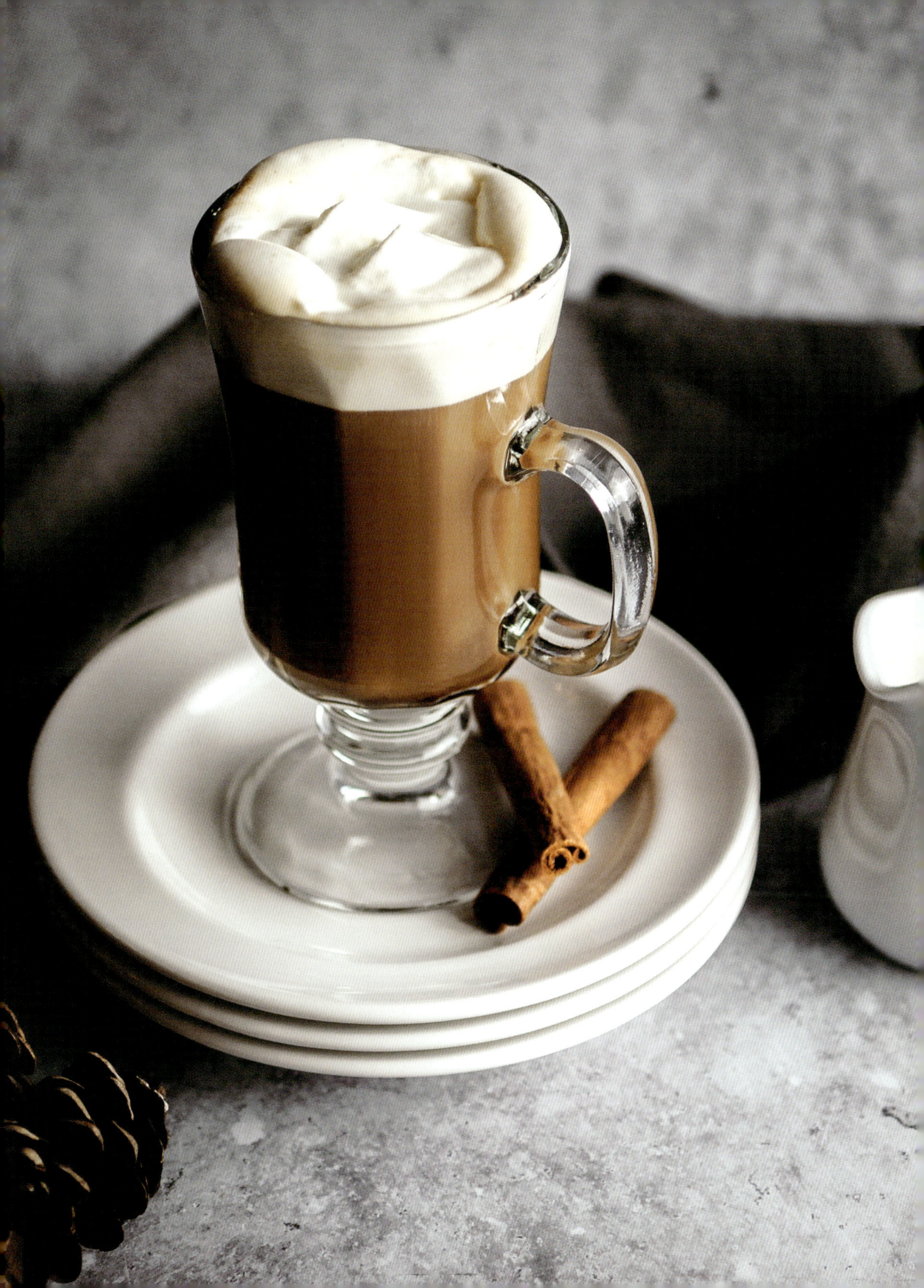

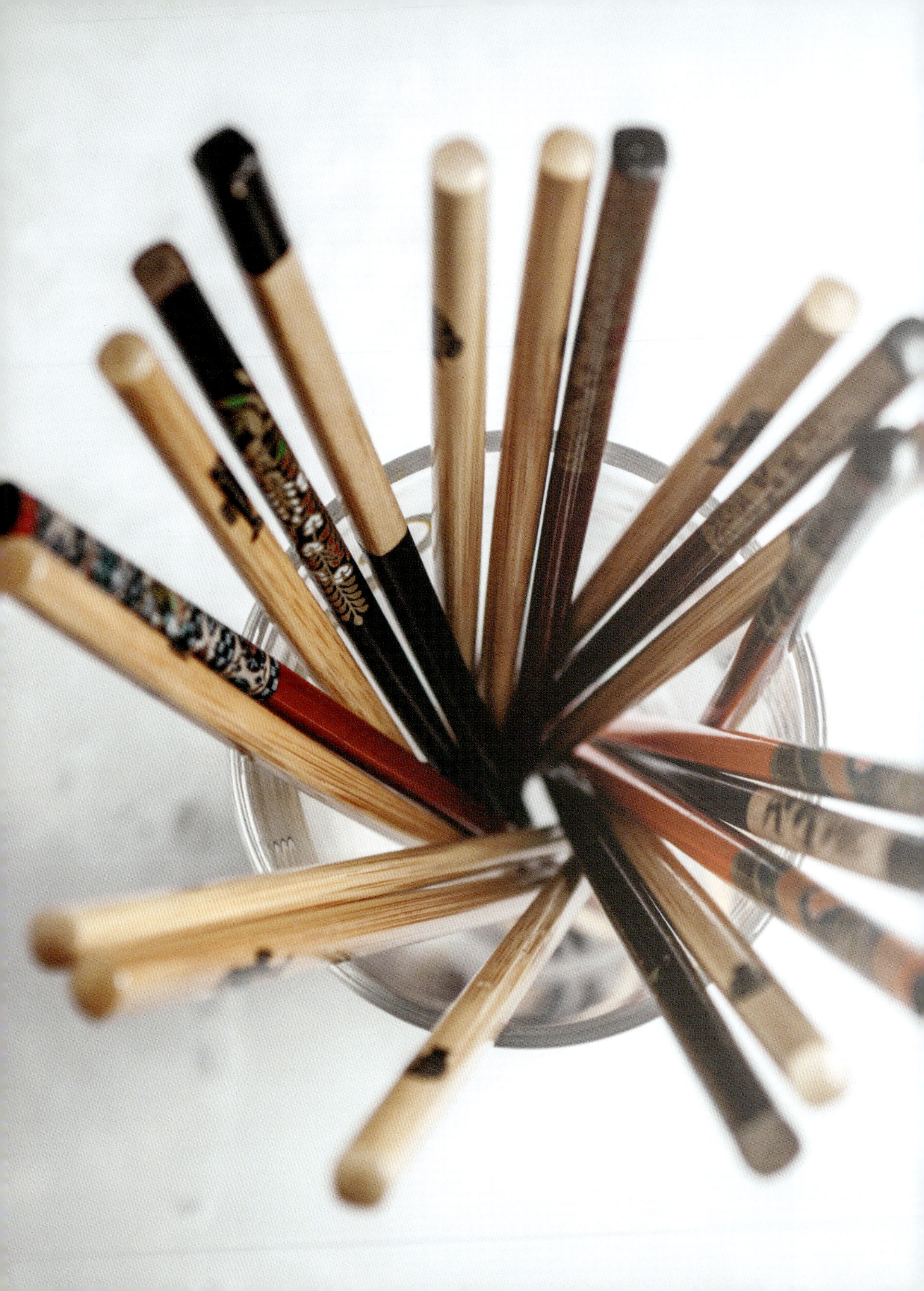

All-Season *Dim Sum*

Tea (*Cha*) 206

Cantonese Pork and Shrimp Dumplings
(*Siu Mai*) 208

Pork and Cabbage Dumplings
(*Jiaozi*) 211

Spring Rolls (*Chun Juan*) 214

Scallion Pancakes
(*Cong You Bing*) 216

Steamed Buns (*Bao*) 218

Red-Braised Pork Belly
(*Hong Shao Rou*) 221

Marbled Tea Eggs
(*Cha Ye Dan*) 224

Chinese Rice Porridge
(*Congee/Jook*) 225

Taiwanese Pan-Fried Rice Vermicelli
(*Chow Mei Fun*) 228

Garlicky Asian Greens
(*Yu Choy Sum*) 231

Stir-Fried Vegetables, Glass Noodles, and Tofu
(*Lo Han Jai*) 232

Egg Custard Tarts
(*Dan Tat*) 235

New England offers a variety of restaurant brunch experiences throughout the cities and suburbs: hearty Irish breakfasts, Greek diner fare served in vintage train cars, quaint Turkish breakfasts at upscale cafes. But there's one brunch-specific cultural experience that continues to thrive across the region, crossing ethnic, class, and generational lines: Chinese *dim sum*.

Dim sum refers to a wide range of Chinese small plates meant for sharing that are served for *yum cha* (brunch or, more specifically, "tea lunch"). This Cantonese custom is thought to have originated in the tea houses of the southern port city of Guangzhou (Canton) in the late nineteenth century. *Dim sum* was popular with spice traders and travelers along the Silk Road, and the practice soon expanded to Hong Kong and beyond. *Dim sum* dishes arrive in succession, like Asian tapas, and are always served with tea for good digestion. They tend to run savory (think dumplings and noodles), but they can also be sweet, like Egg Custard Tarts (*Dan Tat*). Cantonese dishes tend to highlight the rice and seafood of the southern coastal region where the practice began, but I've included some *dim sum* favorites from other regions of China and Taiwan, too.

Today, the Chinese are New England's third-largest immigrant group, and Boston has the third-largest Chinatown in the country after New York City and San Francisco. If you went to college in Boston anytime in the past fifty years, you likely learned that *dim sum* was the cheapest way to get a bellyful of delicious food and an equally fun social experience for weekend brunch. I can tell you, it still holds great appeal in one's later years. At some restaurants, *dim sum* is served from rolling carts pushed around the dining room. At other places the food is made fresh to order, brought to the table in bamboo steamers, small plates, and platters to share.

Here's a collection of some of my favorite *dim sum* dishes that work well in a home kitchen, including Cantonese Pork and Shrimp Dumplings (*Siu Mai*) and Steamed Buns (*Bao*). It's not an exhaustive list—certain popular items like Shrimp Dumplings (*Har Gao*) are far beyond my fine motor skills at this time. Others, like Fried Sesame Balls with Lotus Seed Filling (*Jian Dui*) and Salted Egg Yolk Lava Buns (*Liu Sha Bao*) require hard-to-find ingredients and more logistics than I think is convenient in the home kitchen, especially in the morning. I'll save those for my Chinatown outings. But Spring Rolls (*Chun Juan*), Scallion Pancakes (*Cong You Bing*), and Chinese Rice Porridge (*Congee/Jook*) are certainly within the reach of the average home cook.

I hope the following dishes will help fulfill your *dim sum* cravings at home and compel you to dive deeper into this unique brunch experience. For a list of the essential pantry ingredients to create these *dim sum* recipes, see page xv.

Dim Sum Menu Ideas

Chinese New Year's Brunch: Tea. Cantonese Pork and Shrimp Dumplings (*Siu Mai*). Red-Braised Pork Belly (*Hong Shao Rou*) or Pork Belly Buns (*Bao*) with Rice. Egg Custard Tarts (*Dan Tat*).

Taiwanese Dim Sum: Tea. Pork and Cabbage Dumplings (*Jiaozi*). Taiwanese Pan-Fried Rice Vermicelli (*Chow Mei Fun*). Garlicky Asian Greens (*Yu Choy Sum*).

Cozy, Casual Dim Sum: Tea. Scallion Pancakes (*Cong You Bing*). Chinese Rice Porridge (*Congee/Jook*). Marbled Tea Eggs (*Cha Ye Dan*).

Vegan Dim Sum: Tea. Spring Rolls (*Chun Juan*). Stir-Fried Vegetables, Glass Noodles, and Tofu (*Lo Han Jai*) with rice. Mandarin Oranges.

Tea (Cha)

New Englanders have been drinking Chinese tea since colonial times—the tea famously dumped into Boston Harbor in 1773 to protest British taxation without representation hailed from China. Tea is always served with dim sum, *typically brewed in little teapots at the table. Below are instructions for how to brew the different types of loose-leaf tea (the leaves can be brewed multiple times), or use tea bags instead and follow the instructions on the box.*

SERVINGS: 4–6

Jasmine (*Heung Pin*): A mellow, caffeine-free green tea scented with jasmine flowers that pairs well with most *dim sum* dishes. Preheat the pot by filling it with hot water and then dumping it out. Add 1 teaspoon loose-leaf tea per 1 cup of hot water (175°F–190°F) to the teapot. Let steep 3–5 minutes before straining out the leaves.

Black Tea (*Po-Lay*): A bold, fermented tea that pairs well with fried foods. Preheat the pot by filling it with hot water and then dumping it out. Add 1 teaspoon loose-leaf tea per 1 cup of almost boiling water (205°F–212°F) to the teapot. Let steep 4-5 minutes before straining out the leaves.

Chrysanthemum (*Gook Fa*): A light, caffeine-free herbal tea that pairs well with seafood. Preheat the pot by filling it with hot water and then dumping it out. Rinse about 20 flower buds to remove debris, and add them to the teapot. Pour boiling (212°F) water over the top and let steep for 5–7 minutes. Removing the flower buds is optional.

Oolong (*Tit Kun Yam*): A well-rounded, slightly floral tea. Preheat the pot by filling it with hot water and then dumping it out. Add 1 teaspoon loose-leaf tea per 1 cup of almost-boiling (185°F–205°F) water to the teapot. Let steep 4–5 minutes before straining out the leaves.

Yum Cha Etiquette

- The person closest to the teapot should pour the tea for the rest of the group first before pouring their own.
- When someone pours you tea, tap near the cup twice with the pointer and middle finger to signal thanks (this gesture symbolizes kneeling).
- For more tea, set the lid on top of the pot slightly askew so the server knows you need a refill.

Cantonese Pork and Shrimp Dumplings (*Siu Mai*)

These open-faced, purse-shaped steamed dumplings, filled with pork, shrimp, and shiitake mushrooms, are absolutely delicious. The skins are yellow from yolk in the dough, and the tops can be garnished with fish roe, finely diced carrots, or peas. These are good to start with if you've never made dumplings before because the shaping of the parcels is somewhat free-form and far simpler than pleating potstickers. To simplify the process, you can use store-bought gyoza wrappers (or the special round siu mai *wrappers, if you can find them). But I've also included a recipe for homemade* siu mai *wrappers, which are much thinner than potsticker dough. It's a fun group project for two or three people to form a dumpling assembly line: one to roll, one to fill, one to shape. I highly recommend steaming these in a traditional bamboo steamer. It's quick, no mess, allows you to cook multiple layers at once, and the dumplings can be served directly from the steamer basket. You can buy bamboo steamers inexpensively online or at your local Asian market.*

SERVINGS: MAKES ABOUT 32

Filling

- 3 large, dried shiitake mushrooms (or 6 fresh shiitakes)
- ½ pound raw large shrimp, peeled, deveined
- ½ pound ground pork
- 2 scallions (white and light green parts only), thinly sliced
- 1 teaspoon peeled, grated fresh ginger
- 1 large egg white (yolk reserved for wrappers)
- 1 tablespoon soy sauce

For the filling: Soak the dried shiitake mushrooms in hot water for 30 minutes to soften. Meanwhile, add the shrimp to the bowl of a food processor. Pulse the motor 10–15 times (or coarsely chop by hand), until the shrimp are coarsely ground but not yet a smooth paste. Transfer the shrimp mixture a large bowl.

Add the ground pork, scallions, ginger, egg white, soy sauce, rice wine, cornstarch, sesame oil, salt, sugar, and pepper to the shrimp mixture. When the mushrooms are soft, squeeze out the excess water and coarsely chop or pulse in the food processor until coarsely ground. Add the mushrooms to the shrimp mixture. Mix everything together with a spoon or your hands until well combined. Cover and refrigerate at least 30 minutes or overnight.

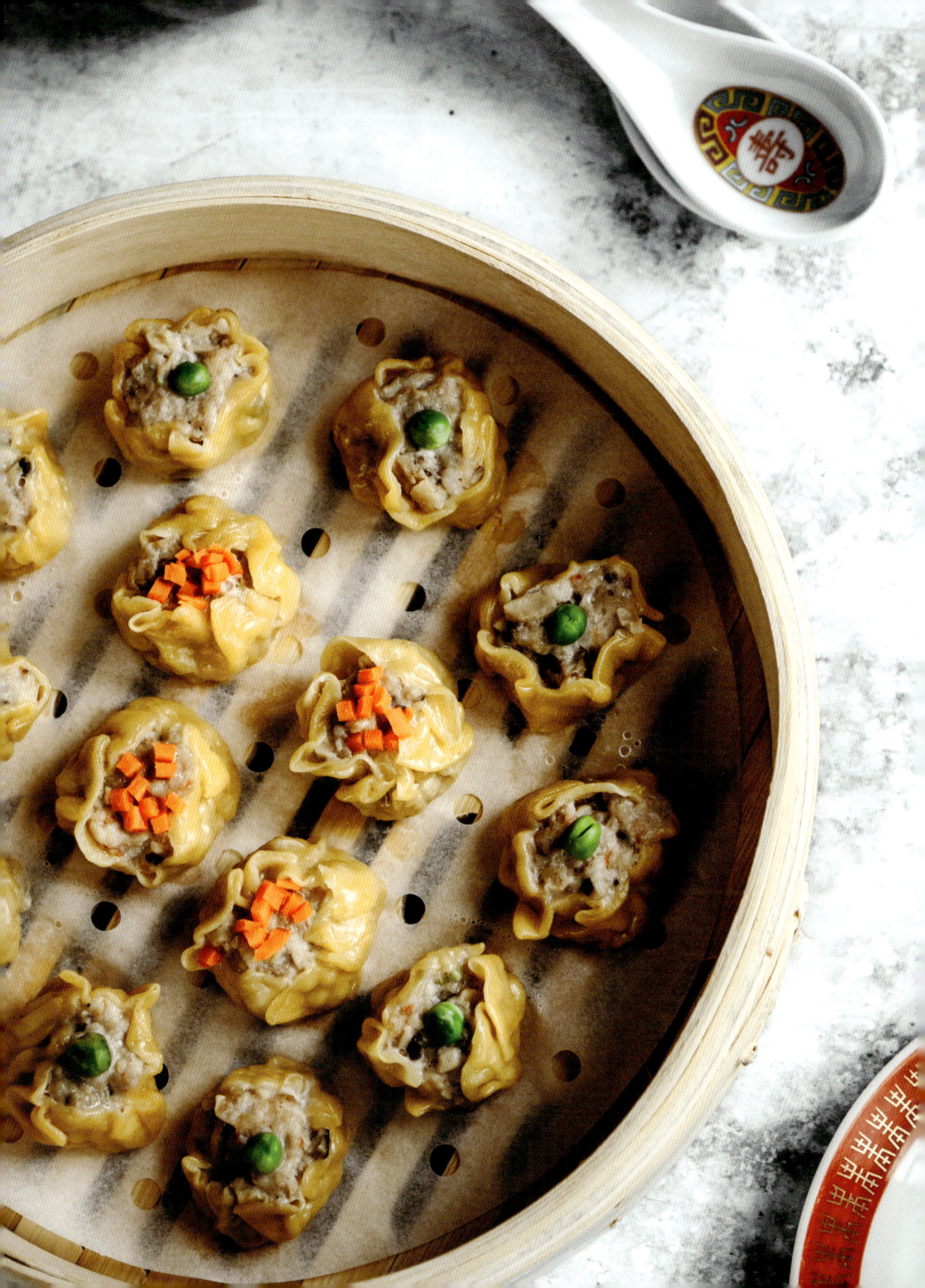

1 tablespoon rice wine or dry sherry

1 tablespoon cornstarch

½ teaspoon sesame oil

¼ teaspoon salt

Pinch of sugar

Pinch of ground white pepper (or black pepper)

Dough

⅔ cup all-purpose flour

2 large egg yolks

3 tablespoons water

Pinch of salt

Cornstarch, for dusting

Garnish

¼ cup finely diced raw carrot or whole frozen peas

Dipping Sauce

Soy sauce

Rice vinegar (or white vinegar)

Splash chili oil

For the dough: Stir together the flour, yolks, water, and salt with a fork in a small bowl. Turn the dough onto a surface dusted with cornstarch and knead 3–5 minutes, until smooth. Form the dough into a log about 12 inches long; cut it into quarters. Dust with cornstarch, cover with plastic wrap, and let rest at room temperature for 20 minutes.

On a cornstarch-dusted surface, roll each piece of dough into a rope about 8 inches long. Cut it into 8 (1-inch) pieces with a knife or bench scraper. Cover the dough with plastic wrap to keep it from drying out. One at a time, set the pieces of dough on the cut end and flatten into a circle. With a floured rolling pin, roll each piece out, rotating as you go, into a very thin circle about 3 inches in diameter. Place about 2 teaspoons of filling into the center. Gather up the edges to form a cup shape. Tap the top and bottom lightly to flatten. (My son finds it helpful to use cornstarch-dusted mini-muffin tins to help with shaping.)

Set the dumplings directly on the racks of a bamboo steamer lined with perforated circles of parchment paper or cabbage leaves to prevent sticking (or cover on a cornstarch-dusted pan if you plan on freezing them). Leave some space in between for steam to flow. Garnish with frozen peas or finely diced carrots by pressing the garnishes gently on top of the dumplings.

To steam the dumplings, set a sauté pan the same diameter as the bamboo steamer with 1 inch of water over medium heat until simmering. Reduce the heat to medium-low and set the bamboo steamer with lid on top of the sauté pan. Steam 7–10 minutes. If you don't have a bamboo steamer, you can also use a metal steamer basket in the sauté pan or a cooling rack set over the top of the pan. Spray with oil to prevent sticking. Cover with a lid to cook. Remove the steamer basket from the sauté pan and let sit, covered, until ready to serve.

For the dipping sauce: Combine equal parts soy sauce and rice vinegar (with an optional splash of chili oil) in little ramekins on the table.

Pork and Cabbage Dumplings (*Jiaozi*)

This recipe was adapted from an old Saveur *recipe for Taiwanese dumplings I've been using for twenty years. It makes a lot because the dumplings are meant to be made ahead of time and frozen. That way you can reach into the freezer and pull out exactly the number you need. The assembly is a project, but you'll thank yourself later. I've included instructions for how to make your own dumpling wrappers—these are much thicker than gyoza wrappers—but you can save time by using premade wrappers. For a vegetarian version, replace the pork with sauteed shiitake mushrooms.*

SERVINGS: MAKES ABOUT 40

Filling

- 1 tablespoon canola or vegetable oil, plus more for frying
- ½ pound Napa cabbage, thinly sliced
- 1 teaspoon kosher salt, divided
- 1 pound ground pork
- 1 cup sliced garlic chives or scallions
- 2 tablespoons peeled, finely chopped fresh ginger
- 2 tablespoons soy sauce
- 2 teaspoons toasted sesame oil

Wrappers

- 3 cups all-purpose flour
- ¼ teaspoon fine sea salt
- 1–1¼ cups water

For the filling: Heat the oil in a large nonstick sauté pan over medium heat. Add the sliced cabbage and toss with ¼ teaspoon of the salt. Sauté, stirring frequently, until the cabbage wilts a bit, 2–3 minutes. Remove from the heat and let cool.

In a medium mixing bowl, add the pork, chives or scallions, ginger, soy sauce, sesame oil, and remaining ¾ teaspoon salt. Once the cabbage is cool, squeeze out any excess water by the handful. Add the cabbage to the pork mixture. Mix well with your hands until all the ingredients are well dispersed. Cover with plastic wrap and refrigerate at least 1 hour or overnight.

For the wrappers: Add the flour and salt to a large mixing bowl. Gradually add 1 cup of water to the center of the bowl, mixing with a fork or chopstick until the dough can no longer be stirred. If you find yourself with too much dry flour around the edges, you can stir in up to ¼ cup more water. The dough will be very shaggy. Using floured hands, knead the dough on a lightly floured surface until smooth, about 5 minutes. Transfer to a clean, lightly oiled bowl, cover with plastic wrap, and refrigerate for at least 30 minutes and up to 3 hours.

To assemble: Divide the dough into 4 pieces. With your hands, roll each into a 1-inch-thick rope. Cut the ropes into 1-inch pieces with a knife or bench scraper. Cover the dough with plastic wrap to keep it from drying out. One at a time, set a piece of dough on the cut side and flatten it into a circle. With a floured rolling pin, roll each piece out, rotating as you go, into a circle about 3½ inches in diameter.

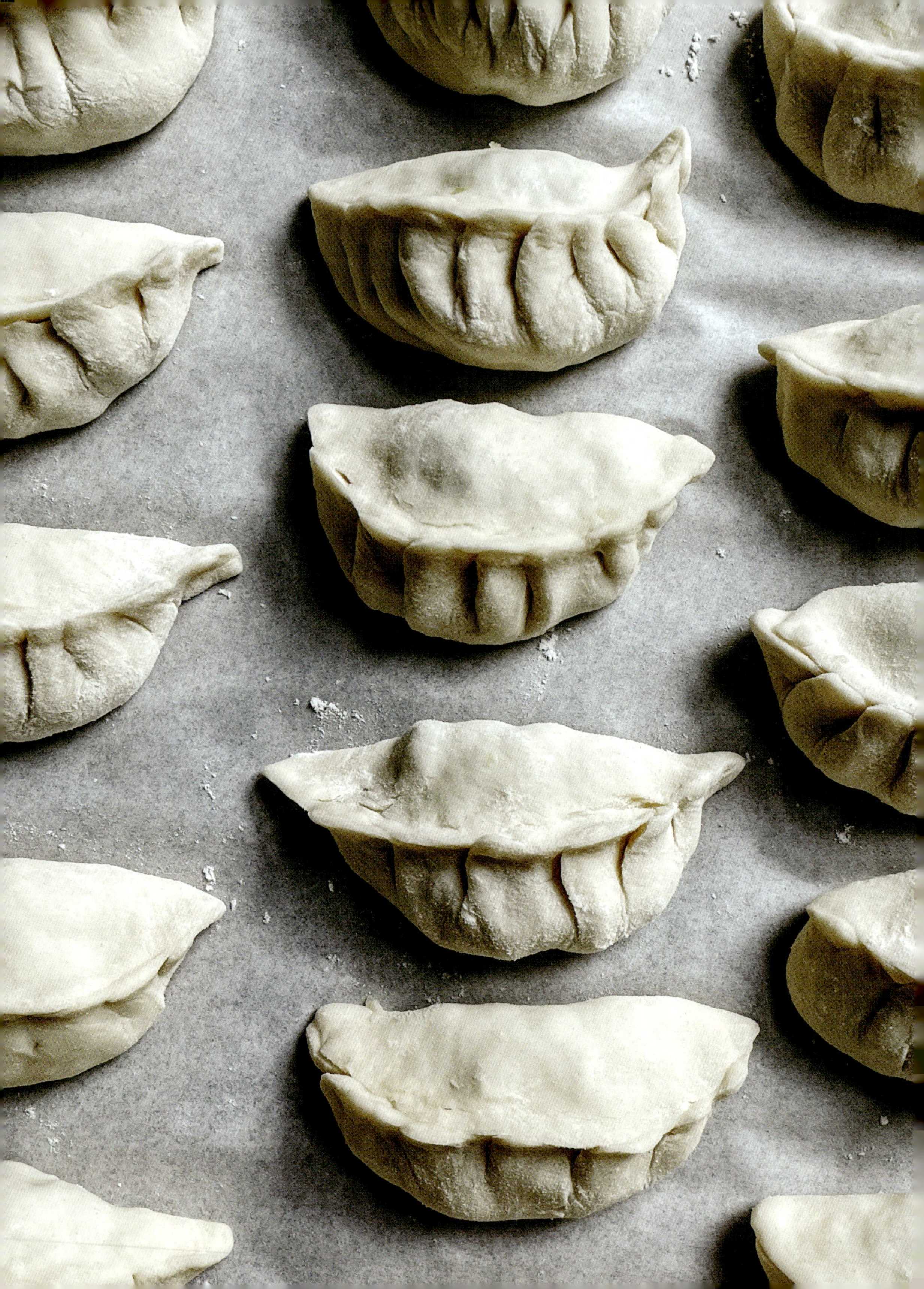

Dipping Sauce

Soy sauce

Rice vinegar (or white vinegar)

Splash chili oil

Place about 2 teaspoons of filling in the center of each wrapper and fold the dough over to form a half-circle. Pinch the top closed in the middle. Pleat the edges together with your fingers toward the center: two on the left and two on the right. (There are lots of different ways to pleat the edges. I find this one to be the easiest for beginners, but do whatever feels best, including starting your pleats on one side and working your way to the other side.) If the edges don't stick, use a little water in between to seal. Transfer to a parchment-lined or floured baking sheet. Cover the full sheet with plastic and freeze overnight. Once frozen, the dumplings can be transferred to freezer bags and stored in the freezer until ready to use.

To pan-fry the dumplings (my favorite way), heat 3 tablespoons of canola or vegetable oil in a large skillet over medium heat. Working in batches of no more than 8, add the fresh or frozen dumplings flat side down and cover with a lid. Cook the dumplings until they turn golden on the bottoms, about 4–6 minutes for fresh dumplings and 8–10 minutes for frozen. Reduce the heat to medium-low, add ¼ cup of water to the pan, and quickly cover (the oil will sizzle aggressively once the water is added). Continue cooking, covered, until the filling is cooked through and the bottoms have browned more deeply but aren't burned, 4–6 minutes for fresh and 8–10 minutes for frozen. Remove to a plate lined with paper towels. Cover with a bowl to keep warm.

To steam the dumplings, set a bamboo steamer basket over a sauté pan half-filled with water. The advantage of this setup is that you can cook multiple layers of dumplings at once. Line each basket with a circle of parchment paper or whole cabbage leaves to prevent sticking (make sure there is still space for the steam to circulate). Set the heat to medium-low and bring to a simmer. Add the dumplings, cover, and steam for 10–15 minutes. You can also use a metal steamer basket in the pan or a cooling rack set over the top of the pan. Spray with oil before adding the dumplings and cover.

For the dipping sauce: Combine equal parts soy sauce and rice vinegar in little ramekins around the table, with a splash of chili oil if desired.

Spring Rolls (Chun Juan)

Be warned, these spring rolls are totally addictive, and not as hard to make as you might think. This recipe makes a lot because they disappear fast, but you can freeze any extra for the future. I like to use wheat flour egg roll wraps, which fry up crispy and blistered, but you could also use translucent rice paper wraps. The sweet and hot chili sauce is the perfect accompaniment.

SERVINGS: MAKES 18–20

- 6 medium dried shiitake mushrooms, stems removed
- 1 ounce mung bean glass noodles
- 2 tablespoons vegetable, peanut, or canola oil, plus more for frying
- 2 cloves garlic, minced
- 6 cups finely shredded Napa cabbage (about 1 medium cabbage)
- 1 cup grated carrots, packed (about 2 large)
- 2 teaspoons soy sauce
- ½ teaspoon fine sea salt
- ¼ teaspoon ground white or black pepper
- 1 large egg
- 1 package egg roll wrappers (20)

Soak the dried mushrooms in a bowl half full of hot water for 30 minutes, or until soft enough to chop. (To keep them submerged, nest a glass bowl on top, taking care that the weight of the bowl doesn't overflow the water.)

Soak the noodles in a separate bowl of hot water according to the package instructions, usually 7–15 minutes. Meanwhile, prepare the vegetables and set them aside. Drain the noodles and cut them into 2-inch lengths with kitchen shears. Drain the mushrooms (reserving the soaking liquid) and chop them finely.

Heat 2 tablespoons oil in a large wok or nonstick sauté pan over medium-high heat. Add the garlic and stir-fry 10 seconds, until fragrant but not browning. Add the cabbage and stir-fry quickly to incorporate the garlic and oil. Continue cooking 2–3 minutes, tossing constantly, until the cabbage starts to wilt. If the pan gets dry, you can add a bit of the mushroom soaking liquid to help things along. Add the carrots, mushrooms, and noodles. Stir well. Add the soy sauce, salt, and pepper. Cook 1–3 minutes more, until the cabbage is fully wilted. Remove from the heat and let cool. For best results, let the mixture chill, covered, in the refrigerator for at least 1 hour so it holds together better.

To assemble, arrange an egg roll wrapper in a diamond configuration with a corner pointing toward you. Beat the egg in a small bowl. Brush beaten egg on the top inch of the top corner. Place 2–3 tablespoons of filling about 1 inch from the bottom corner. Roll the bottom corner of the wrapper over the filling. Bring the left corner over past the midline, followed by the right corner. Continue rolling up toward the

Sauce

¼ cup maple syrup

2 tablespoons soy sauce

2 teaspoons rice vinegar

1–2 teaspoons sambal oelek (optional)

top, letting the egg wash seal the top corner. The spring roll should be about 3 inches wide. (If the wrapper tears, you might be overfilling it. Be sure to keep the wrappers covered with plastic wrap while you work. The finished rolls should be covered as well to prevent drying out and cracking.)

For the sauce: Whisk together the maple syrup, soy sauce, rice vinegar, and sambal oelek in a small bowl.

In a large sauté pan, heat 1 inch of oil to about 350°F over medium heat. In batches of 5 or 6, shallow-fry the spring rolls until golden brown on one side, about 2½ minutes. Flip and brown the second side for about 2½ minutes. Drain on a paper towel–lined plate. Serve immediately with the sweet chili dipping sauce.

These are best eaten fresh as soon as they're made, but they can be covered and stored in the refrigerator for 2–3 days and reheated in the toaster oven.

Scallion Pancakes (Cong You Bing)

These flaky and delicious scallion pancakes are a dim sum *staple. Their flaky savoriness reminds me of a cross between Indian naan and Middle Eastern chapati, a world away from sweeter New England–style pancakes. This recipe is adapted from Ellen Leong Blonder's cookbook* Dim Sum: The Art of Chinese Tea Lunch. *Scallions are the traditional filling, but you can also try the pancakes with sliced chives or chopped garlic scapes.*

SERVINGS: MAKES 6 PANCAKES

1½ cups all-purpose flour, plus more for dusting

¼ teaspoon kosher salt, plus more for the filling

½ cup hot (not boiling) water

1 tablespoon vegetable or peanut oil, plus more for the pan

1 bunch scallions (about 6), white and light green parts only, thinly sliced

Toasted sesame oil

In a large bowl, mix the flour and salt. Make a well in the middle. Add the water and oil. With a fork, slowly incorporate the flour into the liquid until combined. Turn the dough onto a lightly floured surface and knead with flour-dusted hands for 5 minutes, until the dough is firm and smooth. Form it into a ball, dust with flour, and cover with plastic wrap or a small bowl domed over the top. Let rest 30 minutes.

Preheat the oven to 200°F. Line a baking sheet with two layers of paper towels.

Cut the dough into 6 equal portions. On a lightly floured surface, roll out one piece of dough into a 7-inch circle. (Keep the remaining pieces of dough covered to prevent them from drying out.) Brush with a thin film of toasted sesame oil to within ¼ inch of the edges. Sprinkle with a pinch of salt. Scatter one-sixth of the scallions over the oil.

Fold the dough in thirds, like a business letter. Fold the short ends over slightly to seal in the scallions, then loosely roll from one short end to the other. Stand the dough up on a coiled end and gently smoosh it into a fat round with your hand. Set it aside, covered, to rest while you finish the others. When ready to cook, gently roll each pancake into a 5-inch circle and keep covered.

Heat a nonstick pan or cast iron skillet over medium heat. When hot, add 1 teaspoon of vegetable or peanut oil and swirl. Cook the pancakes, one at a time, 3–5 minutes, until golden brown on one side. Lift the pancake, add another teaspoon of oil, and cook the other side until golden brown, another 3–5 minutes. Transfer the pancake to the prepared pan and keep warm in the oven. Repeat for the other pancakes, making sure to replenish the oil for each side. Cut each pancake into 4–6 wedges and serve hot. For a dipping sauce, you can combine equal parts soy sauce and rice wine vinegar or Chinkiang black vinegar in a small bowl.

Steamed Buns (*Bao*)

Bao *refers to* baozi, *steamed, yeast-leavened breads that can be rolled and stuffed with various fillings, like barbecue pork (Char Siu Bao), or formed into puffy, taco-like shapes and filled with succulent pork belly (Gua Bao), as I've done here. Pork belly buns originated in Fujian, the coastal region of China right across the strait from Taiwan. They're traditionally served with chopped peanuts and pickled mustard greens (a type of Chinese sauerkraut), but I also like them with quick-pickled radishes and cilantro. The dough is adapted from Hannah Che's* The Vegan Chinese Kitchen. *Her beautiful book is a great resource for Chinese recipes whether you're vegan or not. For best results, let the dough rise overnight. Then you can start braising the meat (or mushrooms, if you prefer) in the morning, shaping the dough during the second half of the process. A bamboo steamer is highly recommended. You can buy them inexpensively online or at your local Asian market.*

SERVINGS: 6

Buns
- 1 cup warm (not hot) water
- 1 tablespoon granulated sugar
- 1¼ teaspoons active dry yeast
- 3 cups all-purpose flour
- ½ teaspoon kosher salt
- 1 teaspoon baking powder
- 1 teaspoon vegetable oil, plus 1 tablespoon for assembly

Filling
- 1 recipe Red-Braised Pork Belly (page 221) or other filling

For the buns: Stir together the warm water, sugar, and yeast in a measuring cup. Let sit 5–10 minutes, until foamy.

In the bowl of a stand mixer fitted with the dough hook attachment (or in a large bowl by hand), combine the flour, salt, and baking powder. Gradually mix in the yeast mixture on low speed until the dough starts to clump. Add the oil last, continuing on low speed until the dough comes together. Increase the speed to medium and knead with the dough hook (or by hand) 5–8 minutes until smooth and elastic. Oil a clean bowl, roll the dough around in it, cover, and let rise in the refrigerator overnight (at least 8 hours). Or, if your filling is already made, it can rise at room temperature until doubled in bulk, 1–1½ hours.

The next morning, start the pork belly, allowing approximately 4 hours to cook.

Pickled Radish

4 ounces peeled daikon radish, quartered lengthwise and thinly sliced, or 4–6 pink radishes, thinly sliced

1 scallion, trimmed, thinly sliced

2 tablespoons rice vinegar

Dash of sesame oil

Pinch salt and freshly ground white pepper

Toppings

Cilantro leaves (optional)

Pickled mustard greens (optional)

Chopped peanuts (optional)

For the pickled radish: Combine the radish, scallion, vinegar, sesame oil, salt, and pepper in a small bowl. Mix to combine. Cover and set aside until ready to serve.

Line a bamboo steamer with circles of parchment paper with a few holes to allow the steam to circulate. (If you remember how to make paper snowflakes from childhood, that will get the job done, just make the cutouts very small.)

Turn the dough out onto the counter and knead for 5 minutes to force out all the air bubbles. The dough should be very smooth. With a sharp knife or bench scraper, cut the dough ball into quarters, and each quarter into thirds. You should have 12 pieces. Roll each piece into a ball and cover with plastic wrap. One by one, with a rolling pin, roll each piece of dough into an oval about 5 inches long and 3 inches wide. If one side is prettier than the other, arrange that side face down and brush the uglier top side with a thin layer of vegetable oil. Fold in half like a jaw closing. Set on the parchment paper of the prepared steamer and cover with plastic wrap while repeating for the others. Space the *bao* at least 1 inch apart so they have room to expand. Let rise 15–20 minutes, until slightly puffed. (If you can't fit them all in your steamer, you can do them in batches. Just put the second batch in the refrigerator until ready to steam.)

Put the lid on the steamer basket full of *bao*. Add 1 inch of water to a similarly sized skillet or wok and set the steamer basket on top. The round base of the steamer basket should rest on the sloping interior sides of the pan. The water should not touch the bottom of the steamer basket. Turn the heat to medium-high and allow the water to come to a simmer to create steam. Then reduce the heat to medium-low to maintain a constant simmer. Steam 8 minutes with the lid closed. Remove the steamer basket from the skillet with oven mitts. Let sit off heat with the lid on for 5 more minutes. Repeat for any remaining batches. Cover to keep warm. (These can be steamed again for a few minutes to reheat, if necessary.)

To assemble: Open up the buns and stuff them with pork belly and your choice of toppings: pickled radish, cilantro leaves, pickled mustard greens, or chopped peanuts. You can reheat individual buns in the microwave by wrapping them in a damp paper towel and heating them in 10-second intervals on high until warm.

Steamer Hack

If you don't have a bamboo steamer or any other kind of steamer setup, you can improvise one with a medium to large skillet, a large metal cooling rack, and a domed lid. Add 1 inch of water to the skillet and set over medium heat until the water starts to simmer. Set the cooling rack on top so it's suspended above the water by the edges of the pan. The water should not touch the cooling rack. Spray the rack with oil. Set the buns on the rack, being sure to stay within the edges of the pan. Set the domed lid on top to trap most of the steam. (This is not an airtight setup—some steam will escape—but it will trap enough steam to cook the buns if you add an extra minute or two to the cooking time.) You can remove the cooling rack (keeping the lid on top) with oven mitts and set it on a heatproof surface for the final 5-minute rest.

Red-Braised Pork Belly (Hong Shao Rou)

This luscious pork belly is a must-try for any dim sum lover. Give it the whole three hours to braise; you'll be rewarded with meltingly tender meat, a rich and glossy sauce, and a house that smells incredible. You can use the pork as a filling for Pork Belly Buns (Gua Bao) or serve it over rice. This dish is traditionally made in a clay pot, but I use a heavy Dutch oven with a lid to get a similar result. Rock sugar is often used in traditional Chinese braises, but that's not easy to find, so I opted to make my own rock caramel, which takes about five minutes (or you can substitute brown sugar). This recipe calls for two kinds of soy sauce: regular light soy sauce, which is what most folks have in their fridge for stir-fries, and dark soy sauce, which is thicker, richer, and often labeled "mushroom" soy sauce. It's worth the effort to find this special sauce, which gives the meat and braising liquid a deep, dark color and depth of flavor you won't want to miss.

SERVINGS: 6

First Braise

- 2½ pounds boneless pork belly, skin trimmed, cut into 1-inch cubes
- 1½ cups Shaoxing rice wine (or other dry white wine), divided
- 1½ cups water
- 3 scallions, trimmed
- 4-inch piece fresh gingerroot, unpeeled, sliced ¼ inch thick
- 2 star anise
- 2 strips mandarin orange peel (2 × ½-inch), bitter white pith scraped off
- 1 bay leaf
- Freshly ground white pepper, to taste

For the first braise: Set a large Dutch oven over medium heat. Add the pork belly cubes to the dry pan and season with white pepper to taste. (Avoid adding salt—the soy sauce added later will provide plenty of seasoning.) Brown the pork without stirring, 5–7 minutes. Flip the pork pieces and brown 5 minutes more on a second side until there's a golden-brown residue on the bottom of the pan. Transfer the pork to a plate. Pour off the excess fat from the pan into a small bowl. Return the pot to the heat, reduce the heat to medium-low, and deglaze with ½ cup of the rice wine. Use a wooden spoon or spatula to scrape the residue from the bottom of the pan. Then add the rest of the wine and the water.

Slice the white and light green parts of the scallions thinly. Add to a small bowl, cover, and refrigerate, reserving them to garnish the final dish. Add the dark green scallion tops to the pot, along with the ginger slices, star anise, orange peel, and bay leaf. Return the browned pork belly to the pot. Turn the heat to medium-high, partially cover with the lid, and bring to a jaunty simmer. Reduce the heat to medium-low, cover the pot entirely, and simmer gently for 1½ hours.

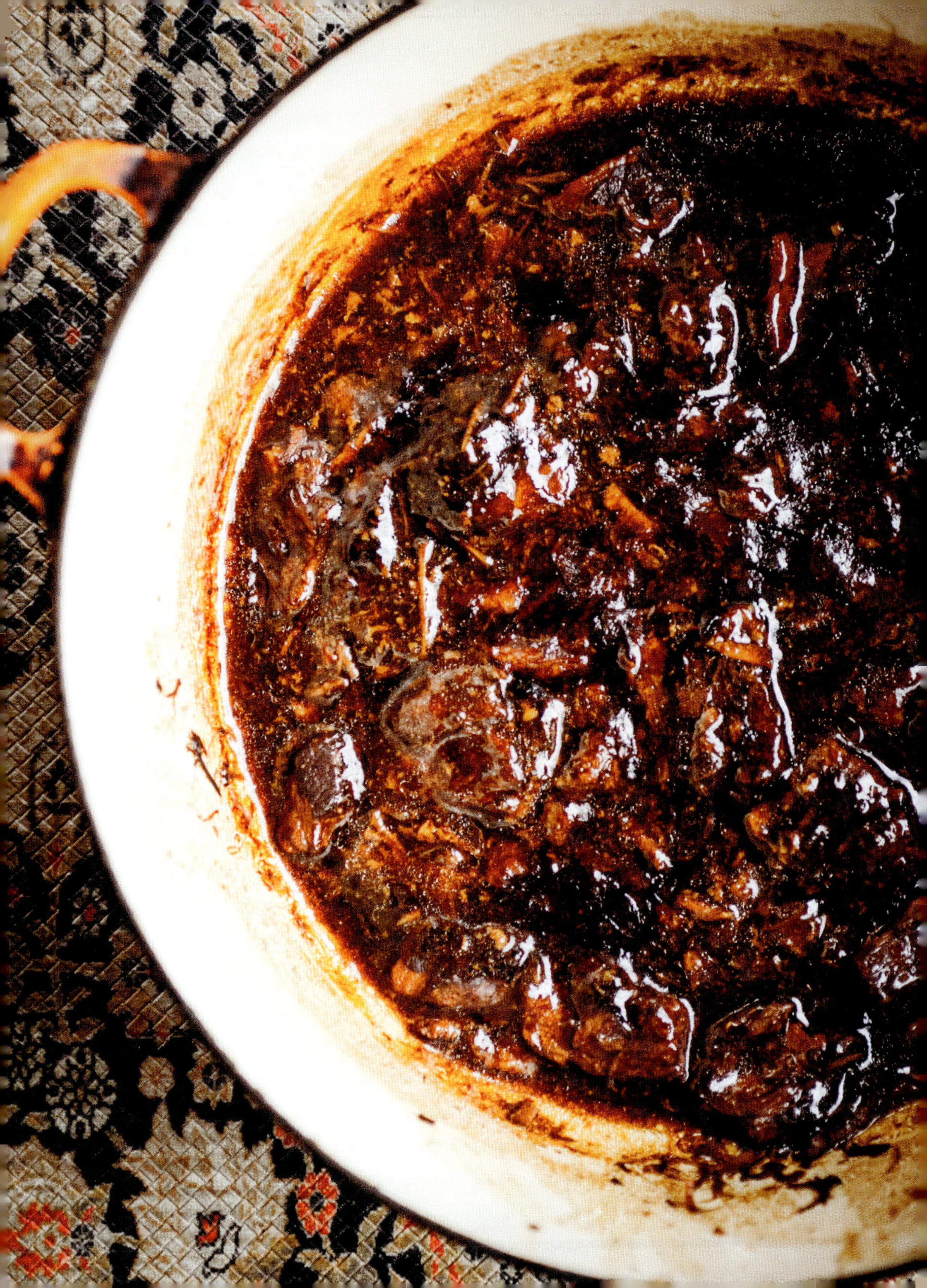

Rock Caramel

⅓ cup granulated sugar

Second Braise

¼ cup light soy sauce

2 tablespoons dark (mushroom) soy sauce

2 tablespoons rock caramel (or 2 tablespoons light brown sugar, firmly packed)

Finish

2 tablespoons cornstarch

2 tablespoons cold water

For the rock caramel: Line a small, rimmed baking pan with parchment paper and place near the stove. Add the sugar to a small, heavy-bottomed saucepan over low heat. Shake to disperse the crystals evenly across the bottom of the pan. Without stirring, allow the sugar to melt, gently swirling the pan and reducing the heat as necessary to make sure all the solid sugar melts before the resulting syrup takes on too much color. Once the sugar has melted, cook a minute or two longer, swirling frequently, until the sugar syrup turns golden and then a medium amber color, 5–10 minutes. Remove the pan from the heat before the syrup burns and pour it onto the prepared baking sheet. Do not touch, as the mixture will be very hot. Let cool completely until hardened, about 20 minutes.

Break the cooled caramel into pieces that fit in a zip-top bag (careful—they're sharp) and crush them with a meat mallet or can. Measure out 2 tablespoons (save the extra in a small jar for next time).

When the first braise is finished, remove the pot from the heat. Transfer the pork and aromatics to a plate temporarily while you pour the braising liquid into a large (at least 2-cup) measuring cup or medium bowl. Let the liquid sit undisturbed for 5–10 minutes so the fats and liquid separate. Spoon off and discard as much of the clear, rendered pork fat from the top as you can. Return the pork, aromatics, and braising liquid to the pan.

For the second braise: Stir in the two types of soy sauce and 2 tablespoons of the rock caramel (or brown sugar). Return the pot to a simmer over medium heat. Cover, reduce the heat to medium-low, and gently simmer for 1½ hours more.

When the pork is tender and fragrant, remove the lid and stir. Remove the scallions, ginger, star anise, orange peel, and bay leaf with tongs. In a small bowl, whisk together the cornstarch and water. Move the pork belly to the side of the pot and stir the mixture into the sauce. Stir everything together, return to medium-low heat, and simmer until glossy and slightly thickened so the sauce coats the meat nicely, just a few minutes more.

Remove from the heat and let cool slightly with the lid off. Taste the sauce for seasoning. Serve the meat and sauce over rice and sprinkle with the reserved scallions. Or let cool and use the filling for the Pork Belly Buns (*Gua Bao*) on page 218.

Marbled Tea Eggs (Cha Ye Dan)

These beautiful eggs are gently cracked all over, then soaked in a fragrant blend of tea, spices, and soy sauce. The result is a delightfully seasoned hard-boiled egg with lovely sepia-colored crazing reminiscent of antique porcelain. Eat them for breakfast, as a snack, or alongside congee (next page), noodles, or rice bowls. Since eggs are a symbol of fertility in Chinese culture, they're often served during Chinese New Year, the fifteen-day lunar festival that starts on the second new moon after the winter solstice. For best results, use dark soy sauce in addition to regular soy sauce to bring out the color on the surface of the eggs. Make these one or two days ahead of time to the give the eggs enough time to develop their flavor.

SERVINGS: MAKES 8–12

- 8–12 large eggs
- 3 tea bags of black or green tea (or 3 tablespoons loose tea)
- 2 star anise
- 1 cinnamon stick
- ½ teaspoon black peppercorns (or Szechuan peppercorns)
- 1 (2-inch) strip orange peel (with white pith scraped off)
- 2 tablespoons dark soy sauce
- 1 tablespoon soy sauce or tamari

Gently set the eggs in a medium saucepan that can fit them all in one layer along the bottom. Add water to cover the eggs by 1 inch. Cover the pot with the lid and bring to a simmer over medium-high heat. Remove the pot from the heat and let sit covered for 12 minutes.

Using a slotted spoon, immediately transfer the eggs to a large bowl of ice water to cool.

Meanwhile, add the remaining ingredients to the pot of cooking water to create the marinade. Return the pot to medium heat and bring to a gentle simmer over low heat.

Once the eggs are cool enough to handle, tap each egg on the counter over its entire surface. Don't peel the eggs—the cracks are where the marinade will penetrate the shells to create the marbling effect.

Remove the tea bags from the pot. With a slotted spoon, add the eggs back to the bottom of the pot. Remove the pan from the heat and let sit uncovered until cool. Cover the pot and let the eggs steep in the marinade in the refrigerator for 12–24 hours.

Remove the eggs from the marinade after 24 hours to prevent them from getting too salty, but don't peel them until ready to eat. Serve cold, warm, or at room temperature.

Eggs can be covered and stored in the refrigerator for up to 1 week.

Chinese Rice Porridge (Congee/Jook)

The first time I tried chicken congee, *a Chinese savory rice porridge, was at* dim sum *with a group of friends at Myers + Chang in Boston. It was the tastiest homemade chicken and rice soup you can imagine, warm and fragrant with ginger. It was so delicious, I rushed home to look up the recipe in the* Myers + Chang at Home *cookbook to figure out how to make it. Since then, I've settled on a scaled-back version that never fails to satisfy me with its comforting flavor and texture. I use chicken breast here, but chicken thighs would be equally tasty. I'd also highly recommend trying this with your leftover turkey bones from Thanksgiving or any turkey or chicken stock you might have (just swap a few cups in for equal amounts of water). Then try it again during the February doldrums if you want to be filled with warmth and optimism. For a vegetarian version, mushrooms are the way to go. Use dried mushrooms (just a few ounces will do) like shiitake or porcini for the broth, then stir in some fresh sautéed mushrooms at the end.*

SERVINGS: 6

Congee

- 1 pound chicken breast or thighs (bone-in or boneless)
- 8 cups water
- 3 garlic cloves, peeled, crushed with the side of a knife
- 1 (2-inch) piece fresh gingerroot, peeled, sliced thinly lengthwise
- 2 teaspoons kosher salt
- 1 cup short-grain rice

For the congee: Add add the chicken, water, garlic, ginger, and salt to a large, heavy pot (hold off on the rice for now). Cover and bring the water to a boil over medium-high heat. Once boiling, remove the lid and lower the heat to maintain a gentle simmer. Poach the chicken 5–12 minutes, until fully cooked (internal temperature of 170°F). Remove the chicken to a plate and let cool. With a slotted spoon, remove the ginger and garlic.

Stir the rice into the cooking liquid. Return to a simmer and cook, stirring every 10–15 minutes to prevent the rice from sticking to the bottom of the pan—45 minutes to 1 hour for regular short-grain rice and 1½–2 hours for sushi or arborio rice. Add more water as necessary to keep the mixture loose.

All-Season Dim Sum

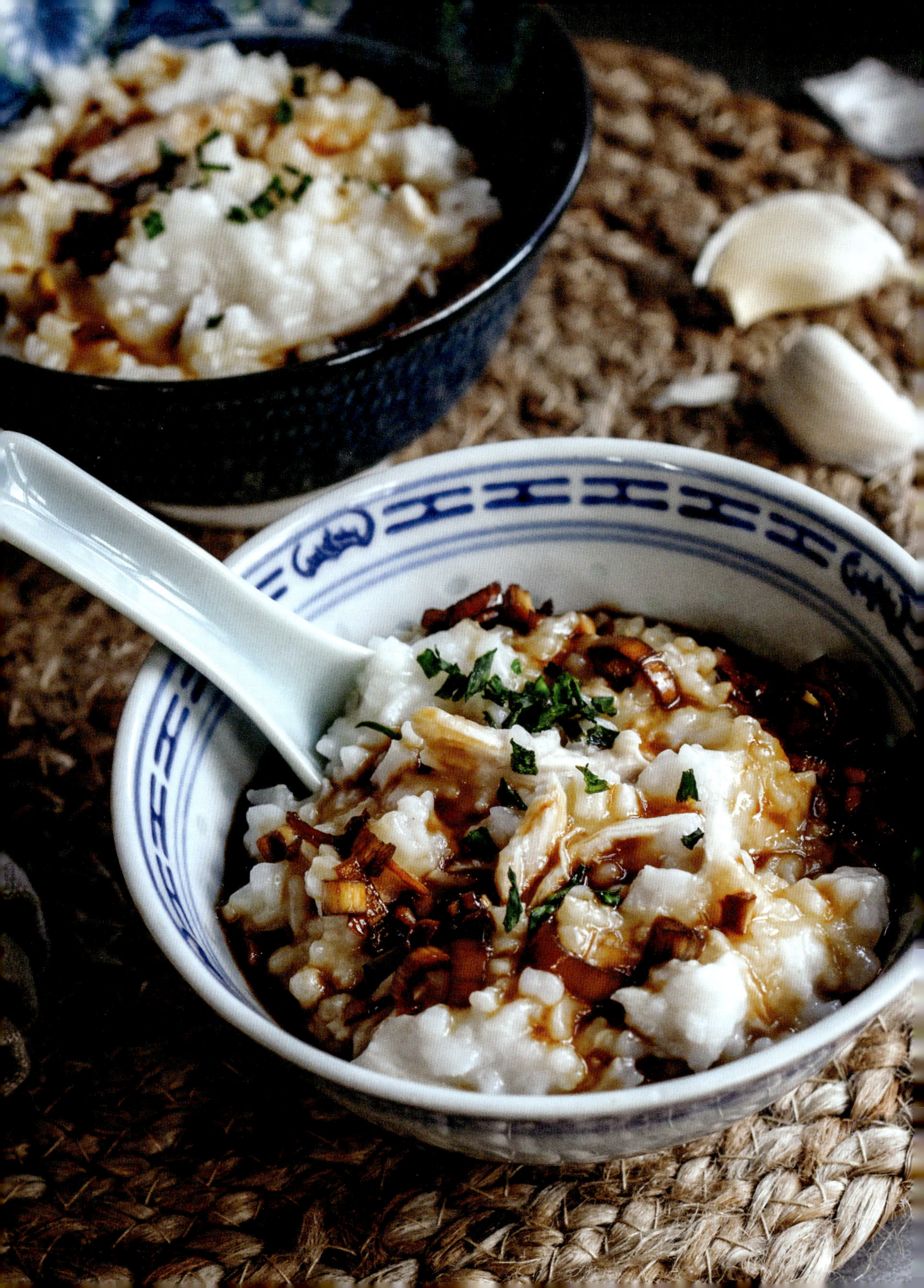

Sauce

⅓ cup soy sauce or tamari

¼ cup rice vinegar

1 bunch scallions, thinly sliced, white and light green parts only

¼ teaspoon toasted sesame oil (optional)

Pinch of fine sea salt

Garnish

Sriracha

Chopped fresh chives or cilantro

For the sauce: Stir together the soy sauce, rice vinegar, sliced scallions, sesame oil, and salt. Remove the bones and shred the chicken into bite-sized pieces with a fork and knife. When the rice is ready, stir in the chicken. Season to taste with salt and pepper.

Portion the congee into rice bowls with a teaspoon or two of the scallion sauce. Pass additional sauce, Sriracha, and chopped fresh herbs at the table if desired.

Leftovers can be stored, tightly covered, in the refrigerator for 3–4 days.

Taiwanese Pan-Fried Rice Vermicelli (Chow Mei Fun)

Here's an authentic Taiwanese recipe contributed by my dear friend I-Wen. I spent three weeks in Taiwan with her and her family in high school, and it was an exciting, immersive cultural experience I'll never forget. This recipe was passed down from I-Wen's mother-in-law to her husband, Oliver, to their younger daughter. She explains that pan-fried rice noodles symbolize a bountiful harvest and prosperous year ahead. It's a great dish to serve for the Lunar New Year celebration, special occasions, or an everyday meal. You can add garlic, onion, mung bean sprouts, or bamboo shoots according to personal preference. For best results, use the thinnest rice vermicelli you can find.

SERVINGS: 4–6

Noodles

- ½ pound thin rice vermicelli
- 6 dried (or fresh) shiitake mushroom caps
- 2 tablespoons small, dried shrimp
- 3 large eggs
- 3 tablespoons vegetable oil, divided
- 2 scallions, trimmed, sliced
- ½–1 pound thinly sliced pork tenderloin, pork loin, pork belly, or ground pork
- 1 pound (4–5 cups) Napa cabbage, thinly sliced
- 1 medium carrot, peeled, grated
- 2 stalks celery, thinly sliced
- Salt and white pepper, to taste

For the noodles: Soak the vermicelli in a large bowl of warm water for 20 minutes (be sure to check the instructions on the package—thicker noodles may require parboiling). Soak the dried mushrooms and dried shrimp in hot tap water in separate bowls until softened (10–20 minutes).

In a medium bowl, whisk the eggs with a pinch of salt and white pepper. Set a wok or other large nonstick skillet over medium heat. Add 1 tablespoon of the oil. Once heated, swirl to coat the bottom and sides of the pan. Add the eggs to the pan and cook over medium-low heat, stirring occasionally, until fully scrambled but not rubbery, about 2–3 minutes. Turn off the heat, transfer the eggs to a bowl, and set aside.

Slice the scallions thinly, using only the white and light green parts. Drain the dried shrimp and noodles. Set aside. Squeeze the excess water from the dried mushrooms, slice them thinly, and set aside. Save the mushroom soaking liquid to use when cooking the noodles.

New England Brunch

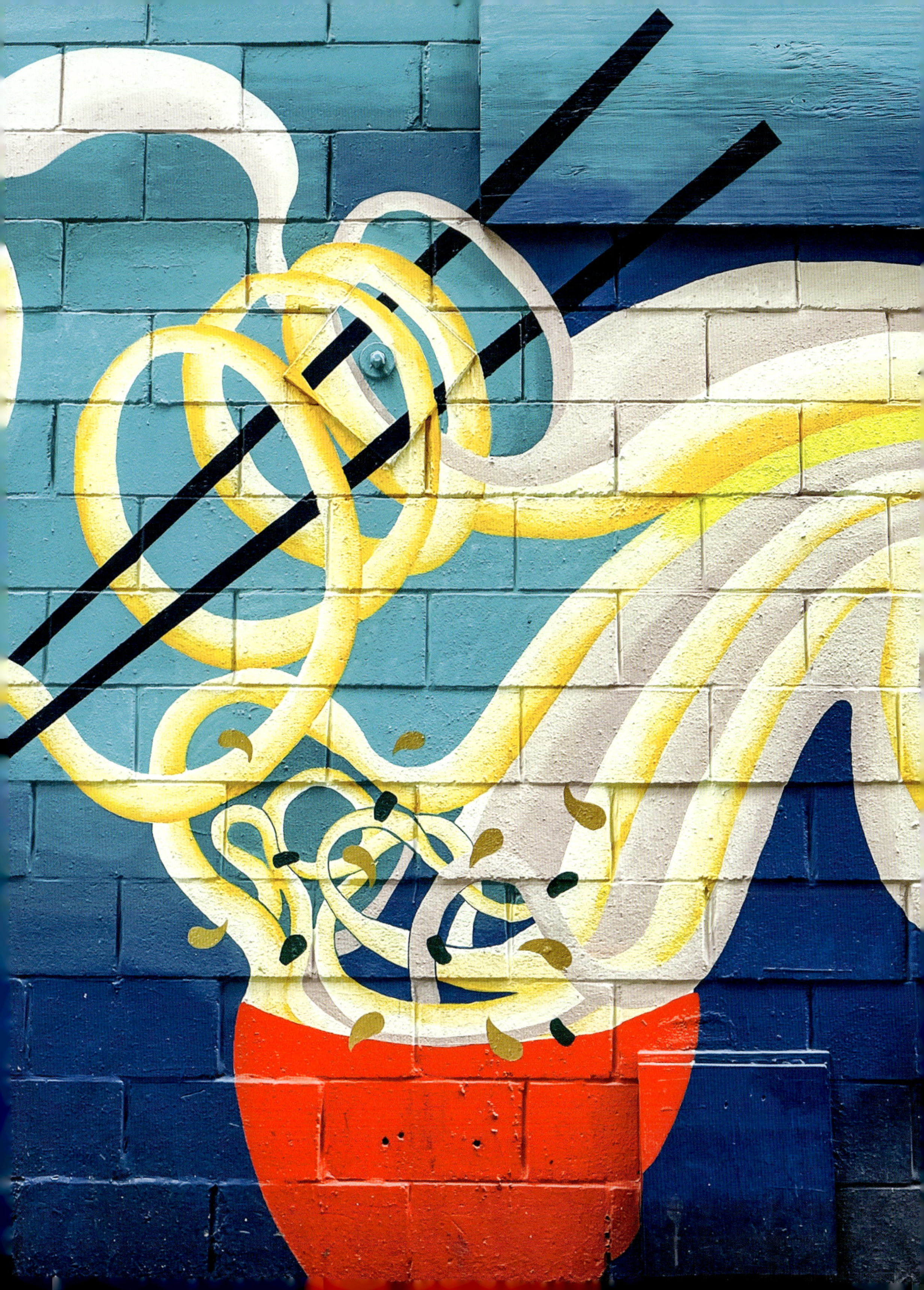

Sauce

2 tablespoons soy sauce or tamari

1 tablespoon black vinegar (or Worcestershire sauce)

1 tablespoon rice wine

1 teaspoon toasted sesame oil

½ teaspoon granulated sugar

½ teaspoon table salt or fine sea salt

½ teaspoon ground white pepper (or black pepper)

¼–½ cup water, as needed

For the sauce: Whisk together the soy sauce, black vinegar, rice wine, and sesame oil in a small bowl. Set aside.

Add the remaining 2 tablespoons of oil to the wok or skillet over medium-high heat. Swirl to coat. Add the mushrooms, shrimp, and sliced scallions to the pan. Stir-fry until aromatic, about 30 seconds. Add the pork and toss well. Stir in the sauce along with the sugar, salt, white pepper, and ¼ cup of the mushroom soaking liquid or water. Bring everything to a boil. Add the soaked rice noodles and mix well. Reduce the heat to medium and continue cooking, stirring frequently, until the pork and noodles are mostly cooked and the sauce is nearly absorbed. Add more liquid if the pork is still pink and the noodles are crunchy, or if the noodles are dry and sticking to the bottom of the pan.

Once the noodles and pork are mostly cooked, add the cabbage and carrots to the noodles and cover the pot to steam for a few minutes until the vegetables are wilted. Finally, stir in the celery and scrambled eggs. Remove from the heat and adjust the seasonings if desired. Serve immediately.

Garlicky Asian Greens (*Yu Choy Sum*)

I've never met an Asian green I didn't like, but there are so many different kinds, they can be a little intimidating: How do you cook them and what do they taste like? My advice, besides just diving in with wild abandon, is to start with Yu Choy Sum. *It's a type of Chinese broccoli that, for me, is the perfect green: crunchy stems that aren't too thick with plenty of leafy greens and a little flower blossom that looks like a tiny broccoli floret. Another option are pea shoots (Dou Miao), the young, tender stems, leaves, and tendrils of the pea plant. Both greens cook down crisply tender and delicious with a little bit of garlic and soy sauce in less than five minutes.*

SERVINGS: 4–6

- 1 pound *yu choy* or pea shoots, cut into 2-inch lengths
- 1 tablespoon canola, vegetable, or peanut oil
- 3 garlic cloves, peeled, chopped
- 1 tablespoon soy sauce

Wash the greens well and drain, but keep the water clinging to the leaves.

In a large sauté pan, heat the oil over medium heat. When the oil is shimmeringly hot, add the garlic and stir-fry about 15 seconds, until fragrant but not browning. Add a few handfuls of the greens to the pot and stir them around to mix with the garlic. Add the rest of the greens and stir well. Add the soy sauce. Cover and reduce the heat to low. Cook 1–3 minutes for pea shoots and 3–5 minutes for *yu choy*, until the greens are wilted and the stems still have some crispness. Stem thickness varies, so check often for doneness with a fork. If the pan dries out, add a tablespoon of water so the garlic doesn't burn.

Uncover and transfer the greens to a serving bowl with tongs. Pour the cooking liquid over the greens and serve.

Leftovers can be covered and stored in the refrigerator for 4–5 days and reheated in the microwave.

Stir-Fried Vegetables, Glass Noodles, and Tofu (*Lo Han Jai*)

This dish, often listed on menus as Buddha's Delight, is a delicious and efficient way to use up your CSA or garden-grown vegetables at home. Quickly sauté bok choy, broccoli, snow peas, carrots (or any other vegetables you might have) with glass noodles and serve over rice with sesame-crusted tofu. This vegan dish is exceedingly fresh and satisfying. The only limitations are the size of your wok. Don't start cooking until you have all your ingredients assembled and prepared—the cooking happens lightning-fast so the veggies stay bright green and crisp. If you can't find the mung bean threads, you can substitute sweet potato cellophane noodles or very thin rice vermicelli, the latter of which most grocery stores carry.

SERVINGS: 4–6

Fried Tofu

Canola oil, for frying

½ pound extra-firm tofu, cut into triangles about ¼ inch thick

1 tablespoon black sesame seeds

1 tablespoon white sesame seeds

Sauce

2 tablespoons soy sauce

1 teaspoon toasted sesame oil

Dash of Sriracha (optional)

For the tofu: Add about ¼ inch of canola oil to a large nonstick skillet. Heat over medium-high heat until hot but not smoking. Slice the block of tofu into 4 thin slabs. Stack them back up nicely and cut the stack in half. Cut each square stack diagonally into triangles.

In a small shallow bowl, stir the sesame seeds together until well dispersed. Separate the tofu triangles and toss them in the seeds to coat (the seeds should stick to the moist exteriors). Gently add the tofu to the hot oil and fry on one side until golden, 3–5 minutes. You don't want the sesame seeds to burn, but a little toastiness is okay. Flip each piece over with tongs and fry the second side until golden, 3–5 minutes. Remove the fried tofu to a paper towel–lined plate and sprinkle with salt. (You can also air-fry the tofu if you prefer.) Set aside until ready to serve.

For the sauce: Whisk together the soy sauce, sesame oil, and a little squirt of Sriracha in a small bowl. Set aside.

For the stir-fry: Set your rice to cook. Soak the mung bean threads per the instructions on the package (usually soak in warm water for 10–15 minutes). Meanwhile, prepare all the vegetables and set aside in separate bowls.

Drain the noodles and use kitchen shears or scissors to cut the bundles into thirds. Set by the stove with the vegetables.

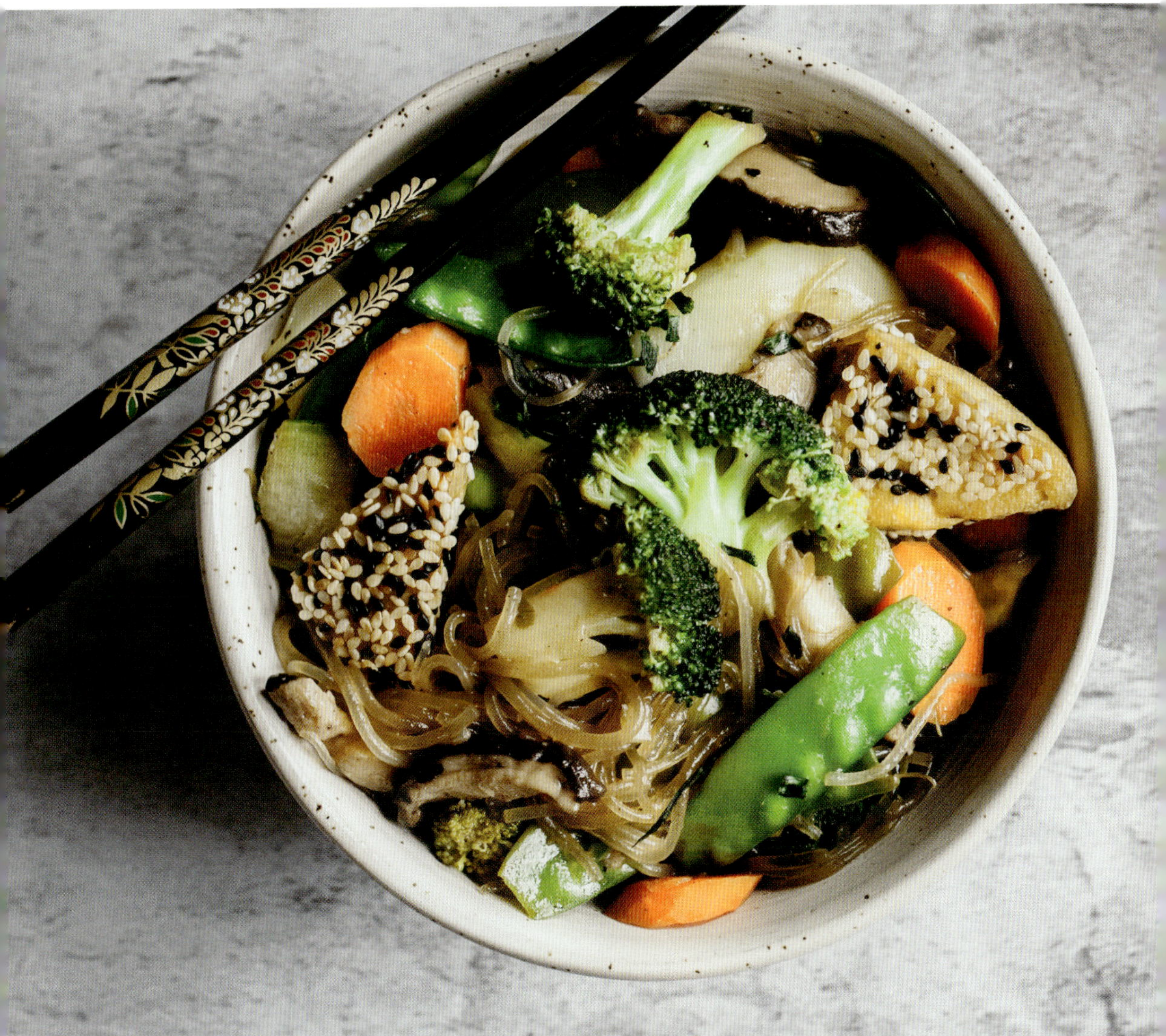

Stir-Fry

- 1 (3-ounce) package mung bean thread glass noodles
- 1 (2-inch) piece fresh gingerroot, peeled, minced or grated with a fine-planed zester
- 4 cloves garlic, peeled, minced or grated with a fine-planed zester
- 4 scallions, trimmed, white and light green parts sliced, dark green parts cut into 1-inch lengths
- 2 cups fresh shiitake mushrooms caps sliced into ¼-inch pieces
- 2 tablespoons rice wine
- 6 ounces snow peas
- 6 ounces carrots (about 2 medium), peeled, thinly sliced
- 1 pound broccoli, cut into bite-sized florets no more than 1 inch across
- 1 pound bok choy or baby bok choy, sliced into ¾-inch pieces
- 5 tablespoons grapeseed or canola oil, divided
- ¾ cup vegetable or mushroom stock (or water)
- Kosher salt and white or black pepper, to taste
- Jasmine rice

In your largest wok or nonstick sauté pan, heat 2 tablespoons of the oil over high heat until hot but not smoking. Add the ginger and stir-fry 20 seconds until fragrant. Add the garlic as well as the white and light green scallions (reserve the dark green parts for the end). Fry for 15–20 seconds. Add the mushrooms and stir-fry for about 2 minutes, until they start to soften. Add the rice wine and continue frying until the liquid evaporates. Transfer to a bowl and set aside.

Set the wok back over high heat and add 1 tablespoon of oil. Before it starts to smoke, add the snow peas and carrots. Stir-fry 1 minute, until they soften just slightly but are still bright and crisp. Transfer to a bowl and set aside.

Set the wok back over high heat and add 1 tablespoon of oil. Add the broccoli and stir-fry 2 minutes. Return the broccoli to its bowl and set aside. Add 1 tablespoon of oil to the wok and stir-fry the bok choy 1 minute. Add the broccoli back to the wok with the bok choy. Add the noodles and toss well. Pour the soy sauce mixture along with the vegetable stock. Stir well, then cover. Reduce the heat to medium-low and steam until the vegetables are crisp-tender but the broccoli is still bright green, 3–5 minutes. Remove the lid and crank the heat back up to high. Add the snow peas, carrots, and dark green scallion tops. Cook, tossing frequently, for 1–2 minutes more, until most of the liquid cooks off but before the vegetables lose their vibrance. Remove from the heat. Season with pepper.

Serve immediately over rice with the fried tofu triangles, passing additional soy sauce and Sriracha at the table.

Leftovers can be stored in the refrigerator for 2–3 days and reheated in the microwave.

Egg Custard Tarts (*Dan Tat*)

These delicious dim sum *pastries originated in Macau, where Portuguese spice traders arrived in China in the sixteenth century.* Pasteis de nata *(Portuguese egg custard tarts) are very similar, and the influence is clear. These are a must-try—so simple, yet so delicious. You can make this recipe even easier by using store-bought puff pastry and rolling it out as thinly as possible. Or look for special premade egg custard tart shells in the frozen section of your local Asian supermarket. Either the Hong Kong–style or Portuguese-style tart shells will work.*

SERVINGS: MAKES 9–12

Pastry

1 cup all-purpose flour

2 tablespoons cornstarch

1 tablespoon confectioners' sugar

¼ teaspoon fine sea salt or table salt

½ cup (1 stick) cold unsalted butter, cut into 8 pieces

3–5 tablespoons ice water, or as needed

Filling

½ cup milk

½ cup granulated sugar

1 teaspoon vanilla extract

2 large eggs, plus 1 large egg yolk

Preheat the oven to 400°F. Spray 12 individual tart molds with nonstick spray (or use a standard 12-cup muffin tin). Set a rimmed 12 × 17-inch baking sheet in the oven to preheat.

For the pastry: Mix the flour with the cornstarch, confectioners' sugar, and salt in a medium bowl. Add the butter and work it into the flour mixture with your hands, pinching the butter apart and rubbing it into the flour until the butter pieces are the size of peas. Add 3 tablespoons ice water and stir with a fork. Add more ice water a little at a time, tossing, until the dough holds together when gently squeezed. Use only as much water as you need.

Gather the dough mixture together on the counter and gently fold the dough over itself two or three times until it holds together. Flour your counter and rolling pin well. Roll out the dough into a 6 × 6-inch circle. Fold in thirds, like a business letter, then in thirds again, until you have a compact square of dough. Wrap the dough in waxed paper or plastic wrap. Chill 20 minutes in the refrigerator while preparing the other ingredients.

For the filling: Heat the milk in a measuring cup in the microwave until hot but not boiling (about 1 minute on high). Stir the sugar into the milk until it dissolves. Add the vanilla and set aside. In a medium bowl, beat the eggs well with a fork. Gradually stir the milk mixture into the eggs with a spoon until combined. Pour through a fine-meshed strainer back into the measuring cup.

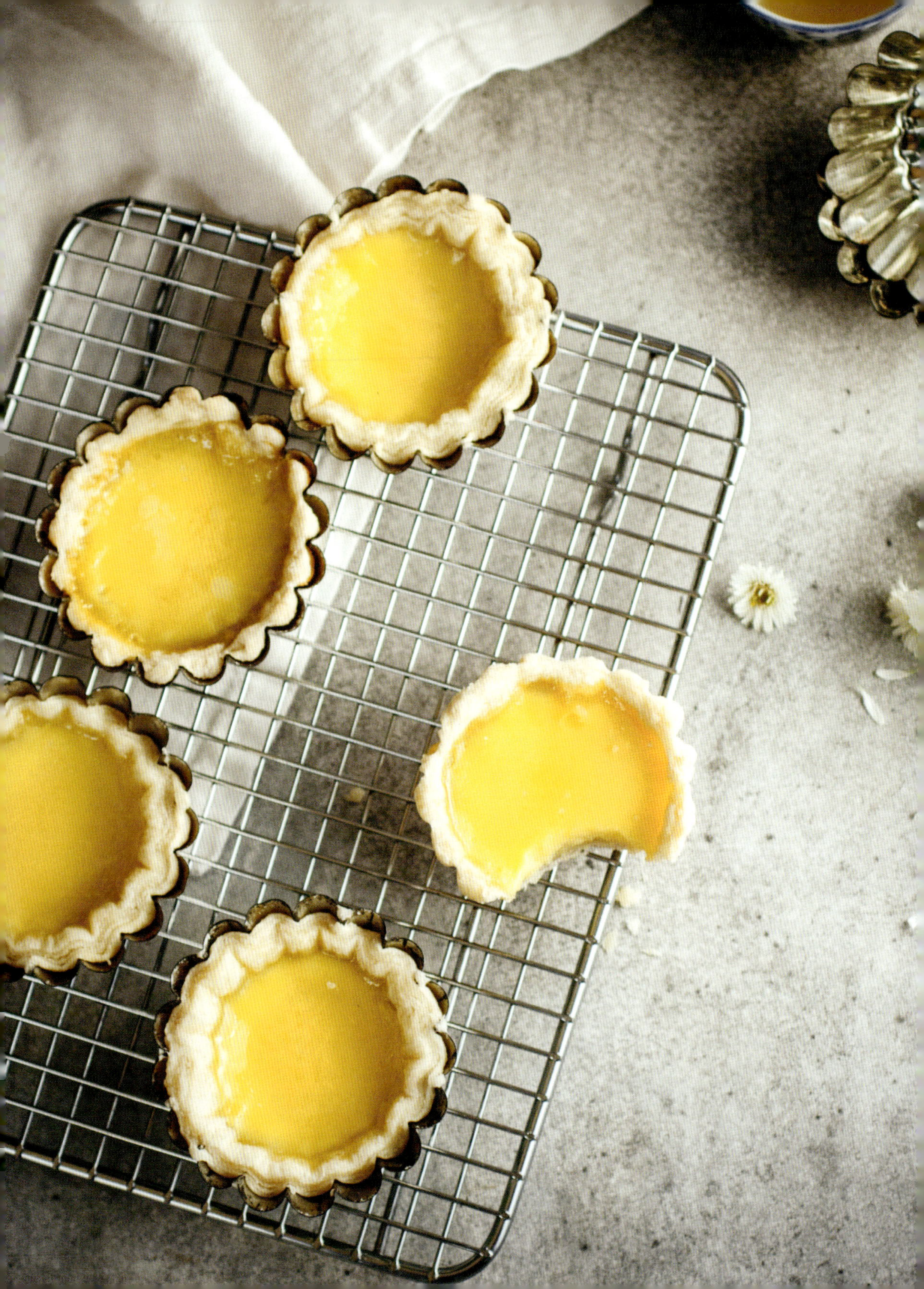

On a lightly floured counter, roll out the dough as thinly as possible, ⅛–1⁄16 inch thick. Using a 3¾-inch biscuit cutter, cut out 9–12 rounds of dough. Press them into the prepared molds or muffin pan wells, pressing them firmly into the bottom and up the sides to the top. Remove the hot sheet pan from the oven. Carefully transfer the molds or the muffin tin to the preheated sheet pan. Pour the custard filling into the cups just below the top of the crust. Skim any bubbles off the tops with a spoon. Place the pan on the middle rack of the oven and bake 10 minutes.

Reduce the oven temperature to 325°F. Rotate the pan a half-turn for even browning and bake 15–20 minutes more. When done, the crust should be golden and the custard puffed and smooth, not browning, wrinkling, frothing, or curdling. Check often toward the end of baking.

These are delicious the day they're made, but they're also very tasty the next day, well chilled. Cover and store in the refrigerator for 3–5 days.

Acknowledgments

I'm so grateful to my literary agent, Amaryah Orenstein, for her steadfast support, expertise, and diplomacy. I was thrilled to work with Globe Pequot again after a great experience with *New England Desserts*. Thanks to my editor, Greta Schmitz, Meredith Dias, and the whole team. I love my job.

I need to thank Carolyn and Bob Manchek, Erin and Chris Puranananda, Leslie Routman, Shona Simkin and Chris Tipper, Juliet and Ed Harrison, and Karen Walsh and Ben Schwartz for their friendship and delicious meals shared over the years. And a special thanks to my parents for their love and encouragement.

I'm indebted to all my recipe-testers who mobilized to make sure these recipes taste as good as they look. They include Pam Aghababian, Dave and Claire Akeson, Christine Bergsma, Colleen Bradley-MacArthur, Amy Brown, Sue Chester, Katie and Richard Chudy, Jen Costa, Kathy Creighton, Jim DeFilippi, Amy DiMatteo, Lauren Doherty, Dana Elisofon, Nicole Fiore, Nan Fornal, Tara R. Greco, Allison Grinberg-Funes, Mimi Gross, Cathy Lee Gruhn, Juliet Harrison, Chloe Tazon Ho, Amy Viens Hutchinson, Max and Nathaniel Inman, Sarah and Stuart Jang, Erin and Jane Jensen, Sharon Marie Grazioso Katz, Kate Kendall, Michele Kosboth, Chandreyee Lahiri, Kayla Leader, Roberta Lerman, Sarah Lewis, Sara Londot, Camilla M. Mann, Cynthia and Quinn Martini, Trish Michael, Leah Mitchell, Cynthia Moran, Erin Puranananda, Elaine Raquel, Melinda J. Rinehart, Amy Rothman, Carolyn Schofield, Ben Schwartz, Rachel and Paige Seremeth, Shona Simkin, Mindy Spiegel, Marika St. Amand, Alison and Megan Tarmy, Sally Theran, Karen Walsh, and Eileen Wozek.

I relied on many resources for the *dim sum* chapter of this cookbook. My oldest friend, I-Wen Chang, contributed a Taiwanese family recipe from her husband, Oliver. Jacqueline Church, who runs Boston Chinatown Tours, provided an amazing, curated culinary experience I won't forget. I also read and cooked from many wonderful cookbooks as I explored Chinese, Cantonese, and Taiwanese cooking in more depth, including *Myers + Chang at Home* by Joanne Chang and Karen Akunowicz, *Dumpling Daughter* by Nadia Liu Spellman and Sally Ling, *Dim Sum* by Ellen Leong Blonder, *The Vegan Chinese Kitchen* by Hannah Che, and *Chinese-Ish* by Rosheen Kaul and Joanna Hu. These are all excellent resources for continuing your journey into traditional and creative *dim sum* recipes.

I appreciate my son Nathaniel for spending part of his February school vacation as my photography assistant, prepping ingredients and cleaning up with only a minimal amount of complaining. Thanks also to my son Max for recipe-testing and keeping my Spotify playlists funky and up to date from Boulder, Colorado. *I'm so proud of you both!*

To my husband, Rich, who survived a major heart attack while on a business trip: *I feel lucky that we get to continue our adventures together. Life is more fun with you in it.*

Finally, I'd like to recognize all the local farmers and food producers throughout New England that keep us eating well, especially those who make sustainability a priority. These include Waltham Fields, Chestnut Farms, Codman Farm, Drumlin Farm, Carver Hill Orchard, Land's Sake Farm, Newton Community Farm, Red Fire Farm, Spring Brook Farm, Tougas Family Farm, and Winter Moon Roots. There have been many challenges to overcome, and we're indebted to your commitment to the communities you serve. Farm on!

New England Resources

Local Farms, Orchards, and Farmers' Markets
localharvest.org

Connecticut
guide.ctnofa.org/

Maine
mainefarmersmarkets.org

Massachusetts
massfarmersmarkets.org/markets

New Hampshire
nofanh.org/farm-and-food-map

Rhode Island
nofari.org

Vermont
nofavt.org

Baer's Best Beans, South Berwick, ME
baersbest.com
Dried heirloom beans like Jacob's cattle, yellow-eye, soldier, and Marfax

Bouchard Family Farms, Fort Kent, ME
ployes.com
French Acadian buckwheat flour and *ployes* mix

Coombs Family Farm, Brattleboro, VT
coombsfamilyfarms.com
Maple syrup, maple sugar

Eureka Farms, Palmyra, ME
eurekafarmsmaine.com
Dried heirloom beans, maple syrup

Formaggio Kitchen, Cambridge, MA
formaggiokitchen.com
Cheese, chocolate, baking supplies

Heiwa Tofu, Rockport, ME
heiwatofu.com
Organic tofu

HMart, Cambridge, Burlington, Quincy, MA
hmart.com
Korean, Chinese, and other Asian food and cooking supplies

Kenyon's Grist Mill, Usquepaugh, RI
kenyonsgristmill.com
Traditional white stone-ground flint cornmeal for johnnycakes

Kimball Farm, Carlisle, Lancaster, Westford, MA; Jaffrey, NH
kimballfarm.com
Maple syrup, maple sugar, honey, jam, and other New England products

King Arthur Flour, Norwich, VT
kingarthurbaking.com
Flour, malted milk powder, baking supplies

Maine Grains, Skowhegan, ME
mainegrains.com
Organic beans and grains—oats, rye, wheat, corn, spelt, barley, buckwheat, and graham flour

Penzeys Spices, Arlington, MA; Hartford, Norwalk, CT
penzeys.com
Spices, cocoa, vanilla

Index

Acadian Buckwheat Crepes with Creamy Mushrooms, 136–37
Algonquin tribes, ix, 91
almonds
    Cranberry Almond Scones, *164*, 164–65
Anadama Bread, 176–77, *177*
anise
    Crepes with Strawberry Anise Compote, 9, *10*, 11
apple cider
    Mulled Pumpkin Cider, *152*, 153
apples, *110*
    Apple Fritters, 109–10
    Apple Streusel Danish Pastry, 172, *173*, 174–75
    Caramel Apple Sticky Buns, *114*, 115–17
    Cranberry Applesauce, 195
Asparagus Chive Frittata, 32–33

bacon, 40
bagels
    Cinnamon Raisin Bagels, 166, *167*, 168
    Homemade Bagels, *118*, 118–20
    Pumpernickel Bagels, 30–31
Bailey's Irish Coffee, 200, *201*
baking tips, xix–xx, xxi
basil
    Warm Tomato Basil Bisque, 147
Bavarian Cream Doughnuts, 27
beans, xv
    Boston Baked Beans, ix, 180–84, *182*
    Portuguese Kale Soup, *142*, 142–43
    Three Sisters Succotash, 91
beef, corned
    Red Flannel Hash with Horseradish Cream, 188, *189*, 190
beets, 188, *189*, 190
bell pepper. *See* red bell pepper
beverages
    Bailey's Irish Coffee, 200, *201*
    Bloody Mary Mix, 47
    Blueberry Lemonade, *96*, 96–97

    Concord Grape Fizz, 148, *149*
    Cranberry Mimosas, 198, *198*
    dim sum tea, 206–7, *207*
    Lavender Lemon Martinis, 100
    Mint Watermelon Gimlets, *98*, 98–99
    Mulled Pumpkin Cider, *152*, 153
    Peach-Berry Sangria, 95
    Pumpkin Eggnog, 199
    Spiced Pear Sangria, *150*, 151
    Strawberry Rhubarb Sangria, 48, *49*
Blackberry Marjoram Scones, *72*, 72–73
Black Raspberry Ricotta Dutch Baby, *58*, 58–59
Bloody Mary Mix, 47
blueberries
    Blueberry Buttermilk Pancakes, 60, *61*
    Blueberry Doughnuts, 7
    Blueberry Lemonade, *96*, 96–97
    Classic Blueberry Muffins, *54*, 54–55
    Wild Blueberry Maple Syrup, 69
bok choy, 232, *233*, 234
Boston Baked Beans, ix, 180–83, *182*, 184
Boston Cream Doughnuts, 24, *25*, 26–27
brandy
    Peach-Berry Sangria, 95
    Spiced Pear Sangria, *150*, 151
brie cheese
    Broccoli and Brie Quiche, 78, *79*, 80–81
broccoli
    Broccoli and Brie Quiche, 78, *79*, 80–81
    Stir-Fried Vegetables, Glass Noodles, and Tofu, 232, *233*, 234
Brown Bread Muffins, 180
brown sugar, xii, xiv
    Caramel Apple Sticky Buns, *114*, 115–17
Brussels Sprouts and Pancetta Hash, *138*, 138–39
buckwheat, xiv
    Acadian Buckwheat Crepes with Creamy Mushrooms, 136–37
burrata
    Cherry Tomato Burrata Salad, 94

butter, xix
   Whipped Maple Cardamom Butter, 4
buttermilk, xx, *82*, 82–83, 180
   Blueberry Buttermilk Pancakes, 60, *61*

cabbage
   bok choy, 232, *233*, 234
   Pork and Cabbage Dumplings, 211, *212*, 213
   Spring Rolls, 214–15
   Taiwanese Pan-Fried Rice Vermicelli, 228, 230
cakes
   Cranberry Orange Coffee Cake, *112*, 112–13
   New England Cornmeal Custard Cake, *162*, 162–63
   Zucchini Earl Grey Tea Cake, 70–71, *71*
Cantonese ingredients, xv–xviii
Cantonese Pork and Shrimp Dumplings (*Siu Mai*), 208, *209*, 210
capers
   Cod Cakes with Preserved Lemon and Dill Sauce, *92*, 92–93
   Eggplant and Red Pepper Shakshuka, 84–85
Caramel Apple Sticky Buns, *114*, 115–17
cardamom, 28–29
   Ginger-Cardamom Syrup, *150*, 151
   Whipped Maple Cardamom Butter, 4
carrots, 188, *189*, 190, 214–15
   Stuffed Carrot Cake Muffins, 19, *20*, 21
Cava
   Concord Grape Fizz, 148, *149*
   Spiced Pear Sangria, *150*, 151
Cheddar Thyme Biscuits, 185
cheese. *See also* cream cheese; Gruyère cheese; ricotta
   Broccoli and Brie Quiche, 78, *79*, 80–81
   Cheddar Thyme Biscuits, 185
   Cherry Tomato Burrata Salad, 94
   mascarpone, 9, *10*, 11
   parmesan, 88, *89*, 90, 144–45
   Pecorino Romano, 88, 136–37
   Sausage and Stuffing Strata, 140–41
   Spinach and Feta Phyllo Crisp, 45–46
cherries
   Sweet Cherry Puff Tarts, 66, *67*, 68
Cherry Tomato Burrata Salad, 94
chicken, x, *x*
   Chicken Salad, 44
   Chinese Rice Porridge, 225, *226*, 227
chili paste, xvii

chili peppers, 197
   Sweet and Spicy Skillet Cornbread, *82*, 82–83
Chinese Rice Porridge (*Congee/Jook*), 225, *226*, 227
chives, 44
   Asparagus Chive Frittata, 32–33
chocolate
   Boston Cream Doughnuts, 24, *25*, 26–27
   Chocolate-Covered Strawberries, 28–29
   Chocolate Honey-Dipped Doughnuts, 7
cinnamon, 19, *20*, 21, 70–71, *71*, *150*, 151
   Apple Fritters, 109–10
   Cinnamon Raisin Bagels, 166, *167*, 168
   Cinnamon Raisin English Muffins, 35
   Cinnamon Sugar Cannoli Popovers, *122*, 123–24
   Dirt Bombs, *12*, 12–13
   Maple Walnut Cinnamon Rolls, 158, *159*, 160
Classic Blueberry Muffins, *54*, 54–55
cocktails. *See* beverages
cocoa powder, 30–31
Cod Cakes with Preserved Lemon and Dill Sauce, *92*, 92–93
coffee
   Bailey's Irish Coffee, 200, *201*
compotes
   Rhubarb, 22–23, *23*
   Strawberry Anise Compote, 9, *10*, 11
Concord Grape Fizz, 148, *149*
corn, 86
   Lobster, Corn, and Potato Pot Pie, 127, *128*, 129
   Rhode Island Johnnycakes with Shrimp, Zucchini, and Sweet Corn, 86–87
   Three Sisters Succotash, 91
cornmeal, xiv, *72*, 72–73, 176–77, *177*, 180
   Corn Muffins, 3
   Cranberry Cornmeal Pancakes, 121
   New England Cornmeal Custard Cake, *162*, 162–63
   Rhode Island Johnnycakes with Shrimp, Zucchini, and Sweet Corn, 86–87
   Sweet and Spicy Skillet Cornbread, *82*, 82–83
cranberries, 9, *10*, 11
   Cranberry Almond Scones, *164*, 164–65
   Cranberry Applesauce, 195
   Cranberry Baked French Toast with Maple Cream, 169, *170*, 171
   Cranberry Cornmeal Pancakes, 121
   Cranberry English Muffins, 35
   Cranberry Orange Coffee Cake, *112*, 112–13
   Cranberry Walnut Granola, 161

cranberry juice, 9, *10*, 11
    Cranberry Mimosas, 198, *198*
cream. *See* milk and cream
cream cheese
    Apple Streusel Danish Pastry, 172, *173*, 174–75
    Maple Walnut Cinnamon Rolls, 158, *159*, 160
    Pumpkin Breakfast Bars, *130*, 130–31
    Stuffed Carrot Cake Muffins, 19, *20*, 21
    Sweet Cherry Puff Tarts, 66, *67*, 68
    Vegetable Schmear, 120
    Whipped Cream Cheese, 108
crepes
    Acadian Buckwheat Crepes with Creamy Mushrooms, 136–37
    Crepes with Strawberry Anise Compote, 9, *10*, 11
Crispy Hash Browns, 41
cucumbers
    Saltwater Pickles, 77

dates, 19, *20*, 21
dill, 45–46
    Cod Cakes with Preserved Lemon and Dill Sauce, *92*, 92–93
    Saltwater Pickles, 77
dim sum, 204–37
    pantry essentials, xv–xviii
Dirt Bombs, *12*, 12–13
doughnuts, 8
    Boston Cream Doughnuts, 24, *25*, 26–27
    Jelly Doughnuts, *62*, 62–64
    Old-Fashioned Sour Cream Doughnuts, 5–7, *6*

Eggplant and Red Pepper Shakshuka, 84–85
egg roll wrappers, 214–15
eggs, xx. *See also* French toast
    Asparagus Chive Frittata, 32–33
    Broccoli and Brie Quiche, 78, *79*, 80–81
    Egg Custard Tarts (*Dan Tat*), 235, *236*, 237
    Eggplant and Red Pepper Shakshuka, 84–85
    Herbed Lobster Benedict, *36*, 36–38
    Marbled Tea Eggs, 224
    Pumpkin Eggnog, 199
    Sausage and Stuffing Strata, 140–41
    Simple Scrambled Eggs, 39
    Spinach, Pancetta, and Tomato Strata, 141
English Muffins
    Herbed Lobster Benedict, *36*, 36–38
    recipe, 34–35

feta
    Spinach and Feta Phyllo Crisp, 45–46
fish. *See* seafood
flour, xix, xxi
    rye, xiv, 30–31, 180
    wheat, xiv, 106, *107*, 108
Focaccia with Rosemary, Red Onion, and Olives, *134*, 134–35
French toast
    Cranberry Baked French Toast with Maple Cream, 169, *170*, 171
    Pear-Nutella Baked French Toast, 125–26

Garlicky Asian Greens (*Yu Choy Sum*), 231
gin
    Lavender Lemon Martinis, 100
    Mint Watermelon Gimlets, *98*, 98–99
ginger, 221, *222*, 223, 225, *226*, 227
    Gingerbread Muffins, 180
    Ginger-Cardamom Syrup, *150*, 151
    Rhubarb Yogurt Parfaits with Ginger Granola, 22–23, *23*
granola
    Cranberry Walnut Granola, 161
    Pumpkin Spice Granola, 111
    Rhubarb Yogurt Parfaits with Ginger Granola, 22–23, *23*
grape juice
    Concord Grape Fizz, 148, *149*
Grape-Nuts cereal, 22–23, *23*
Gruyère cheese
    Asparagus Chive Frittata, 32–33
    Rosemary Gruyère Popovers, 191

hazelnuts, 125–26
Herbed Heirloom Tomato Tart with Whipped Ricotta, 88, *89*, 90
Herbed Lobster Benedict, *36*, 36–38
Hollandaise sauce, *36*, 36–38
Home Fries, 196–97
Homemade Bagels, *118*, 118–20
honey, xiv, *82*, 82–83
horseradish, 47
    Horseradish Cream, 188, *189*, 190

immigrants, vii, ix, xi–xii, 204
Indigenous people, ix–x, xi, 91, 105, 184
Irish cream liqueur, 200, *201*

Jam, Mixed-Berry, 65, *65*
Jelly Doughnuts, *62*, 62–64
juniper berries
    Parsnip and Juniper Latkes, 192, *193*, 194

Kabocha Butter, *178*, 178–79
kale
    Kale Caesar Salad with Squash Croutons and Pepitas, 144–45
    Portuguese Kale Soup, *142*, 142–43

Lavender Lemon Martinis, 100
leeks, 45–46
lemon, *58*, 58–59, 95
    Blackberry Marjoram Scones, *72*, 72–73
    Blueberry Lemonade, *96*, 96–97
    Cod Cakes with Preserved Lemon and Dill Sauce, *92*, 92–93
    Hollandaise sauce, *36*, 36–38
    Lavender Lemon Martinis, 100
lettuce and greens, 231
    Cherry Tomato Burrata Salad, 94
    Simple Spring Pea Salad, 42, *43*
lime, *98*, 98–99
linguica, *142*, 142–43
lobster, *75*
    cooking, 76
    Herbed Lobster Benedict, *36*, 36–38
    Lobster, Corn, and Potato Pot Pie, 127, *128*, 129
    Lobster Salad Sliders, 74

maple syrup and sugar, xii, 22–23, 161
    Maple Breakfast Sausage, 186
    Maple Cream, 169, *170*, 171
    Maple Walnut Cinnamon Rolls, 158, *159*, 160
    Whipped Maple Cardamom Butter, 4
    Wild Blueberry Maple Syrup, 69
Marbled Tea Eggs (*Cha Ye Dan*), 224
marjoram
    Blackberry Marjoram Scones, *72*, 72–73
mascarpone, 9, *10*, 11
menu ideas, 2, 53, 105, 156, 205
milk/cream, xx, 9, *10*, 11, 127, *128*, 129, 147
    Acadian Buckwheat Crepes with Creamy Mushrooms, 136–37
    Bailey's Irish Coffee, 200, *201*
    Boston Cream Doughnuts, 24, *25*, 26–27

Cranberry Baked French Toast with Maple Cream, 169, *170*, 171
Maple Cream, 169, *170*, 171
New England Cornmeal Custard Cake, *162*, 162–63
Pumpkin Eggnog, 199
Whipped Cream Cheese, 108
mint, 95
    Mint Watermelon Gimlets, *98*, 98–99
Mixed-Berry Jam, 65, *65*
molasses, xii, 176–77, *177*
    Boston Baked Beans, ix, 180–84, *182*
    Brown Bread Muffins, 180
    Pumpernickel Bagels, 30–31
muffins. *See also* English Muffins
    Brown Bread Muffins, 180
    Classic Blueberry Muffins, *54*, 54–55
    Corn Muffins, 3
    Dirt Bombs, *12*, 12–13
    Gingerbread Muffins, 180
    Stuffed Carrot Cake Muffins, 19, *20*, 21
Mulled Pumpkin Cider, *152*, 153
mung bean noodles
    Spring Rolls, 214–15
    Stir-Fried Vegetables, Glass Noodles, and Tofu, 232, *233*, 234
mushrooms, xviii. *See also* shiitakes
    Acadian Buckwheat Crepes with Creamy Mushrooms, 136–37
mushroom soy sauce, xvi, 221, *222*, 223

New England
    foodways history, vii, ix–xii
    pantry essentials, xii, *xiii*, xiv–xv
    seasons, v–vii, 2, 52, 104, 156
New England Cornmeal Custard Cake, *162*, 162–63
Nutella
    Pear-Nutella Baked French Toast, 125–26
nuts, xiv–xv, 28–29. *See also* walnuts
    Caramel Apple Sticky Buns, *114*, 115–17
    Cranberry Almond Scones, *164*, 164–65
    hazelnuts, 125–26

oats, xiv
    Cranberry Walnut Granola, 161
    Pumpkin Breakfast Bars, *130*, 130–31
    Pumpkin Spice Granola, 111
    Rhubarb Yogurt Parfaits with Ginger Granola, 22–23, *23*

oils, high-heat, xvi
Old-Fashioned Sour Cream Doughnuts, 5–7, *6*
olives
    Focaccia with Rosemary, Red Onion, and Olives, *134*, 134–35
onion, red
    Focaccia with Rosemary, Red Onion, and Olives, *134*, 134–35
orange
    Cranberry Orange Coffee Cake, *112*, 112–13

pancakes
    Black Raspberry Ricotta Dutch Baby, *58*, 58–59
    Blueberry Buttermilk Pancakes, 60, *61*
    Cranberry Cornmeal Pancakes, 121
    Pumpkin Whole Wheat Pancakes, 106, *107*, 108
    Scallion Pancakes, *216*, 216–17
pancetta
    Brussels Sprouts and Pancetta Hash, *138*, 138–39
    Spinach, Pancetta, and Tomato Strata, 141
panko bread crumbs, *92*, 92–93, 144–45
pantry essentials, xii, *xiii*, xiv–xviii
Parsnip and Juniper Latkes, 192, *193*, 194
Peach-Berry Sangria, 95
pear
    Pear-Nutella Baked French Toast, 125–26
    Spiced Pear Sangria, *150*, 151
peas
    Simple Spring Pea Salad, 42, *43*
    Stir-Fried Vegetables, Glass Noodles, and Tofu, 232, *233*, 234
pea shoots, 231
peppercorns, white, xviii
peppers. *See* chili peppers; red bell pepper
phyllo dough, 45–46
Pickled Radish, 219
Pickles, Saltwater, 77
popovers
    Cinnamon Sugar Cannoli Popovers, *122*, 123–24
    Rosemary Gruyère Popovers, 191
pork. *See also* pancetta; sausage
    Boston Baked Beans, ix, 180–84, *182*
    Cantonese Pork and Shrimp Dumplings, 208, *209*, 210
    Pork and Cabbage Dumplings (*Jiaozi*), 211, *212*, 213
    Red-Braised Pork Belly, 221, *222*, 223

Sheet Pan Bacon, 40
Steamed Buns, 218–20
Taiwanese Pan-Fried Rice Vermicelli, 228, 230
Portuguese Kale Soup, *142*, 142–43
Portuguese Sweet Rolls, 16, *17*, 18
potatoes
    Crispy Hash Browns, 41
    Home Fries, 196–97
    Lobster, Corn, and Potato Pot Pie, 127, *128*, 129
    Parsnip and Juniper Latkes, 192, *193*, 194
    Red Flannel Hash with Horseradish Cream, 188, *189*, 190
Prosecco
    Cranberry Mimosas, 198, *198*
    Peach-Berry Sangria, 95
    Strawberry Rhubarb Sangria, 48, *49*
puff pastry, 127, *128*, 129
Pumpernickel Bagels, 30–31
pumpkin
    Mulled Pumpkin Cider, *152*, 153
    preparation and baking, 133
    Pumpkin Breakfast Bars, *130*, 130–31
    Pumpkin Eggnog, 199
    Pumpkin Spice Doughnuts, 7
    Pumpkin Whole Wheat Pancakes, 106, *107*, 108
pumpkin seeds, 111
    Kale Caesar Salad with Squash Croutons and Pepitas, 144–45
pumpkin spice
    Pumpkin Breakfast Bars, *130*, 130–31
    Pumpkin Spice Doughnuts, 7
    Pumpkin Spice Granola, 111

quiche
    Broccoli and Brie Quiche, 78, *79*, 80–81
    Summer Squash and Red Pepper Quiche, 81

radishes, 42, *43*
    Pickled Radish, 219
raisins
    Brown Bread Muffins, 180
    Cinnamon Raisin Bagels, 166, *167*, 168
    Cinnamon Raisin English Muffins, 35
raspberries
    Black Raspberry Ricotta Dutch Baby, *58*, 58–59
    Peach-Berry Sangria, 95

red bell pepper
    Eggplant and Red Pepper Shakshuka, 84–85
    Home Fries, 196–97
    Summer Squash and Red Pepper Quiche, 81
Red-Braised Pork Belly (*Hong Shao Rou*), 221, *222*, 223
Red Flannel Hash with Horseradish Cream, 188, *189*, 190
Rhode Island Johnnycakes with Shrimp, Zucchini, and Sweet Corn, 86–87
rhubarb
    Rhubarb Yogurt Parfaits with Ginger Granola, 22–23, *23*
    Strawberry Rhubarb Sangria, 48, *49*
    Strawberry Rhubarb Scones, *14*, 14–15
rice, xviii
    Chinese Rice Porridge, 225, *226*, 227
    Stir-Fried Vegetables, Glass Noodles, and Tofu, 232, *233*, 234
rice noodles
    Taiwanese Pan-Fried Rice Vermicelli, 228, 230
rice wine, xvii
    Red-Braised Pork Belly, 221, *222*, 223
ricotta
    Black Raspberry Ricotta Dutch Baby, *58*, 58–59
    Cinnamon Sugar Cannoli Popovers, *122*, 123–24
    Herbed Heirloom Tomato Tart with Whipped Ricotta, 88, *89*, 90
rosemary
    Focaccia with Rosemary, Red Onion, and Olives, *134*, 134–35
    Rosemary Gruyère Popovers, 191
rum, xv
    Pumpkin Eggnog, 199
rye, xiv
    Brown Bread Muffins, 180
    Pumpernickel Bagels, 30–31

sage
    Squash and Sage Scones, *132*, 132–33
salt, xix
Saltwater Pickles, 77
sausage
    Maple Breakfast Sausage, 186
    Portuguese Kale Soup, *142*, 142–43
    Sausage and Stuffing Strata, 140–41
    Sausage Gravy, 187
Scallion Pancakes (*Cong You Bing*), *216*, 216–17

scones
    Blackberry Marjoram Scones, *72*, 72–73
    Cranberry Almond Scones, *164*, 164–65
    Squash and Sage Scones, *132*, 132–33
    Strawberry Rhubarb Scones, *14*, 14–15
seafood, 76. *See also* lobster; shrimp
    Cod Cakes with Preserved Lemon and Dill Sauce, *92*, 92–93
    Smoked Bluefish, 146
sesame oil, xvii
Sheet Pan Bacon, 40
shiitakes, xviii
    Cantonese Pork and Shrimp Dumplings, 208, *209*, 210
    Spring Rolls, 214–15
    Taiwanese Pan-Fried Rice Vermicelli, 228, 230
shrimp
    Cantonese Pork and Shrimp Dumplings, 208, *209*, 210
    Rhode Island Johnnycakes with Shrimp, Zucchini, and Sweet Corn, 86–87
Simple Scrambled Eggs, 39
Simple Spring Pea Salad, 42, *43*
Smoked Bluefish, 146
snow peas, 232, *233*, 234
    Simple Spring Pea Salad, 42, *43*
soups
    Portuguese Kale Soup, *142*, 142–43
    Warm Tomato Basil Bisque, 147
sour cream, 92, 92–93, 158, *159*, 160
    Horseradish Cream, 188, *189*, 190
    Old-Fashioned Sour Cream Doughnuts, 5–7, *6*
Sourdough Waffles, 56, *57*
soy sauce, xvi, 221, *222*, 223
Spiced Pear Sangria, *150*, 151
spices, essential, xv
spinach
    Spinach, Pancetta, and Tomato Strata, 141
    Spinach and Feta Phyllo Crisp, 45–46
Spring Rolls (*Chun Juan*), 214–15
squash. *See also* zucchini
    Kabocha Butter, *178*, 178–79
    Kale Caesar Salad with Squash Croutons and Pepitas, 144–45
    Squash and Sage Scones, *132*, 132–33
    Summer Squash and Red Pepper Quiche, 81
    Three Sisters Succotash, 91

Steamed Buns (*Bao*), 218–20
Stir-Fried Vegetables, Glass Noodles, and Tofu (*Lo Han Jai*), 232, *233*, 234
strata
    Sausage and Stuffing Strata, 140–41
    Spinach, Pancetta, and Tomato Strata, 141
strawberries
    Chocolate-Covered Strawberries, 28–29
    Crepes with Strawberry Anise Compote, 9, *10*, 11
    Strawberry Rhubarb Sangria, 48, *49*
    Strawberry Rhubarb Scones, *14*, 14–15
Stuffed Carrot Cake Muffins, 19, *20*, 21
substitutions, for baking, xix–xx
sugar, xi, xxi. *See also* brown sugar; maple syrup and sugar; molasses
sugar snap peas
    Simple Spring Pea Salad, 42, *43*
Summer Squash and Red Pepper Quiche, 81
sunflower seeds, 111
Sweet and Spicy Skillet Cornbread, *82*, 82–83
Sweet Cherry Puff Tarts, 66, *67*, 68

Taiwanese Pan-Fried Rice Vermicelli (*Chow Mei Fun*), 228, 230
tarts
    Egg Custard Tarts, 235, *236*, 237
    Herbed Heirloom Tomato Tart with Whipped Ricotta, 88, *89*, 90
    Sweet Cherry Puff Tarts, 66, *67*, 68
tea, xvi
    dim sum, 206–7, *207*
    Marbled Tea Eggs, 224
    Zucchini Earl Grey Tea Cake, 70–71, *71*
Three Sisters Succotash, 91
thyme
    Cheddar Thyme Biscuits, 185
tofu
    Stir-Fried Vegetables, Glass Noodles, and Tofu, 232, *233*, 234
tomatoes, *36*, 36–38
    Cherry Tomato Burrata Salad, 94
    Herbed Heirloom Tomato Tart with Whipped Ricotta, 88, *89*, 90
    Spinach, Pancetta, and Tomato Strata, 141
    Warm Tomato Basil Bisque, 147
tomato juice, 47
triple sec, 48, *49*, 198, *198*
turnips, *157*, 188, *189*, 190

V8 vegetable juice, 47
vegan menu ideas, 105, 205
Vegetable Schmear, 120
vermouth, 100
vinegar, xvii–xviii

Waffles, Sourdough, 56, *57*
walnuts
    Cranberry Walnut Granola, 161
    Maple Walnut Cinnamon Rolls, 158, *159*, 160
    Pumpkin Breakfast Bars, *130*, 130–31
    Stuffed Carrot Cake Muffins, 19, *20*, 21
    Zucchini Earl Grey Tea Cake, 70–71, *71*
Warm Tomato Basil Bisque, 147
watermelon
    Mint Watermelon Gimlets, *98*, 98–99
weight conversions, xxi
wheat flour, xiv
    Pumpkin Whole Wheat Pancakes, 106, *107*, 108
Whipped Cream Cheese, 108
Whipped Maple Cardamom Butter, 4
Wild Blueberry Maple Syrup, 69
wine. *See also* Cava; Prosecco; rice wine
    Peach-Berry Sangria, 95
    Strawberry Rhubarb Sangria, 48, *49*

yeast, xix
yogurt, xx, 45–46
    Rhubarb Yogurt Parfaits with Ginger Granola, 22–23, *23*

zucchini, 81, 91
    Rhode Island Johnnycakes with Shrimp, Zucchini, and Sweet Corn, 86–87
    Zucchini Earl Grey Tea Cake, 70–71, *71*

About the Author

Born in Maine, bred in New Hampshire, and a Massachusetts resident for more than thirty years, **Tammy Donroe Inman** is a New England writer, trained chef, and Boston-based cooking instructor. Her first cookbook, *Wintersweet: Seasonal Desserts to Warm the Home*, was praised by *USA Today*, the *Wall Street Journal*, the *Boston Globe*, *Edible Boston*, and the *Kitchn*. Her second cookbook, *New England Desserts: Classic and Creative Recipes for All Seasons*, won New England Book of the Year at the 2022 Readable Feast Awards. After earning her chops in the test kitchen of *Cook's Illustrated* magazine and the television show *America's Test Kitchen*, she spent nearly twenty years writing about food and developing recipes for *Fine Cooking*, *Parents*, *Yankee*, the *Boston Globe*, *Boston* magazine, *Cape Cod Life*, and *Serious Eats*. She taught hands-on cooking classes for adults and children at the Newton cooking school, Create a Cook, for five years. Inman has been interviewed by NPR's *All Things Considered*, *CBS Evening News*, and the *Atlantic* about her perspective on food. She was also the force behind the beloved *Food on the Food* blog. She lives outside Boston with her husband (her two sons have flown the coop), two high-maintenance cats, and a well-worn pair of roller skates. To learn more, visit tammydonroe.com.